BORDER JUMPING AND MIGRATION CONTROL IN SOUTHERN AFRICA

BORDER JUMPING AND MIGRATION CONTROL IN SOUTHERN AFRICA

Francis Musoni

Indiana University Press

This book is a publication of

Indiana University Press
Office of Scholarly Publishing
Herman B Wells Library 350
1320 East 10th Street
Bloomington, Indiana 47405 USA

iupress.indiana.edu

Manufactured in the United States of America

Library of Congress Cataloging-in-Publication Data

Names: Musoni, Francis, author.
Title: Border Jumping and Migration Control in Southern Africa/
    Francis Musoni.
Description: Bloomington, Indiana : Indiana University Press, 2020. |
    Includes bibliographical references and index.
Identifiers: LCCN 2019980962 (print) | LCCN 2019021140 (ebook) | ISBN
    9780253047144 (hardback : alk. paper) | ISBN 9780253047151 (pbk. : alk.
    paper) | ISBN 9780253047175 (ebook)
Subjects: LCSH: Zimbabwe—Emigration and immigration—History—20th century.
    | South Africa—Emigration and immigration—History—20th century. |
    Zimbabwe—Boundaries. | South Africa—Boundaries. | Border
    crossing—Zimbabwe. | Border crossing—South Africa. | Zimbabweans—South
    Africa—Social conditions.
Classification: LCC JV9006.15 .M87 2020 (ebook) | LCC JV9006.15 (print) | DDC
    325.68—dc23
LC record available at https://lccn.loc.gov/2019980962

1 2 3 4 5   25 24 23 22 21 20

In loving memory of my father—a former migrant, educator, and community leader.

Contents

Preface

THIS BOOK WAS conceived around the 2008 outbreak of xenophobic violence in South Africa that left more than fifty migrants dead and thousands others displaced. My original idea was to study the historical construction of foreignness among Zimbabweans in South Africa. I hoped such a study would provide some historical context that was missing in the largely presentist discussions of the violence, which affected migrants from Zimbabwe, Mozambique, and other parts of sub-Saharan Africa, whom South Africans collectively referred to as *makwerekwere* (foreigners). However, I changed my mind a year later after a few days of research at the National Archives of Zimbabwe in Harare led me to a huge file labeled "Illegal Recruiting of Native Labour, 1925–1951." In that file, which contained hundreds of documents from various units of the colonial government in Zimbabwe, were reports of the Criminal Investigation Department. One of those reports made reference to a statement dated November 8, 1941, that was ostensibly written by someone identified as "Native" Davidson. It read as follows:

> It was my intention today to proceed to Mafeking. I have no Pass to Leave the Territory, nor have I any papers authorising my entry to the Union of South Africa, but I have made arrangements to travel on a goods train which is travelling to the Union this morning. Sometime ago, when I expressed an intention of going to the Union of South Africa, I was told by one of my friends, a native named Jack *alias* Faison, who works in the Railway Telegraph Office, Bulawayo, that he could arrange that I be taken down South by one of the Europeans employed on the Railways. He mentioned that the charge would be about £2-0-0, and that many natives had been taken down South by this particular person. On the 31st October, 1941, I paid £2-0-0 to native Jack, who said he would hand it to the European concerned. He told me that this European works on the trains which travel down South. I saw Jack alias Faison again on Wednesday 5 November, and he told me that he had handed the money to the European. I don't know the name of the European. Jack told me to be ready on Saturday morning the 8th November, at the station, and he would give me a note, which had been left with him, to give to me, for purposes of identification, when I joined the goods train. I was told by Jack that he would show me the train on which I was to travel, and there, an arrangement would be made with the European as to how I was to travel (ie in goods truck or compartment, or on the engine, or in the guards' van). I was not able to go up to the station today, as I was detained by the police, on a native pass charge.[1]

Although the prevalence of "illegal migration" across the Zimbabwe–South Africa border featured prominently in media and scholarly discussions of the 2008 xenophobic violence, it had never occurred to my mind that there could be a long history of this phenomenon. Not even a single one of the historical studies of migration in Southern Africa, which I had read since my undergraduate years in Zimbabwe, addressed this issue. While a few works made passing reference to work-seeking migrants who sneaked out of colonial Zimbabwe and went to South Africa, they did very little to examine how such people crossed the border between the two countries.

This book contributes to Southern African historiography and migration studies by examining the historical dynamics of cross-border movements that evaded official measures of controlling migration from colonial and postcolonial Zimbabwe to South Africa. It covers the period from 1890, when the British-sponsored settlers occupied the Zimbabwean plateau and created a separate colony from the then Boer-controlled Transvaal colony on the southern side of the Limpopo River, to around 2010. Although I discuss why people left Zimbabwe at any given moment over the course of that period and why they went to South Africa, the main objective of the book is to understand why and how travelers crossed the border between the two countries without following official channels. In that respect, this book is as much a study of "illegal" migration as it is about the making of the Zimbabwe–South Africa border. It is also about statecraft and the politics of emigration and immigration control in Zimbabwe and South Africa.

In terms of methodology, the book relies on historical research at the National Archives of Zimbabwe in Harare, the National Archives of South Africa in Pretoria, the British Library in London, and the University of Johannesburg's (Doornfontein Campus) Special Collections, as well as ethnographic fieldwork in the Zimbabwe–South Africa border zone. In addition to the file referred to earlier, my research at the National Archives of Zimbabwe involved reading hundreds of official documents from the colonial period, especially those produced by the Native Affairs Department and the British South Africa Police. These two departments were at the forefront of the settler administration's effort to mobilize a pool of cheap labor for the colony from the 1890s to the 1950s; therefore, they produced a huge corpus of documents relating to the movement of Africans within and out of Southern Rhodesia during that period.

At the National Archives of South Africa, the most relevant materials came from the Government Native Labor Bureau, particularly the office of the Director of Native Labor, who played a significant role as a link between the government and employers organizations such as the Transvaal Chamber of Mines and the Lowveld Farmers Association. As was the case in colonial Zimbabwe, the police in South Africa also produced documents regarding the movements of African foreign workers, especially after the introduction of the Immigrants Regulation Act in 1913. At the University of Johannesburg's Doornfontein Campus, my research focused on archives of the Witwatersrand Native Labor Association, the organization that recruited migrant workers on behalf of companies affiliated with the Chamber of Mines. The bulk of the materials in these archives are in the form of circulars, minutes of management meetings, and correspondence between the association's management and officials in various state departments. More information about the politics of migration control in South Africa came from the Union of South Africa's parliamentary debates, which I found at the British Library in London.

While archival records in Zimbabwe, South Africa, and London provided a glimpse of migrants' experiences of crossing the border through unofficial channels, I learned a lot from the fieldwork I conducted in the border region. This research took place in three segments: a five-month continuous stay in the area (from March to July 2010), two weeks in June 2012, and then three weeks during summer 2013. For the most part, my field research consisted of oral interviews with former migrants and residents of Zimbabwe's border district of Beitbridge, which was simultaneously a major source of and transit zone for migrants en route to South Africa. I also collected a lot of information through focused group discussions with Zimbabwean deportees and voluntary returnees who sought temporary shelter and other kinds of assistance at the International Organization for Migration's (IOM's) office in Beitbridge and Musina (formerly Messina) Town on the South African side of the border.

In addition to the interviews, I learned about historical and contemporary dynamics of "clandestine" mobility between these countries from personal observations as I moved around with the IOM staff, especially the team that conducted the "Health and Safe Migration Awareness" campaigns in the border areas. I also accompanied a number of IOM Beitbridge staff members on several trips to the Refugee Reception Center in Musina. This place is where hundreds of "undocumented" migrants (mostly Zimbabweans) received various kinds of assistance, including food handouts, clothes, and blankets as well as paperwork to apply for asylum permits and other kinds of documentation to "legalize" their stay in South Africa. With the support and guidance of staff at the IOM Musina office, I was able to drive along the security patrol road adjacent the South African border fence and got to see several holes through which migrants and smugglers entered and/or left South Africa. Furthermore, my informal conversations with the IOM staff and other people I met in various settings on both sides of border yielded crucial information for this book. For example, I watched several of the 2010 FIFA World Cup soccer matches at the Beitbridge Country Club, which was a popular drinking spot for residents of Beitbridge town and for stop-by travelers to or from South Africa. Quite often, conversations at the club strayed from soccer to matters of "bread and butter," which revolved around the border economy and its politics.

In an attempt to capture broader historical changes that shaped the development of this phenomenon, I use place and country names that were in use at different periods that I cover in different sections of the book. For example, I use *Southern Rhodesia* in reference to present-day Zimbabwe from the 1890s to 1965. Between 1965 and 1979, the country was officially known as *Rhodesia* before it was renamed *Zimbabwe* at the end of colonial rule in 1980. Different names have also been used in reference to the area on the southern side of the border. From the mid–nineteenth century to the formation of the Union of South Africa in 1910, the area was part of the Transvaal colony. Although the Union of South Africa officially ended with the proclamation of the Republic of South Africa in 1961, there were no significant changes in the country's name after 1910. In line with these changes, some sections of the book use the *Transvaal*, whereas others use *South Africa* to refer to the same area. I also use phrases such as the *Transvaal–Southern Rhodesia* border, the *Southern Rhodesia–South Africa* border, the *Rhodesia–South Africa* border, and the *Zimbabwe–South Africa* border to refer to the same boundary in different sections of the book, depending on the historical periods covered in those sections. In the same vein, I use *Nyasaland* and *Northern Rhodesia* and *Portuguese East Africa* to refer to colonial Malawi, Zambia, and Mozambique, respectively.

Note

1. National Archives of Zimbabwe, S1226, Statement Made by "Native" Davidson at Criminal Investigation Department Office, Bulawayo, November 8, 1941.

Acknowledgments

THIS BOOK IS a result of almost ten years of research and writing during which I received support from numerous people and institutions in different parts of the world. I owe my deepest gratitude to my PhD advisor Clifton Crais for his mentorship, which has continued since I completed my studies at Emory University. In addition to teaching me the art of asking the "so what" type of questions, he also read and critiqued several drafts of the chapters in this book. It was under his guidance that I also developed a strong interest in understanding the state not as a thing but as a result of contested processes. While this book is not necessarily a study of the state, it benefited from a critical historical reading of statecraft and conceptions of mobility and border control in Zimbabwe and South Africa. I am also grateful to Regine Jackson, who kindly agreed to direct an independent study on "migration theory" and to David Eltis for putting together a minor field on "coerced migration" for my qualifying exams at Emory university. The readings and discussions I had with both of them broadened my understanding of various aspects of migration as an economic, political, and sociocultural phenomenon. Gyanendra Pandey helped me to think critically about the politics of the "subalterns" and how they relate to mainstream politics, while Bruce Knauft, Corrine Kratz, and the late Ivan Karp introduced me to the anthropological way of thinking about the state, migration, borders, politics, culture, and power. Combining historical and anthropological methods enabled me to develop a better understanding of my research and how to approach it. As members of my dissertation committee, Kristin Mann and Pamela Scully gave me timely encouragement and helpful comments on earlier drafts of the book. They also wrote letters in support of my applications for research funding and jobs. Without their support, I would not have made it into the University of Kentucky as a member of the faculty. Fellow graduate students, who include Andrea Arrington, Katherine Fidler, Jane Hooper, Daniel Domingues da Silva, John Thabiti Willis, Ugochukwu-Smooth Nzewi, Sunandan K. N, Molly McCullers, Husseina Dinani, Jill Rosenthal, Durba Mitra, Robyn Pariser, and Kara Moskovitz provided the camaraderie that made my stay at Emory enjoyable.

The bulk of the writing of this book took place after I joined the history department at the University of Kentucky as an assistant professor. I want to express my heartfelt gratitude to my colleagues for giving me a chance when I barely knew what it meant to work in America's higher education system and for patiently guiding me through the labyrinth over the past few years. The comments I received when I presented draft chapters under the department's Works-in-Progress seminars helped me to package my ideas and arguments in ways that made it possible for non-Africanists to understand the complicated history of border jumping across the Zimbabwe–South Africa border. Special thanks go to Karen Petrone and Mark Kornbluh for not just supporting my research and teaching activities but also providing timely intervention when the process of changing my immigration status became more complicated than I had anticipated. I am very thankful for their support.

This book also greatly benefited from the comments I received from Tim Scarnecchia, Blair Rutherford, and Martin Murray, who read earlier versions of the entire manuscript, and from Luise White, Loren Landau, Eliakim Sibanda, Tapiwa Mucherera, JoAnn McGregor, Diana Jeater, Munya Munochiveyi, Anna Hüncke, Nedson Pophiwa, Olivia Klimm, Andrea Arrington, Husseina Dinnani, Kara Moskovitz, Alois Mlambo, Lea Kalaora, Zoe Groves, Maxim Bolt, and Wendy Urban-Mead, who read parts of the book as draft chapters or conference papers. The feedback I got from participants at several meetings of the African Studies Association, where I presented drafts of chapters in this book, was very helpful. I am also grateful to the British Zimbabwe Society, the Southern African Historical Society, the North Eastern Workshop on Southern Africa, the African Borderlands Research Network, the Southeastern Regional Seminar in African Studies, and the Association of Borderlands Studies for the feedback I received at the conferences they organized. I also owe special thanks to the Department of Historical and Heritage Studies at the University of Pretoria and the Center for African Studies at the University of Florida for opportunities to present chapters of the book and receive helpful feedback. Researchers at the African Center for Migration and Society (formerly the Forced Migration Studies Program) at the University of the Witwatersrand, which I have called my academic home in South Africa since 2006, have also been supportive of my work on this book and other projects.

Without the materials I accessed at the National Archives of Zimbabwe in Harare, the National Archives of South Africa in Pretoria, the British Library in London, and the University of Johannesburg's (Doornfontein Campus) Special Collections, it would have been impossible to write this book. I owe a special debt of gratitude to the staffs at these very important institutions. Many thanks to Natasha Erlank and Dunbar Moodie, who provided the information and connections that helped me to access the rich archives of the Witwatersrand Native Labor Association and its successor, called the Employment Bureau of Southern Africa, in the Special Collections of the University of Johannesburg's (Doornfontein Campus) Library. Victor Maronga and Boniface Hlabano, along with their families, opened their homes to me on several occasions when I visited Johannesburg and Pretoria to conduct research for this book or attend conferences, and Irene Staunton and Murray McCartney always made their cottage available to me whenever I was in Harare. I am so grateful for their hospitality. I am also thankful for the research assistance provided by David Siyasongwe, Busani Mhlanga, Anusa Daimon, and Nicholas Nyachega and for the moral and intellectual support I received from numerous friends, especially Gerald Mazarire, Awet Weldemichael, Mhoze Chikowero, Terence Mashingaidze, Clement Masakure, Douglas Mpondi, Enocent Msindo, Joseph Mujere, and Ivan Marowa.

Furthermore, I would like to acknowledge the support I got from the offices of the International Organization for Migration (IOM) in Harare, Beitbridge, and Musina. Special thanks go to the Chief of Mission of the IOM Harare office, Marcelo Pisani, for taking me in as an affiliate during the time I conducted field research in the Zimbabwe–South Africa border zone. Katie Kerr and Peter Mudungwe helped with the process of obtaining affiliation, and Nick van der Vyver hosted me at the IOM offices in Beitbridge. In addition to introducing me to local government representatives in the border district, Nick allowed me to join IOM teams on several of their field trips. It was during those trips that I met most of the people I interviewed for this project. I am also thankful for the support I got from the staffs at the IOM office and the Refugee Reception Center in Musina. The bulk of the ethnographic materials I use in this book came from my interviews and informal interactions with migrants and residents of the border towns of Beitbridge and Musina. I extend my special thanks to them. Thanks to Simon Muleya, the district administrator for Beitbridge, for providing introductory letters that I carried as I traveled in the border area. Special thanks to Thupeyo Muleya, Gift (Papi) Mbedzi, Remember Ndou, and the management of the Beitbridge Country Club for the warm welcome that made my stays in Beitbridge town enjoyable.

Funding from Emory University's Laney Graduate School, the Institute of African Studies, the Race and Difference Initiative, the Institute of Critical International Studies, and the Joseph Mathews Fellowship sponsored the first phase of my research in Zimbabwe and South Africa, which lasted from July 2009 to July 2010. Subsequent trips in 2012 and 2013 benefited from funding provided by the history department, College of Arts and Sciences, and Office of the Vice President for Research at the University of Kentucky. I am grateful for the generosity of these institutions. Last, but not least, I would like to salute my father, who died around the time this project was born; my mother and siblings; and my wife, Everjoy, and our children, Nyasha, Anopa, and Taonashe, for their understanding and unconditional support, which eased the pain of writing and rewriting this book.

An earlier version of chapter 2 appeared as an article in the *African Studies Review* (Francis Musoni, "The Ban on 'Tropical Natives' and the Promotion of Illegal Migration in Pre-Apartheid South Africa," *African Studies Review* 61, no. 3 (2018): 156–177, doi:10.1017/asr.2018.73).

Acronyms and Abbreviations

ANC	African National Congress
BL	British Library
BSAC	British South Africa Company
BSAP	British South Africa Police
CID	Criminal Investigation Department
DHA	Department of Home Affairs
ESAP	Economic Structural Adjustment Program
ETD	emergency travel document
GNU	Government of National Unity
IOM	International Organization for Migration
MDC	Movement for Democratic Change
MK	Umkhonto we Sizwe
MP	member of parliament
NASA	National Archives of South Africa
NAZ	National Archives of Zimbabwe
NRC	Native Recruiting Corporation
PAC	Pan African Congress
RC	registration certificate
RENAMO	Resistência Nacional Moçambicana
RLB	Rhodesia Labour Bureau
RMS	Railway Motor Services
RNLA	Rand Native Labour Association
SACP	South African Communist Party
SADC	Southern African Development Community
SADF	South African Defense Forces
SAIMR	South African Institute for Medical Research
SAMP	Southern Africa Migration Project
SANDF	South African National Defense Forces
SAPS	South African Police Services
SAR	South African Railways
SME	small to medium enterprises
TEBA	The Employment Bureau of Southern Africa
UDI	Unilateral Declaration of Independence
WNLA	Witwatersrand Native Labour Association
ZANLA	Zimbabwe African National Liberation Army

ZANU	Zimbabwe African National Union
ZANU-PF	Zimbabwe African National Union- Patriotic Front
ZAPU	Zimbabwe African People's Union
ZDP	Zimbabwe Dispensation Program
ZIPRA	Zimbabwe People's Revolutionary Army

BORDER JUMPING AND MIGRATION CONTROL IN SOUTHERN AFRICA

Introduction

WHILE INTERNATIONAL MIGRATION has been a major focus of debates in many parts of the world since the early twentieth century, global attention to cross-border movements that seek to evade official channels of migration control increased significantly over the past few years. The reasons for this attention vary from security concerns fueled by the 2001 bombing of the World Trade Center in New York City by individuals linked to Al-Qaeda—a terrorist organization whose activities rely on cross-border movements of its operatives—to the rise of anti-immigration movements in many parts of the world. In the United States, for example, debates around this issue became more complicated than ever when presidential candidate Donald Trump made a pledge to prevent illegal migration from Mexico by building a wall along the border between the two countries and then went on to win the 2016 election. In addition to these developments, widely circulated media reports and images from the Mediterranean region, where thousands of people from Africa and the Middle East (including young children) have died while trying to enter Europe through unofficial channels, have also contributed to ongoing debates around this topic.[1]

Away from the spotlight of international media outlets, hundreds of Zimbabweans died while many others faced various forms of violence as they tried to escape from a double-dip recession that engulfed their country during the first decade of the twenty-first century. At least three million people—about 25 percent of Zimbabwe's entire population—are believed to have left the crisis-ridden country between 1999 and 2008.[2] Although the majority of people who left Zimbabwe relocated to South Africa, many others regularly traveled between the two countries as cross-border traders or subsistence shoppers. By 2009, when I began research for this book, the Beitbridge border post between Zimbabwe and South Africa had become one of Africa's busiest inland ports of entry. Long queues of people and vehicles were a common sight at this place where travelers often spent several hours awaiting clearance by Zimbabwean and South African border officials. Although some travelers followed official channels for crossing the border, others swam across the Limpopo River and crawled under or jumped over the South African border fence. Some of those who sought to avoid the official border post enlisted the help of unregistered transport operators, locally referred to as *malayitsha* or *omalayisha*, and human smugglers (*maguma-guma*), who removed portions of the border fence and charged fees for the use of the "alternative gates" they created.[3] However, the malayitsha and maguma-guma often assaulted, raped, and even killed travelers they interacted with in the border zone. As such, the Zimbabwe–South Africa border—particularly the no-man's land between the Limpopo River, which separates these countries, and the border fence on the South African side—also became a hotbed of crime and violence associated with border jumping.[4]

Although a substantial body of literature exists on "illegal migration" in Southern Africa, the bulk of the studies on this phenomenon come from geographers, anthropologists, sociologists, and political scientists who focus predominantly on the post-1990s period.[5] This book takes a different approach by exploring the history of border jumping from Zimbabwe to South Africa since the border's inception as a colonial boundary, between what was then known as the *Transvaal* (now the Limpopo province of South Africa) and what became Southern Rhodesia (now Zimbabwe) in the 1890s, to the early 2000s. Arguing that the practice of evading state-centered measures of controlling migration between the two countries is as old as the border itself, I tell the story of how border jumping in this region came to be so prevalent and violent. At the center of this history are multilevel contestations over the meaning of this border and movements across it. On one level, the study explores contestations between policy makers and employers of unskilled workers in Zimbabwe and South Africa, who had different and at times conflicting understandings of cross-Limpopo mobility. On another level, we see migrant workers, cross-border shoppers, and traders from colonial and postcolonial Zimbabwe and other areas north of the Limpopo River doing everything they can to defy state-centered controls of mobility by entering South Africa through unofficial channels. Moreover, I probe the contribution of corrupt state officials, labor recruiters, and the malayitsha and maguma-guma who facilitated border jumpers' breaches of various measures of border enforcement and migration control that both countries have deployed at different times.

By focusing on contestations about the meaning of the border and attempts to control people's movements from Zimbabwe to South Africa, this study challenges the argument that conditions of insecurity in the migrants' countries of origin are the major causes of "illegal" migration that features prominently in scholarly and policy discussions of migrations in many parts of the world. In the case of Southern Africa, scholars, journalists, and policy makers often point at the Mozambican civil war and the rising rates of unemployment and poverty that have prevailed in other countries of the region from the 1990s onward as the major drivers of illegal migration to South Africa.[6] In challenging this view, my study invites readers to make a distinction between factors that push people out of their countries of origin and those that cause or promote illegal crossings of international boundaries. For example, although various factors in colonial and postcolonial Zimbabwe compelled many people to leave on short- or long-term trips to South Africa, such factors did not cause travelers to cross the border between the two countries through illegal, irregular, or informal channels. In fact, most people whose experiences I discuss in this book resorted to border jumping only after they were denied documents such as passbooks, visas, or permits that would have allowed them to use official channels.

My study also engages with the view that "illegal immigration" is a sign that the receiving country has failed to secure its borders.[7] This argument is at the center of ongoing immigration debates in the United States, the United Kingdom, and other countries with large immigrant populations. In South Africa, this view is common among opposition politicians and other government critics who argue that the postapartheid administration has weakened the country's borders by withdrawing the military from border patrol units.[8] Although this argument has some merits, the story I tell suggests that tightening border control measures does not eradicate border jumping; it only makes border jumping more violent and risky. Over the more than 120 years studied in this book, state officials on both sides of the Zimbabwe–South Africa border made several attempts to harden the border, but border jumpers responded to each and every initiative by devising new strategies to dodge the revised policies. Rather than eliminating border jumping, the attempts to tighten border control in these countries actually encouraged and promoted it. In making this point, my study resonates with works in other areas of the world where tightening border enforcement and immigration control measures encouraged migrants to use unofficial channels to cross borders. Joseph Nevins's study of Operation Gatekeeper, a boundary enforcement strategy that the Clinton administration launched in 1994, reveals that militarization of the United States–Mexico border did not eliminate illegal migration between the countries. By 1998, the United States had installed floodlights on sections of the border in addition to deploying helicopters that hovered over the border area, monitoring people's movements. Despite these and other measures put in place since then, the United States–Mexico border has remained a site of intense contestation.[9] A similar scenario has unfolded along the border between Morocco and Spain, where border jumping and smuggling turned violent and more complicated over the past decade despite Spain's attempts to fortify the Melilla border fence. Instead of ending border jumping, the tightening of border controls in this region gave rise to what Ruben Andersson has aptly called "an illegal migration industry" that thrives on a wide variety of factors and actors in Africa and Europe.[10]

This book also builds on a growing body of scholarship on Africa's borders and borderlands.[11] Existing work often uncritically adopts and deploys state-centered notions of legality and illegality in characterizing cross-border movements. In contrast, my study advances the idea that Africa's boundaries and borderlands are products of historical contestations and negotiations. In line with this argument, I show that the contestations and other interactions that take place both in and away from this in-between space either produce or fuel illegal activities, such as bribing border enforcement agents and cutting South Africa's border fence. These activities do not just exceed the intended master plan of the border but rather encourage and promote border jumping. Furthermore, instead of viewing the Zimbabwe–South Africa boundary as simply a marker of territorial and political limits between the two states, this book provides a nuanced analysis of this border as a socially constructed space where local and global forces converge to produce history.[12]

Border Jumping as an Analytical Concept

Just a decade ago it was almost the convention in migration studies to use the phrase *illegal migration* in reference to cross-border movements that did not conform to official channels of moving from one country to another. Since then, the use of this term has become quite controversial. Although many such movements breach some countries' migration laws, scholars, policy makers, journalists, and the public sometimes use the term *illegal migration* in situations where existing laws do not specifically make such movements illegal. The use of this juridical term also implies that people who cross international boundaries without following official channels automatically become criminals who deserve detention, deportation, or other forms of punishment. As Russell King and Daniela DeBono put it, *illegal migration* "carries a pejorative connotation and reveals an explicit criminalisation of the migrant's situation of either entry or residence, or both."[13]

Owing to the controversies surrounding this term, other scholars and the general public have resorted to the use of adjectives such as *informal* or *irregular* when talking about migrants who cross borders without following official channels. However, these terms also suggest that border crossings that do not follow legal or formal channels always take place in a disorderly manner. Furthermore, these terms imply that something is intrinsically wrong, undesirable, or abnormal about people who engage in such movements.[14] In other circles, the same phenomenon is often referred to as *undocumented migration*, which reflects the condition of most migrants who cross borders without presenting or obtaining identity and travel documents at international border posts. However, many migrants classified as undocumented do have documents, except that "they just aren't the right ones for where they are living and what they are doing."[15] Equally problematic are terms such as *unauthorized* and *unpermitted*, which are in popular use among scholars, journalists, migrants rights advocates, and policy makers. Border crossings that avoid official channels usually take place without official authorization; however, it is also quite common for border agents to facilitate such movements in return for monetary rewards and other kinds of favors.

In this book I use the term *border jumping* to refer to border crossings that avoid officially designated channels of movement from Zimbabwe to South Africa. Although this term also comes across as somewhat derogatory and thus controversial, I use it here without any negative connotations. While conducting research for this study in 2009 and 2010, I noticed that most border residents, migrant workers, cross-border traders, and other travelers I interacted with commonly used the term *border jumpers* to refer to themselves or their acquaintances who swam across the Limpopo River and jumped over the fence on the South African side of the border. Such people did not see anything pejorative in the use of this term. Given the livelihood challenges that Zimbabweans faced during the first decade of the twenty-first century, being able to evade official controls at the border was associated with a sense of defiance. There was something heroic about being a border jumper in this region. More important, border jumping is increasingly becoming a popular concept among other scholars of migration in Southern Africa.[16]

By using this contemporary, "vernacular" term, my objective is to understand multiple perspectives of the contestations that produced and sustained a historical phenomenon that I explore in this book. Unlike other terms, which give the impression that something is abnormal about border crossings that avoid official channels, *border jumping* makes it possible to simultaneously capture both the state's concerns and the sentiments of nonstate actors who often challenge the legitimacy of borders and state-centered efforts of controlling movements between countries. In a similar fashion, terms such as *clandestine crossings* and *illicit flows* are also common among migration scholars. These terms could imply viewing movements from the state's perspective while concurrently considering the views of the migrant workers, transnational traders, and other travelers who take pride in evading official measures of controlling cross-border mobility.[17] However, they give the impression that border crossings that happen outside of official channels are hidden away from state authorities.

I also find *border jumping* the most appropriate term for exploring the changes and continuities in the nature of "illegal" border crossings that I explore in this book. In the first three chapters, I use this term to reference movements of people who left colonial Zimbabwe without identity documents and travel permits at a time when South African authorities did not require foreign Africans to produce such documents to enter the country. This was the case during the twenty years between the British conquest of Zimbabwe in 1890 and the formation of the Union of South Africa in 1910 and throughout much of the period before 1960. During much of that early period, Southern Rhodesian authorities deployed legal and quasilegal measures in an effort to restrict cross-Limpopo mobility. Their counterparts in South Africa leaned toward an open border policy by not actively seeking to restrict immigration from colonial Zimbabwe and other areas in the region.[18] From Southern Rhodesia's perspective, people who left the country during this period without travel permits did so in contravention of the law. For this reason, Southern Rhodesian state officials, business owners, and ordinary colonists used the term *illegal migrants* to refer to such people. However, those movements did not necessarily violate the Transvaal or South Africa's immigration policies. Technically, this movement could be referred to as illegal *emigration* rather than illegal *immigration*.

The book also uses *border jumping* to reference border crossings that occurred when either country introduced laws to regulate cross-border mobility but did very little to enforce them. A good example is when the South African government announced the banning of so-called tropical workers (migrants from areas north of latitude 22° south) in 1913 but continued to welcome such people—before lifting the ban in 1932—if they entered the country through unofficial channels. To a large extent, this approach created a situation similar to what Michel Foucault called "tolerated illegality," which prevailed under the Ancien Regime in France. Although this type of illegality often manifested itself in the form of privileges or exemptions reserved for certain individuals and groups, it was a multifaceted phenomenon. As Foucault puts it, at times tolerated illegality "took the form of massive general non-observance [of laws], which meant that for decades, sometimes for centuries, ordinances could be published and constantly renewed without ever being implemented . . . or quite simply the actual impossibility of imposing the law and apprehending offenders."[19] Sometimes policy contradictions and inconsistencies in the interpretation of laws would make it impossible to enforce laws, creating opportunities for border jumping to thrive. Despite passing laws that illegalized certain kinds of cross-border movements and activities, state officials sometimes saw these phenomena as permissible and even legitimate in some contexts.[20] In South Africa, state officials put some barriers at the front entrance and deliberately left the back door open. They knew that some people entered the country through the back door but did very little to stop them. Consequently, I find it problematic to use *illegal, clandestine, illicit,* or similar terms to describe cross-border movements that did not conform to South African laws during this period.

I also use *border jumping* in reference to border crossings that openly defied South Africa's concerted efforts to control immigration from its northern neighbors during the period from the 1960s to the early 2000s. Successive administrations in South Africa at that time actively sought to control people's movements across the country's borders using a combination of immigration laws and bilateral agreements with neighboring countries. In the same period, state authorities in colonial and postcolonial Zimbabwe deployed various measures in an effort to regulate cross-Limpopo mobility. This effort created a scenario in which the term *illegal migration* could appropriately describe any cross-Limpopo movements that avoided official channels of movements between the two countries. In recognition of this scenario, I occasionally use the term *illegal* when discussing border crossings that were clearly in violation of South Africa's immigration laws during this period. However, I put this term in quotation marks to emphasize the specificity associated with its use in those situations. On rare occasions, I use the term *clandestine*, also in quotation marks, when the nature of movements described warrants the use of that term.

Furthermore, I use *border jumping* to explore the border-crossing experiences of various categories of mobile people (e.g., migrant workers, refugees, cross-border traders, and human smugglers) who, for one reason or the other, did not follow official channels to travel across the Zimbabwe–South Africa border. Whereas other scholars might prefer to treat these groups as subjects of different scholarly discourses, *border jumping* makes it possible to see the common traits in the way people moved between these two countries. For much of the period before the mid-1970s, the majority of people who traveled from Zimbabwe to South Africa through unofficial channels did so in pursuit of employment opportunities in South African mines, farms, and factories. With the outbreak of Zimbabwe's liberation war in the 1970s, the risks of jumping the border—which had become heavily militarized—to look for work in South Africa outweighed the potential gains. However, some residents of Zimbabwe's border districts left the war-torn country and sought refuge among their relatives in South Africa. In this way, the figure of the border jumper changed from a migrant worker to a refugee. As the Zimbabwean economy began to shrink in the early to mid-1990s, cross-border traders became the most visible category of people who traveled between these countries without following official channels. In fact, some of these people crossed the border on a regular basis. Most cross-border shoppers tended to spend only a day or two (sometimes even a few hours) in South Africa. To call such people *migrants* and to characterize their movements between the two countries as *migration* is problematic. I use the term *border jumping* to emphasize the point that such people crossed the border without following the official channels, despite the forces that caused them to travel to South Africa and the length of time they stayed there. They did, indeed, jump the border.

Of Contested Borders and Enforcement Regimes

As of August 2019, about two thirds of the United Nations's 193 member countries were embroiled in territorial disputes of various magnitudes.[21] This means that a large number of geopolitical boundaries were sites of conflicts. If we factor in disputes involving nonstate actors, the number of contested borders will surely rise. I doubt that any geopolitical boundary is free of contestation. Some border contestations or disputes have resulted in widely publicized diplomatic standoffs or military confrontations, whereas many others have escaped public attention. This is because borders in different regions of the world have different statuses in global politics. In addition, the causes of border conflict vary from one locale or region to another. Nevertheless, certain attributes of geopolitical boundaries put them at the center of various kinds of disputes and conflicts that the world has witnessed since the prevailing notions of nation-states with strictly defined boundaries were created in the 1648 Spanish–Dutch Treaty of Westphalia.[22] A quick overview of some of those attributes will help frame discussion of historical contestations over the Zimbabwe–South Africa border in a broader theoretical context.

It is important to note that the majority of borders in today's world came out of violent and coercive processes of nation-state building. As Oscar Martinez observed, "history demonstrates that few boundaries have been created as a result of peaceful negotiations; power politics, military pressures, and warfare have been the determining factors in most cases."[23] This is as true of the United States–Mexico border as it is of boundaries in many parts of Africa, Asia, Latin America, and Europe, where borders have been made and remade as empires and states (large and small) competed and fought for their own existence. Apart from, and partly because of, the coercion that is usually involved in making boundaries, states in many parts of the world deploy armed personnel, walls, and fences along their boundaries. Such measures do not simply serve as physical reminders of the state's presence; they remind the border people and passersby about the state's commitment to exercising its power through violent means.[24] It is also quite common—especially in the current era, characterized by the US-led global campaigns against terrorism—for states to use intrusive surveillance mechanisms to enforce their borders. Robert Pallitto and Josiah Heyman argue that the current "amplified border security regime" has generated debate not simply because of its intrusive nature but also because it has deepened inequalities, as different categories of mobile people are often treated differently at security checkpoints in various places.[25]

In addition to using bilateral and sometimes multilateral agreements to control cross-border mobility, most modern states deploy legal statutes and other kinds of regulatory frameworks. Measures of controlling cross-border mobility not only impose barriers to movements across space but also invariably illegalize and even criminalize certain forms of cross-border activities.[26] For example, it is currently a standard requirement for people to carry passports or other forms of travel documents with visas or permits before they can cross international boundaries. Therefore, anyone who crosses an international boundary without presenting their travel documents for inspection by state officials at a port of entry risks being classified as an "illegal migrant" unless they apply for asylum or other forms of protection. In this respect, some countries treat "illegal" border crossings as criminal offences punishable not just by deportation but also by jail terms or fines. Although nothing appears to be wrong with countries enforcing their laws, migration control policies do not always reflect the interests of minority populations who might not have enough political capital to influence policy formulation. Such people usually find other channels, which may not be legal or formal, to express their opposition to specific measures of border enforcement.[27]

As geographical margins of state systems, borders usually mark spaces of multiple and often competing sovereignties. Heather Nicol and Julian Minghi note that borders are "at the skin of the state at the same time that they are literally and rhetorically at its heart."[28] As Benedikt Korf and Timothy Raeymaekers point out, borders are the "meeting points of clashing ideological projects, through which metropolises and indigenous populations legitimize their claims to political space."[29] In some cases, this scenario provides fertile conditions for tensions to grow between states and communities in border zones that may feel excluded from major decision-making processes; it also sometimes causes tensions between states on opposite sides of the border. The latter outcome is very likely to occur in situations where interstate boundaries are vaguely defined. For example, some of Africa's boundaries that appear on paper are either unmarked on the ground or defined by invisible boundary markers, beacons, small rivers, or other geophysical features that barely present barriers for cross-border travelers. Others are virtually unguarded or guarded by personnel of only one of the two or more countries sharing a border. At times, such personnel may be stationed in "border" towns or other locations far away from the actual boundary.[30]

Some borders are sites of friction because they are not aligned with community-based notions of boundaries. This is the case with most interstate boundaries in Africa, which came out of the European conquest and partition of the continent in the late nineteenth century. As Achille Mbembe argues, precolonial African societies "were not delimited by boundaries in the classical sense of the term, but rather by an imbrication of multiple spaces constantly joined, disjoined, and recombined through wars, conquests, and the mobility of goods and persons."[31] Some scholars refer to this as "mental mapping" to emphasize the idea that boundaries and maps existed in Africa before a group of European powers (mainly Britain, France, Portugal, Germany, Belgium, and Italy) invaded the continent.[32] However, the impact of colonial rule on notions of borders, border enforcement, and cross-border mobility in Africa should not be underestimated. The colonists went to Africa with the Westphalian ideas of strictly defined geopolitical boundaries. To make matters worse, the process of redrawing Africa's boundaries, which the colonists legitimized through the Berlin Act of 1885 (a product of the 1884–85 Berlin Conference), barely took into consideration the African people's interests and conceptions of states and borders.

In saying this, I do not seek to refute Paul Nugent's and other important studies, which show that the African people, in different parts of the continent, embraced colonial boundaries early on and contributed in several ways to their making.[33] What is clear, though, is that the European partitioning of Africa resulted in a mishmash of boundaries that either cut across preexisting cultural communities or grouped together people who previously belonged to different polities. For example, the partition of what was known as Yorubaland in West Africa affected the precolonial kingdoms of Sabe, Ketu, and Ifonyin, whose leaders ended up in the French colony of Dahomey (now Benin) while most of their followers became part of British Nigeria.[34] A similar scenario played out among groundnut cultivators in the Senegambia region where colonial boundaries destabilized preexisting land tenure systems by separating people from their lands. As Ken Swindell notes, some groundnut cultivators found themselves in the British territory of the Gambia while their lands became part of the French colony of Senegal, on the other side of the border.[35] The East African region also has several cases of groups and "nations" that were divided by colonial boundaries, with the Somalis in four different countries (present-day Somalia, Kenya, Ethiopia, and Djibouti) being an obvious example.[36] As colonial states evolved, the European notions of boundaries became entrenched through the implementation of laws and policies that sought to restrict African people's mobility. In this context, people who consciously or otherwise defied colonial orders and bypassed official channels when crossing interstate boundaries became classified as "illegal migrants." Despite the end of European rule in Africa, colonial boundaries remained in place except for minor adjustments here and there. As such, "illegal migration" continued to be a challenge in many parts of the continent where interstate disputes and wars over boundaries abounded.[37]

The Zimbabwe–South Africa border fits very well into this theoretical framework in that the border emerged and evolved as simultaneously troublesome and troubled. Like the majority of interstate boundaries in Africa, this border emerged with the European colonization of the continent. My analysis of the story of border jumping from Zimbabwe to South Africa begins with the British conquest of Zimbabwe—the event that produced this boundary. Evidence shows that the precolonial inhabitants of the Limpopo Valley used stone walls to enforce boundaries, suggesting that they knew something about border jumping; however, the dynamics and significance of this phenomenon changed following the British conquest of the Zimbabwean plateau in 1890.[38] This development did not simply lead to the loss of freedom among the inhabitants of what became Southern Rhodesia; it also resulted in the reconfiguration of the Limpopo River from an ordinary stream to a juridical divide between the British-controlled territory of Southern Rhodesia and the Transvaal (South Africa Republic) under the control of the Boer (Afrikaner) descendants of Dutch sailors who settled at the cape in 1652.

Similar to the West African cases of Yorubaland and Senegambia, this development divided the Venda, Shangaan, Sotho, and other groups astride the Limpopo River into two polities with competing sovereignties. Given this background, the border did not always mean the same thing to policy makers on opposite sides of the Limpopo. From the mid-1890s to the late 1950s, for example, policy makers in Southern Rhodesia deployed several strategies to restrict migration to South Africa while their counterparts across the border covertly and overtly encouraged the free movement of people across the entire region of Southern Africa. People from communities astride the Limpopo, who previously moved freely back and forth across the river, contested the border by disobeying state-sponsored measures of migration control. In doing so, the border people were joined by others from communities further up in Southern Rhodesia, Nyasaland (now Malawi), Mozambique, and other areas who responded to the emerging cash-based (colonial) economies by seeking higher-wage jobs in South Africa.[39]

With the militarization of antiapartheid and anticolonial struggles in both countries in the 1960s, the dynamics of border contestations and cross-border movements shifted. The fear of infiltration by Umkhonto we Sizwe fighters made policy makers and employers in South Africa view migrants from north of the Limpopo as a security threat rather than as a source of cheap labor. They therefore sought ways of working with their counterparts in Southern Rhodesia who also felt threated by unregulated movements of Africans in the region. However, the two countries' newly found common ground cracked in 1980 when the shift from white-minority rule to independence in Zimbabwe severed their friendship. Soon thereafter, the South African government constructed an electrified fence along the border between the two countries. With the end of apartheid rule in South Africa in 1994, relations between the two countries improved somewhat. However, the economic challenges that prevailed in Zimbabwe, and that resulted in hundreds of thousands of its citizens moving to South Africa, have made it difficult for the countries to see the border from the same perspective. As policy makers in these countries continued to quarrel over control of cross-Limpopo mobility during the first decade of the twenty-first century, border jumping emerged as a salient feature of the Zimbabwe–South Africa border culture.

Border Jumpers and the Search for Livelihood

Border jumping, like other forms of mobility, often involves the movement of much more than human beings. Sometimes border jumpers smuggle drugs, guns, and other controlled substances across borders. Quite often, this phenomenon also involves cutting border fences, using forged documents, giving bribes to border officials, and performing many other activities that are legally prohibited in many countries. As a result, in addition to being illegalized and criminalized, border jumping is often viewed with disdain and is sometimes regarded as pathological to the existence of law and order. In some cases, border jumpers are also viewed as victims of restrictive measures of controlling migration in many countries and regions of the world.[40] Although viewing border jumpers as either criminals or victims helps formulate policy interventions, too much focus on either or both of these perspectives occludes other important dynamics of this phenomenon.

In her ethnographic analysis of the forces that gave rise to what she calls "fiscal disobedience" in the Chad basin, Janet Roitman reminds us about the importance of exploring "the reasoning that leads one to engage in illegal practices—or more distinctly, to maintain the status of illegality."[41] In other words, researchers should seek to understand the motives, desires, and long-term goals as well as the agency and creativity of people who engage in this practice. To do that effectively means recognizing that border jumpers are, first and foremost, individuals who are determined to "seize control of their own lives and . . . struggle to establish their own destiny."[42] In line with this view, my work examines how the dynamics of border jumping shifted at various moments from the border's inception in the 1890s to 2010. I show that during the early years of the border's existence, people from areas close to the Limpopo sought to continue preexisting patterns of movement across the river and made up the majority of border jumpers. As the cash-based colonial economy became more entrenched, from the second decade of the twentieth century onward, many people left Southern Rhodesia (through unofficial channels) in search of higher wages and better working conditions in South Africa. When the anticolonial struggles in Zimbabwe turned into full-scale war in the 1960s, most people who jumped the border did so mainly in search of protection in South Africa. As the country's economy began to shrink in the 1990s, cross-border traders (mostly women) made up the majority of border jumpers. Despite wide differences in their premigration status, most people who crossed the Zimbabwe–South Africa border through unofficial channels over the period studied in this book viewed border jumping as a source of opportunity for a better livelihood.

In exploring the shifting dynamics of border jumping between these countries over the past 120 years, I discuss how different regimes of border enforcement and migration control affected differently positioned travelers. Regardless of where a migrant originated, it was crucial to know the routes that went to the border and to figure out how to avoid arrest and other risks. As Akin Fadahunsi and Peter Rosa observed in their study of smuggling across the Nigeria–Benin border, border jumpers had to acquire a certain level of knowledge about both countries' migration control policies in order to evade them.[43] More important, border jumpers needed to know the border landscape and especially where and how to cross the Limpopo River during the rainy season when the water level made it difficult to cross willy-nilly. Each generation of border jumpers came up with strategies that helped people overcome the kinds of challenges they faced along the way. Some strategies succeeded, but others did not work as anticipated.

During much of the period before the 1960s, the most common strategy that travelers used was to follow "secret" footpaths and crossing points that the police and other state functionaries in Southern Rhodesia found difficult to control. For example, when the South African government announced its highly contested ban on "tropical workers" in 1913, some migrants from Southern Rhodesia had to cross into Mozambique's southern districts where they posed as "Portuguese natives" to obtain official documents that allowed them to work in South Africa. A similar scenario unfolded along Zimbabwe's border with Botswana (then known by its colonial name of Bechuanaland), which was not as strictly controlled as the Limpopo boundary. Some people crossed into Bechuanaland and used various strategies to obtain identity documents, purporting to be from that country originally before proceeding to the Transvaal or some other place in South Africa. In some of the cases that I discuss in chapter 3, border jumpers paid drivers of freight trains to disguise their "unauthorized" passengers as part of the crew. In doing so, border jumpers created and utilized what Charles van Onselen refers to as "intelligence networks" to escape from forced labor, low wages, and poor working conditions in Southern Rhodesia.[44]

The strategies of border jumping changed significantly in the post-1960s period, in large part due to shifts in South Africa's migration control policies. Although border jumpers continued to use some of the existing routes and networks, they devised new ways of overcoming an increasingly hardened border. This approach developed particularly after the South African government installed an electrified fence and deployed armed personnel along the borderline. The border jumpers might have easily studied and mastered the routines of the border patrol units, which could not cover the entire stretch of the border at all times, but the electrified fence posed a real danger to people trying to cross the border at places other than the official check points. Through sheer resilience, some border jumpers dug holes under the fence and crawled into South Africa. Others threw blankets, clothes, or other nonconductive materials on the fence and climbed over it, whereas the more cunning ones used wire cutters to create holes in the fence and slip through. As already suggested, it was also common for migrants to utilize the services of informal transport operators and other people who smuggled them across the border, often with the help of corrupt state functionaries. Each individual's decision to use any of these strategies was informed not just by his or her specific situation but also by his or her own understanding of the benefits and risks associated with border jumping.

In examining these strategies and others used by travelers, this book presents the men and women who "illegally" crossed the Zimbabwe–South Africa border as rational thinkers whose actions were informed by their fears, struggles, and desires.[45] Rather than presenting border jumpers simply as lawbreakers, these strategies show that they were smart, savvy, and able to adapt to changing circumstances in Southern Rhodesia/Zimbabwe, South Africa, and the border zone. By engaging in activities that were prohibited by legal statutes or other policy frameworks, border jumpers not only expressed their disgruntlement with the border and how it was enforced but also challenged the legitimacy of the states that sought to regulate people's mobility across the Limpopo River. In the words of Hastings Donnan and Thomas Wilson, border jumpers threatened "to subvert state institutions by compromising the ability of the institutions to control their self-defined domain."[46] This is not to say that subaltern agency (in the form of border jumpers' ingenuity) alone gave rise to border jumping in this region. This phenomenon emerged and thrived against the backdrop of competing interests of and contradictory interactions among travelers, state functionaries, and other actors both in and away from the border zone.

Structure of the Book

Although chronology is key to understanding the story I tell in this book, each chapter is focused on a specific regime of migration control that contributed to the historical evolution of border jumping across the Zimbabwe–South Africa border. The first chapter focuses on the two decades between the colonization of the Zimbabwean plateau in 1890 and the formation of the Union of South Africa in 1910—a fragile period of state formation that witnessed the emergence of a Westphalian type of boundary and the advent of state-centered restrictions of mobility between these two countries. I argue that contestations between Southern Rhodesian authorities, who wanted to restrict migration to the Transvaal, and people from communities astride the Limpopo River, who wanted to continue the patterns of mobility that existed before the 1890s, created the phenomenon of border jumping that is currently prevalent in this region. I also show how state controls of cross-Limpopo mobility created incentives for nonstate actors and corrupt state functionaries to earn money by assisting travelers to cross the border through unofficial channels.

The discussion in chapter 2 explores how South Africa's ban on migrant workers from Zimbabwe and other areas north of latitude 22° south (announced in 1913 and lifted in 1932) stirred contestations among officials in different departments of the South African state, between state officials and employers' groups in South Africa, between government officials in South Africa and their counterparts in Southern Rhodesia, and between cross-Limpopo travelers and border enforcement personnel in both countries. I argue that these multisited contestations encouraged and promoted border jumping, which went on to become a defining feature of diplomatic engagements in Southern Africa. Building on this argument, chapter 3 examines how competition for regional labor (from the mid-1930s to the late 1950s) created tensions between Southern Rhodesian authorities, who sought to impose stringent controls of cross-Limpopo mobility, and their counterparts in South Africa, who preferred an open border policy—fueling border jumping between the two countries.

Chapter 4 examines how the intensification of black people's struggles for independence in South Africa and Zimbabwe shifted the dynamics of mobility between these countries. I argue that the securitization of the border, which began in the 1960s and led to the construction of South Africa's border fence along the Limpopo River between 1985 and 1986, did not stop border jumping. Instead, it made this phenomenon more dangerous than before. In the fifth chapter, the discussion advances by examining the dynamics of border jumping across the Zimbabwe–South Africa border from the 1990s to 2010—a period when the flow of mobility between these countries significantly increased. I argue that South African authorities' decision to impose stringent visa conditions on Zimbabwean travelers at a time when the Zimbabwean economy was in distress encouraged contestations, which in turn fueled border jumping as travelers and human smugglers deployed more sophisticated strategies to evade official measures of controlling migration in the region.

In the conclusion, I emphasize the study's significance in understanding historical and contemporary dynamics of border jumping across the Zimbabwe–South Africa border, arguing that this phenomenon is an understudied legacy of the European partitioning of Africa. The concluding chapter also reiterates the view that border jumping as a product of contestations over borders and regimes of border enforcement—not simply as a result of conditions of insecurity in migrants' countries of origin—helps explain why this phenomenon is prevalent in many regions of the world despite huge investments in the construction of border fences, walls, and other measures for controlling people's mobility across international boundaries.

Notes

1. Ruben Andersson, *Illegality, Inc.: Clandestine Migration and the Business of Bordering Europe* (Oakland: University of California Press, 2014); Reece Jones, *Violent Borders: Refugees and the Right to Move* (London: Verso, 2016). See also, *Europe or Die*, directed by Milene Larsson (New York: Vice News, 2015), https://www.vice.com/en_us/article/exqgek/europe-or-die-all-episodes.

2. Given the prevalence of unrecorded movements of people from Zimbabwe to South Africa, Botswana, and other countries in the region, it is hard to know exactly how many people left the country during this period. For further discussion of this, see Alexander Betts,

Survival Migration: Failed Governance and the Crisis of Displacement (Ithaca, NY: Cornell University Press, 2013); Jonathan Crush and Daniel Tevera, eds., *Zimbabwe's Exodus: Crisis, Migration, Survival* (Cape Town: SAMP, 2010); Robyn Leslie, Sandy Johnston, Ann Bernstein, and Riaan de Villiers, eds., *Migration from Zimbabwe: Numbers, Needs and Policy Options* (Johannesburg: Centre for Development and Enterprise, 2008); JoAnn McGregor and Ranka Primorac, eds., *Zimbabwe's New Diaspora: Displacement and the Cultural Politics of Survival* (New York: Bergham, 2010).

3. *Malayitsha* is a noun derived from the verb *layitsha*, which refers to the act of loading stuff into a big container, cart, or vehicle. In this case, *malayitsha* refers to informal transporters of people and goods across the border. *Maguma-guma* derives from *guma-guma*, which denotes the use of crooked ways to achieve one's objectives. In this case, *maguma-guma* refers to people who use treachery, thievery, and violence in their interactions with travelers. See Tinashe Nyamunda, "Cross-Border Couriers as Symbols of Regional Grievance? The Malayitsha Remittance System in Matabeleland, Zimbabwe," *African Diaspora* 7, no.1 (2014): 38–62; Blair Rutherford, "The Politics of Boundaries: The Shifting Terrain of Belonging for Zimbabweans in a South African Border Zone," *African Diaspora* 4, no. 2 (2011): 207–29.

4. I use the term *border jumping* to refer to so-called "illegal migration" in this region because it vernacularizes and decriminalizes the rhetorical overlay of illegal migration and other terms, such as *undocumented migration, illicit migration,* or *irregular migration*. For a more detailed discussion of this term and its use in this book, see the section entitled "Border Jumping as an Analytical Concept" in this introduction.

5. John O. Oucho, "Cross-Border Migration and Regional Initiatives in Managing Migration in Southern Africa," in *Migration in South and Southern Africa: Dynamics and Determinants*, ed. Pieter Kok, Derik Gelderblom, John Oucho, and Johan Van Zyl (Pretoria: Human Science Research Council, 2006); Jonathan Crush, "Migrations Past: An Historical Overview of Cross-border Movements in Southern Africa," in *On Borders: Perspectives on International Migration in Southern Africa*, ed. David A. McDonald (Ontario: SAMP, 2000); Jonathan Klaaren and Jay Ramji, "Inside Illegality: Migration Policing in South Africa after Apartheid," *Africa Today* 48, no. 3 (2001): 35–47; Anthony Minaar and Mike Hough, *Who Goes There?: Perspectives on Clandestine Migration and Illegal Aliens in Southern Africa* (Pretoria: HSRC, 1996); Jonathan Crush, "The Discourse and Dimensions of Irregularity in Post-apartheid South Africa," *International Migration* 37, no. 1 (1999): 125–51; Sally A. Peberdy, "Border Crossings: Small Entrepreneurs and Cross-Border Trade Between South Africa and Mozambique," *Tijdschnft voor Economische en Social Geografie* 91, no. 4 (2000): 361–378; Jens A. Anderson, "Informal Moves, Informal Markets: International Migrants and Traders from Mzimba District, Malawi," *African Affairs* 105, no. 420 (2006): 375–97; Darshan Vigneswaran, Tesfalem Araia, Colin Hoag, and Xolani Tshabalala, "Criminality or Monopoly? Informal Immigration Enforcement in South Africa," *Journal of Southern African Studies*, 36, no. 2 (2010): 465–81. See also, Francis B. Nyamnjoh, *Insiders and Outsiders: Citizenship and Xenophobia in Contemporary Southern Africa* (Dakar: Council for the Development of Social Science Research in Africa, 2006); Jonathan Crush, Abel Chikanda, and Caroline Skinner, eds., *Mean Streets: Migration, Xenophobia and Informality in South Africa* (Cape Town: Southern African Migration Project, 2015); Norma Kriger, "The Politics of Legal Status for Zimbabweans in South Africa," in *Zimbabwe's New Diaspora and the Cultural Politics of*

Survival, ed. JoAnn McGregor and Ranka Primorac (New York: Berghahn, 2010); James Muzondidya, "*Makwerekwere*: Migration, Citizenship and Identity among Zimbabweans in South Africa," in McGregor and Primorac, *Zimbabwe's New Diaspora*; Loren Landau, "Transplants and Transients: Idioms of Belonging and Dislocation in Inner-City Johannesburg," *African Studies Review* 49, no. 2 (2006): 125–45.

6. See Hussein Solomon, *Of Myths and Migration: Illegal Immigration into South Africa* (Pretoria: University of South Africa, 2003); David A. McDonald and Jonathan Crush, eds., *Destinations Unknown: Perspectives on the Brain Drain* (Pretoria: Africa Institute and SAMP, 2002); Rudo Gaidzanwa, *Voting with Their Feet: Migrant Zimbabwean Nurses and Doctors in the Era of Structural Adjustment* (Uppsala: Nordiska Institute, 1999); David A. McDonald, Lovemore Zinyama, John Gay, Fion de Vletter, and Robert Mattes, "Guess Who's Coming to Dinner: Migration from Lesotho, Mozambique and Zimbabwe to South Africa," *International Migration Review* 34, no. 3 (2000): 813–41.

7. Sandra Lavenex, "Migration and the EU's New Eastern Border: Between Realism and Liberalism," *Journal of European Public Policy* 8, no. 1 (2001): 24–42; Rob T. Guerette and Ronald V. Clarke, "Border Enforcement, Organized Crime, and Deaths of Smuggled Migrants on the United States–Mexico Border," *European Journal on Criminal Policy and Research* 11, no. 2 (2005): 159–74; Sule Toktas and Hande Selimoglu, "Smuggling and Trafficking in Turkey: An Analysis of EU-Turkey Cooperation in Combating Transnational Organized Crime," *Journal of Balkan and Near Eastern Studies* 14, no. 1 (2012): 135–50.

8. Aurelia Segatti, "Reforming South African Immigration Policy in the Post-apartheid Period (1990–2010)," in *Contemporary Migration to South Africa: A Regional Development Issue,* ed. Aurelia Segatti and Loren B. Landau. (Washington, DC: World Bank, 2011. See also, Democratic Alliance, "Secure Our Borders," https://www.da.org.za/policy /secure-our-borders. See also, News24, "Parts of SA-Zim Border Stolen," July 24, 2009, http:// www.news24.com/Africa/News/Parts-of-SA-Zim-border-stolen-20090724.

9. Joseph Nevins, *Operation Gatekeeper: The Rise of the "Illegal Alien" and the Making of the US-Mexico Boundary* (New York: Routledge, 2002).

10. Andersson, *Illegality, Inc.*, 3.

11. Anthony I. Asiwaju, ed., *Partitioned Africans: Ethnic Relations across Africa's International Boundaries, 1884–1984* (New York: St Martin's Press, 1985); William F. S. Miles, *Hausaland Divided: Colonialism and Independence in Nigeria and Niger* (Ithaca, NY: Cornell University Press, 1994); Paul Nugent and Anthony Asiwaju, eds., *African Boundaries: Barriers, Conduits and Opportunities* (New York: Pinter, 1996); Paul Nugent, *Smugglers, Secessionists and Loyal Citizens on the Ghana-Togo Frontier: The Lie of the Borderlands since 1914* (Oxford: James Currey, 2002).

12. For similar analyses, see Dereje Feyissa and Markus Virgil Hoehne, eds., *Borders and Borderlands as Resources in the Horn of Africa* (Suffolk: James Currey, 2010); David B. Coplan, "Border Show Business and Performing States," in *A Companion to Border Studies,* ed. Thomas M. Wilson, and Hastings Donnan (West Sussex: Blackwell, 2012); Benedikt Korf, and Timothy Raeymakers, eds., *Violence on the Margins: States, Conflict, and Borderlands* (New York: Palgrave Macmillan, 2013).

13. Russell King and Daniela DeBono, "Irregular Migration and the 'Southern European Model' of Migration," *Journal of Mediterranean Studies* 22, no. 1 (2013): 3. See also, Nicholas De Genova, "The Production of Culprits: From Deportability to Detainability in the Aftermath of 'Homeland Security'" *Citizenship Studies,* 11, no. 5 (2007): 421–48; Catherine

Dauvergne, *Making People Illegal: What Globalization Means for Migration and Law* (Cambridge: Cambridge University Press, 2008).

14. For a further discussion of these terms and their usage, see De Genova, "Production of Culprits"; David W. Haines and Karen E. Rosenblum, "Introduction: Problematic Labels, Volatile Issues," in *Illegal Immigration in America: A Reference Handbook,* ed. David W. Haines and Karen E. Rosenblum (Westport: Greenwood, 1999).

15. Haines and Rosenblum, "Introduction: Problematic Labels," 4.

16. See, e.g., Maxim Bolt, *Zimbabwe's Migrants and South Africa's Border Farms: The Roots of Impermanence* (Cambridge: Cambridge University Press, 2015); Josphat Mushongah and Ian Scoones, "Livelihood Change in Rural Zimbabwe over 20 Years" *Journal of Development Studies* 48, 9 (2012): 1241–57; Nedson Pophiwa, "Mobile Livelihoods—The Players Involved in Smuggling of Commodities across the Zimbabwe-Mozambique Border," *Journal of Borderlands Studies* 25, 2 (2010): 65–76; Blair Rutherford, "Zimbabweans Living in the South African Border-Zone: Negotiating, Suffering and Surviving," *Concerned African Scholars Bulletin* 80 (2008): 35–42; Sally Peberdy, "Imagining Immigration: Inclusive Identities and Exclusive Policies in Post-1994 South Africa," *Africa Today* 48, no. 3 (Autumn 2001): 15–32; Crush, "Discourse and Dimensions" and "Fortress South Africa and the Deconstruction of Apartheid's Migration Regime" *Geoforum* 30, no. 1 (1999): 1–11.

17. See, e.g., David Spener, *Clandestine Crossings: Migrants and Coyotes on the Texas-Mexico Border* (Ithaca, NY: Cornell University Press, 2009); Itty Abraham and Willem van Schendel, ed., *Illicit Flows and Criminal Things: States, Borders and the Other Side of Globalization,* (Bloomington: Indiana University Press, 2005); Janet Roitman, *Fiscal Disobedience: An Anthropology of Economic Regulation in Central Africa* (Princeton, NJ: Princeton University Press, 2005); Andersson, *Illegality, Inc.*

18. Bill Paton, *Labour Export Policy in the Development of Southern Africa* (London: Macmillan, 1995); Alois S. Mlambo, "A History of Zimbabwean Migration to 1990," in *Zimbabwe's Exodus: Crisis, Migration, Survival,* ed. Jonathan Crush and Daniel Tevera (Cape Town: SAMP, 2010).

19. Michel Foucault, *Discipline and Punish: The Birth of the Prison,* trans. Alan Sheridan (New York: Vintage, 1995), 82.

20. Janet Roitman, "The Ethics of Illegality in the Chad Basin," in *Law and Disorder in the Postcolony,* ed. Jean Comaroff and John L. Comaroff (Chicago: University of Chicago Press, 2006); and "A Successful Life in the Illegal Realm: Smugglers and Road Bandits in the Chad Basin," in *Readings on Modernity in Africa,* ed. Peter Geschiere, Birgit Meyer, and Peter Pels (London: International African Institute, 2008).

21. United Nations, "Peace and Security," https://www.un.org/en/sections/issues-depth /peace-and-security/. See also, Kathleen Staudt, *Border Politics in a Global Era: Comparative Perspectives* (Lanham, MD: Rowman & Littlefield, 2018).

22. Henk Van Houtum, "The Geopolitics of Borders and Boundaries," *Geopolitics,* 10, no. 4 (2005): 672–679.

23. Oscar J. Martinez, *Troublesome Borders* (Tucson: University of Arizona Press, 2006), 4.

24. Jonathan Goodhand, "Epilogue: The View from the Border," in Korf and Raeymakers, *Violence on the Margins.*

25. Robert Pallitto and Josiah Heyman, "Theorizing Cross-Border Mobility: Surveillance, Security and Identity," *Surveillance and Society* 5, no. 3 (2008): 322.

26. Josue D. Cisneros, *The Border Crossed Us: Rhetorics of Borders, Citizenship and Latina/o Identity* (Tuscaloosa: University of Alabama Press, 2014); Hastings Donnan and Thomas M. Wilson, *Borders: Frontiers of Identity, Nation and State* (New York: Berg, 1999); Dauvergne, *Making People Illegal*.

27. Josiah McC. Heyman, "The Study of Illegality and Legality: Which Way Forward?" *Political and Legal Anthropology Review* 36, 2 (2013): 304–7; Chad Richardson and Rosalva Resendiz, *On the Edge of the Law: Culture, Labor, and Deviance on the South Texas Border* (Austin: University of Texas Press, 2006); Sharam Khosravi, *'Illegal' Traveller: An Auto-ethnography of Borders* (Hampshire: Palgrave Macmillan, 2010).

28. Heather Nicol and Julian Minghi, "The Continuing Relevance of Borders in Contemporary Contexts," *Geopolitics* 10, no. 4 (2005): 681.

29. Benedikt Korf, and Timothy Raeymakers, "Introduction: Border, Frontier and the Geography of Rule at the Margins of the State," in *Violence on the Margins*, 14.

30. Ieuan Griffiths, "Permeable Boundaries in Africa," in *African Boundaries: Barriers, Conduits and Opportunities,* ed. Paul Nugent, and Anthony Asiwaju (New York: Pinter, 1996); Timothy Mechlinski, "Towards an Approach to Borders and Mobility in Africa," *Journal of Borderlands Studies* 25, no. 2 (2010): 94–106; Roelof J. Kloppers, "Border Crossings: Life in the Mozambique/South Africa Borderland Since 1975," (DPhil Diss., University of Pretoria, 2005).

31. Achille Mbembe, "At the Edge of the World: Boundaries, Territoriality, and Sovereignty in Africa," *Public Culture* 12, no. 1 (2000): 263; Paul Nugent, "Arbitrary Lines and the People's Minds: A Dissenting View on Colonial Boundaries in West Africa," in Nugent and Asiwaju, *African Boundaries*.

32. Ivor Wilks, "On Mentally Mapping Greater Asante: A Study of Time and Motion," *Journal of African History* 33, no. 2 (1992): 175–90. For further discussion of precolonial notions of borders and frontiers in Africa, see Igor Kopytoff, ed., *The African Frontier: The Reproduction of Traditional African Societies* (Bloomington: Indiana University Press, 1987).

33. Nugent, "Arbitrary Lines." See also, Saadia Touval, "Treaties, Borders, and the Partition of Africa," *Journal of African History* 7, no. 2 (1966): 279–93; Joseph C. Anene, *The International Boundaries of Nigeria, 1885–1960: The Framework of an Emergent African Nation* (London: Longman, 1970); Derrick J. Thom, *The Niger-Nigeria Boundary, 1890–1906: A Study of Ethnic Frontiers and a Colonial Boundary* (Athens: Ohio University Center for International Studies, 1975).

34. Anthony I. Asiwaju, *Western Yorubaland Under European Rule 1889–1945* (London: Longman, 1976); Anthony I. Asiwaju, "The Conceptual Framework," in *Partitioned Africans.*

35. Ken Swindell, "Serawoolies, Tillibunkas and Strange Farmers: The Development of Migrant Groundnut Farming along the Gambia River 1848–95," *Journal of African History* 21, no. 1 (1980): 93–104.

36. Said S. Samatar, "The Somali Dilemma: Nation in Search of a State," in *Partitioned Africans.* For more examples of groups that were divided by colonial boundaries in Africa, see Asiwaju, "Partitioned Culture Areas: A Checklist," in *Partitioned Africans*; Feyissa and Hoehne, *Borders and Borderlands;* William F. S. Miles, "Postcolonial Borderland Legacies of Anglo-French Partition in West Africa," *African Studies Review* 58, no. 3 (2015): 191–213; Ghislaine Geloin, "Displacement, Migration, and the Curse of Borders in Francophone West Africa," in *Movements, Borders and Identities in Africa,* ed. Toyin Falola and Aribidesi Usman (New York: University of Rochester Press, 2009).

37. William F. S. Miles, *Scars of Partition: Postcolonial Legacies in French and British Borderlands*, (Lincoln: University of Nebraska, 2014); Saadia Touval, *The Boundary Politics of Independent Africa* (Cambridge, Massachusetts: Harvard University, 1972).

38. For detailed discussions of precolonial borders and walls in the Limpopo Valley, see Innocent Pikirayi, *The Zimbabwe Culture: Origins and Decline of Southern Zambezian States* (Walnut Creek, CA: AltaMira, 2001); Thomas N. Huffman, *Snakes and Crocodiles: Power and Symbolism in Ancient Zimbabwe* (Johannesburg: Witwatersrand University, 1996); Mphaya H. Nemudzivhadi, "The Attempts by Makhado to Revive the Venda Kingdom, 1864–1895" (PhD diss., Potchefstroom University for Christian Higher Education, 1998). See also, Andrew MacDonald, "Colonial Trespassers in the Making of South Africa's International Borders, 1900 to c.1950," (PhD diss., University of Cambridge, 2012); Enocent Msindo, *Ethnicity in Zimbabwe: Transformations in Kalanga and Ndebele Societies, 1860–1990* (Rochester: University of Rochester Press, 2012).

39. Patrick Harries, *Work, Culture, and Identity: Migrant Laborers in Mozambique and South Africa, c1860–1910* (Portsmouth, NH: Heinemann, 1994); Jonathan Crush, Alan Jeeves, and David Yudelman, *South Africa's Labor Empire: A History of Black Migrancy to the Gold Mines* (Boulder, CO: Westview, 1991); Paton, *Labour Export Policy*.

40. Crush, "Discourse and Dimensions." The same is true with several other informal economic activities such as smuggling, prostitution and street vending, which often exist outside the official regulatory frameworks. For further discussions, see Peberdy, "Border Crossings"; Janet MacGaffey and Remmy Bazenguissa-Ganga, *Congo-Paris: Transnational Traders on the Margins of the Law* (Bloomington: Indiana University Press, 2000); Itty Abraham and Willem van Schendel, "Introduction: The Making of Illicitness," in van Schendel and Abraham, *Illicit Flows and Criminal Things*; Chad Richardson and Michael J. Pisani, *The Informal and Underground Economy of the South Texas Border* (Austin: University of Texas Press, 2012).

41. Roitman, *Fiscal Disobedience*.

42. David Newbury "From 'Frontier' to 'Boundary': Some Historical Roots of Peasant Strategies of Survival in Zaire," in *The Crisis in Zaire: Myths and Realities*, ed. George Nzongola-Ntalaja (Trenton, NJ: Africa World, 1986), 96.

43. Akin Fadahunsi and Peter Rosa, "Entrepreneurship and Illegality: Insights from the Nigerian Cross-border Trade" *Journal of Business Venturing*, 17 (2002): 402. See also, Donna Flynn, "We are the Border: Identity, Exchange, and the State Along the Benin-Nigeria Border," *American Ethnologist* 24, no. 2 (1997): 311–30; Nick Megoran, Gael Raballand, and Jerome Bouyjon, "Performance, Representation and the Economics of Border Control in Uzbekistan," *Geopolitics* 10, no. 4 (2005): 712–40.

44. Charles van Onselen, *Chibaro: African Mine Labour in Southern Rhodesia, 1900 to 1933* (London: Pluto Press 1976).

45. For similar analyses in other regions of the world, see Spener, *Clandestine Crossings*; Khosravi, *'Illegal' Traveller*.

46. Donnan and Wilson, *Borders: Frontiers of Identity*, 88.

1 Colonial Statecraft and the Rise of Border Jumping

In a study of smuggling across the border between Rwanda and the Democratic Republic of the Congo, David Newbury argues that the shift from the idea of a frontier to a geopolitical boundary resulted in the illegalization of activities that had been considered perfectly reasonable and normal.[1] To emphasize this point, Newbury says that the nature of the social and economic activities in the region did not change, "but a profound shift in the political/ideological context [occurred] . . . so that the same activities of at least 200 years' duration and undoubtedly longer than that are classified in a new manner by the state system."[2] A similar scenario unfolded along the Zimbabwe–South Africa border following the British conquest of the Zimbabwean plateau in 1890. This development, which took place at the height of the European scramble for Africa, led to the reconfiguration of the Limpopo River as an interstate boundary and the beginning of state-centered controls of people's movements between Southern Rhodesia (Zimbabwe) and the Transvaal (South Africa). As the region grappled with new ideas of borders and territoriality, people who crossed the Limpopo without following officially designated channels came to be regarded as illegal or clandestine migrants. This view was a huge departure from the previous scenario where communities astride the Limpopo moved back and forth across the river without fear of breaking any state-centered protocol.

Before the colonization of Zimbabwe, the Limpopo Valley had witnessed the development of sociocultural and economic networks that thrived on cross-Limpopo mobility. Among other factors, the existence of the Venda people on both sides of the river helped make cross-Limpopo connections stronger. For example, people from the Zoutpansberg area on the southern side of the Limpopo used to send messengers to the Marungudze (Malungudze) shrine in Beitbridge District to seek spiritual guidance in times of famines, wars, and other difficulties.[3] It was also common (and still is) for the Venda people to marry across the Limpopo. As a result, some men moved permanently onto one side of the river, whereas others established multiple homes (with multiple wives and children) on both sides of the Limpopo. Some parents also used to send their adolescent sons and daughters across the Limpopo to attend initiation schools. Regardless of the side of the river where the initiation rites and classes took place, the initiates sometimes spent more than six weeks in the home area of the elders who presided over their training.[4] In addition, people often moved their livestock back and forth across the Limpopo in search of pastures. Sometimes cattle herders had to migrate temporarily and spend several months in camps along the banks of the Limpopo regardless of which side of the river they came from. Whether people moved from one side of the Limpopo River to another as cattle herders, initiates, brides, bridegrooms, or mere visitors, the Venda did not think of themselves as intruders, foreigners, or even migrants because they regarded the region as unified geographically, socially, and politically.[5]

In ways similar to the Tonga, Nambya and other communities astride the Zambezi River—the focus of JoAnn McGregor's *Crossing the Zambezi*— the Venda developed an intimate understanding of the Limpopo Valley and the river's flowing patterns.[6] In addition to acquiring the skills to build make-shift canoes to cross the Limpopo in flood, they had identified low-risk crossing points, which avoided parts of the river with crocodile-infested pools. In that respect, the Venda knew how and where to cross the Limpopo River during those times of the year when it was dangerous to cross (usually December to March). They also understood the behaviors of different kinds of animals that roamed the valley before construction of the Gonarezhou and Kruger national parks on the Zimbabwean and South African sides, respectively, of the border. As David Siyasongwe, a resident of Beitbridge, pointed out, "if they [the Venda] saw elephants from a distance they would throw dust in the air to determine the direction of the wind. Knowing that the elephant's sense of smell is much stronger than its sense of sight, they would make sure to walk on the side where the wind was blowing."[7] In this way, the Limpopo, which the Venda referred to as *Vhembe*, was not a boundary per se but "just one of the perennial streams that flowed across the Venda territory on their way to the Indian Ocean."[8] With no state-based controls of mobility, the Limpopo's flowing patterns determined when and how people moved back and forth across it.

In the same vein, the Afrikaners who occupied what became the Transvaal colony in northern South Africa in the 1850s viewed the Limpopo not as a marker of territorial limits of their state but as a river within a frontier zone. Commenting on this scenario, Stefanus Du Toit—an Afrikaner participant at the 1883–84 London Convention that restored the Transvaal's autonomy after brief colonization by the British—wrote that although "the Transvaal bound itself to enter into no treaty with the natives to the east and west of the Republic without the sanction of England, the north was, for good reasons, left unmentioned."[9] In Du Toit's thinking, which reflects that of many of his contemporaries, not using the Limpopo to define the northern boundary of the Transvaal meant that the Afrikaners had leeway to expand their territorial possessions and influence as far northward as they wanted. When large-scale gold mining operations began in the Witwatersrand area in the 1880s, the Transvaal officials did not see the need to restrict the entry of migrant workers from the Zimbabwean plateau, Mozambique, Malawi, Zambia, Tanzania, and other places. However, state officials actively sought to restrict the movements of people from the Transvaal to the Cape Colony and Natal, which were under the control of British settlers. Given that the British also tried to regulate people's movements across the borders of the Cape Colony, it is no surprise that "illegal" migration became an issue of concern in pre-1890 South Africa.[10] However, such concerns did not apply to movements across the Limpopo River, which were generally unregulated.

Colonial Conquest and the Rise of the Wage-Based Economy in Zimbabwe

Without the British South Africa Company (BSAC)-sponsored occupation of Zimbabwe on behalf of Britain in September 1890, the history of "illegal" migration across the country's border with South Africa would have been different. Although previous centuries had witnessed other developments that stirred things up in the Limpopo Valley—such as the rise and fall of the Venda Kingdom and the settlement of the Shangani, Ndebele, Sotho, and other groups—the conquest of Zimbabwe significantly changed the character of the region.[11] The greatest impact came from policies implemented by the BSAC administration that disrupted livelihood strategies on the Zimbabwean plateau and changed the meaning of cross-Limpopo mobility. The company's labor mobilization efforts, which introduced the idea of wage-based livelihoods across the territory, were particularly disruptive. Although some people, especially those from the country's border districts, had started working in the Transvaal mines before the 1890s, labor migration was not a major livelihood strategy for Zimbabweans then. It was only after the BSAC sponsored occupation of the territory that wage-based migrations became common among Zimbabweans.[12]

As a profit-oriented entity, the BSAC directed the bulk of the colony's capital resources toward the labor-intensive sectors of mining and agriculture. In that respect, most policies that the company administration implemented in the early years of colonial rule sought to create a reservoir of cheap labor. For example, the company authorities introduced a "native" taxation apparatus that required Africans to pay different kinds of taxes (e.g., hut tax, dog tax, poll tax) with cash. This requirement was intended to force Africans to look for employment in various sectors of the emerging colonial economy so they could earn the money to pay taxes. Whereas most Africans on the Zimbabwean plateau previously worked only to produce food for their subsistence, they now had to work to earn money. The BSAC-administered taxation was also "arbitrary and irregular, appearing more like the levy of a tribute than the collection of a civil tax, as marauding bands of Native Department levies despoiled villages and districts of their crops and livestock."[13] As a technology of governance, taxation not only raised revenue for the colonial administration but also dragged Africans into the wage-based capitalist economy on an unequal footing.

In addition to cash taxation, the early 1890s witnessed the introduction of identity documents and travel passes in Southern Rhodesia. This process began with the BSAC administration compiling what it called the *Registration of Natives Regulations* in 1895. Borrowing several aspects of the pass systems that existed in the Transvaal and other parts of South Africa, the 1895 regulations stipulated that every African male who entered a township or a mining area—both of which were dominated by white settlers—must be registered and in possession of a permit (or pass) authorizing him to be in those areas. The regulations also introduced two categories of passes: one for Africans seeking employment in industrial and mining towns and the other for those taking up jobs as domestic servants in white people's homes anywhere in the colony. Along with these requirements, the administration appointed a "registrar of natives" with the responsibility of issuing passes to Africans as they moved from one part of the colony to another.[14] In most modern states, identification documents serve to distinguish between citizens and noncitizens, whereas in early colonial Zimbabwe, they were mostly used to trace the movement of Africans. As Vazira Fazila-Yacoobali Zamindar argues in her study of the chaos that emanated from the partition of India in 1947, these permits were not mere documents; they were bureaucratic tools for imposing limits on the colonized people.[15]

The introduction of the 1895 regulations coincided with the beginning of a territory-wide land dispossession and community restructuring process that gained momentum after the Ndebele–Shona revolts of 1896–97. As part of this process, the BSAC administration set aside large tracts of the colony's prime lands for white settlers to use as farms and established "native reserves" mostly in areas with low rainfall and poor soils. With total disregard of preexisting community settlement patterns and ethnolinguistic boundaries, the colonists then forcibly relocated tens of thousands of Africans into the reserves. Land dispossession and forced relocations led not only to the loss of arable lands but also to overcrowding, overgrazing, and a general sense of insecurity among Africans in the reserves. It also helped to emasculate the local population to ensure their complete subjugation. More important, these policies created a pool of cheap labor for the emerging colonial economy.[16] Without stable and dependable sources of livelihood, many Africans were forced to look for work on the mines, farms, and other industries in Southern Rhodesia.

It was also common for colonial officials to inflict pain on African people's bodies to force them to sign up for jobs in different sectors of the economy. For example, while bragging about his use of coercion in dealing with Africans in 1895, the native commissioner for Hartley District wrote, "I am forcing the natives of this district to work sorely against their will."[17] As Harry Thomson noted in 1898, this meant flogging Africans to make sure they went out to work. In this regard, Thomson wrote, "I was told that if a boy will not work, or tries to run away, the usual thing is to take him to the native commissioner, and have him given twenty-five, and I found that the word 'twenty five' said in English to any of the boys was sufficient to make them grin in a sickly way—they quite understood what it meant."[18]

In an attempt to supplement local supplies of labor, which kept fluctuating for the larger part of the first and second decades of colonial rule, Southern Rhodesian authorities made arrangements to import foreign workers. Like their counterparts in the Transvaal, Natal, and other parts of South Africa, colonial officials intended to import indentured workers from India and China. However, negative stereotypes of Indians, deriving mostly from the European–Indian interactions in other parts of the world, stirred an anti-Indian attitude among white settlers in Southern Rhodesia and led to the discontinuance of the arrangements.[19] Another arrangement meant to facilitate the importation of Arabs, Shamis, and Somali workers from Djibouti to Southern Rhodesia was also implemented but only briefly because it failed to achieve desired results. Ultimately, Southern Rhodesia turned to its neighboring territories, particularly Nyasaland (Malawi), Northern Rhodesia (Zambia), and Mozambique. However, many early migrant workers from these areas did not stay long in Southern Rhodesia, which they considered a temporary stopover on their way to better-paying jobs in South Africa.[20]

Given that cross-Limpopo mobility had existed for centuries prior to 1890, it might appear unfair to blame the British occupation of Zimbabwe for the prevalence of border jumping across the country's border with South Africa. However, the point I am making in this chapter and throughout the entire book is that the imposition of colonial rule in Zimbabwe changed the political, economic, and ideological context in which cross-Limpopo mobility took place. Although the Venda, Sotho, Ndebele, and other groups of people in Zimbabwe's border districts continued to visit their relatives across the river, which had become a colonial boundary, they did so under different conditions. Because the Limpopo was no longer just another river, the act of crossing it no longer meant the same thing. In addition, the imposition of new demands on life that came with the introduction of a cash-based economy induced new forms of mobility across the Limpopo. In this respect, people used cross-Limpopo mobility in a bid to escape taxation, poverty, overcrowding, or other conditions of insecurity in the native reserves.[21]

The Beginning of State-Centered Restrictions
of Cross-Limpopo Mobility

In what became the first major state-based attempt to stop Zimbabweans from moving to South Africa or to any other country, the BSAC administration introduced the Natives Employment Ordinance in 1899. As the president of the Legislative Council pointed out during the Second Reading of the ordinance, the objective was to "meet the representations which have been addressed to the Administration as to the necessity of controlling and regulating the employment of natives, especially in regard to those natives induced to leave Rhodesia."[22] Whereas the 1895 regulations focused on the control of African workers' movements within the colony, this ordinance targeted those who intended to seek employment elsewhere. Given that South African mines had emerged as the major employers of migrant workers from Southern Rhodesia and other territories in the region, there is no doubt that the ordinance was meant to control cross-Limpopo mobility. It is also very likely that the "representations" that the president of the Legislative Council referred to came from white settlers who owned mines and commercial farms where demand for cheap labor rose steeply during the first decade of colonial rule.[23] Over the years, employers' organizations became major players in the politics of migration control in Southern Rhodesia and South Africa.

A key provision of this piece of legislation was that it required every person working as a labor agent in Southern Rhodesia to register and obtain a license and to provide a security deposit and keep the chief native commissioner's office informed about his operations. While the annual cost of a license to recruit people for work within the colony was set at £1, labor agents who wanted to recruit workers for employment outside Southern Rhodesia were required to pay £50 annually. As for a security deposit, a person applying for a permit to recruit Africans for the local employers had to pay £100, and those intending to engage workers for employment outside the territory paid £250.[24] Just by looking at the differences between these figures, one can tell that the officials wanted to encourage the recruiting of labor for local employers while making it hard for labor agents to send workers out of the colony. The ordinance also gave the Native Affairs Department officials, especially the native commissioners, the authority to apprehend labor agents who recruited people for work in South Africa without the proper licenses. Thus, in addition to laying out the procedures and requirements for employment of Africans within the colony, the Natives Employment Ordinance discouraged the recruitment of locals for work outside Southern Rhodesia. In this way, the ordinance marked the beginning of regulatory frameworks that fueled border jumping across the Zimbabwe–South Africa border.

Yielding to pressure from white settlers who advocated for more stringent controls of Africans' mobility, Southern Rhodesia's Legislative Council introduced the Natives Pass Ordinance in 1902. This legislation did not simply modify previous "native regulations" but caused an overhaul of the colony's native administration system. During the Second Reading of this ordinance in the Legislative Assembly, the attorney general argued that the 1902 pass law was "designed not only to meet the wishes and wants of those interested in the native labour—masters and employers of all kinds, but it was also in the interests of the good governance and proper control of the natives themselves."[25] This statement shows how the interests of business owners began driving Southern Rhodesia's policies toward the local people just as the colonial state was evolving. This outcome is not surprising, given that this colony was founded and administered by a for-profit company. However, such an approach fueled the tension between the state and the local people, whose lives became more difficult following the introduction of this ordinance.

The 1902 law required every male African aged fourteen years and older to obtain a registration certificate containing the details of his name, height, and any visible marks as well as the identities of his ethnic group, chief, headman, and district of residence. Each certificate had a unique identity number assigned to the holder. Although it was considered lawful for such people to move around the districts in which they resided without a permit, the ordinance required them to carry their registration certificates and be prepared to produce them at any given time if asked to do so by state officials.[26] The Natives Pass Ordinance also required African chiefs and village heads, the majority of whom had been coopted as salaried civil servants, to ensure that "all male natives of the age of fourteen years and upwards living or being within their tribal districts are properly registered."[27] Furthermore, it became mandatory for male Africans to obtain traveling passes (also known as *permits of removal*) from pass officers in their districts every time they traveled to other areas. Section 8(1) of the Natives Pass Ordinance says, "Any native desiring to remove from the district in which he shall have been registered to any other district shall before removal obtain a travelling pass in the prescribed form which he shall produce at the proper Pass Office in such last-mentioned district, together with his certificate of registration in order that he may be properly registered in such district."[28]

If the purpose of leaving one's district of habitual residence was to look for employment, the ordinance required that he obtain "a pass to seek work, in the prescribed form which shall be of force for a period not exceeding twenty-one days. Should the Native fail to find work within the period mentioned in his pass he shall proceed to the nearest Pass Office and may obtain an extension for a period not exceeding fourteen days, which shall be noted upon the pass."[29]

It was also a requirement that the pass contain the holder's identity number, as indicated on his registration certificate. As a result, the issuing of identity documents helped with the mobilization of labor and the collection of taxes while taking away African people's anonymity and the power and freedom that came with it. The 1895 regulations required the registration and identification of only those Africans entering designated towns and labor areas, whereas under the 1902 law, every male "adult" had to obtain a certificate of registration. In a way that speaks to "the creation of tribalism" thesis, which Terence Ranger and others have debated extensively.[30] Identity documents also sought to tie different groups of Africans to specific geographical areas in colonial Zimbabwe.

The 1902 law also reflected the BSAC administration's desire to control the mobility of migrant workers brought into Southern Rhodesia from Nyasaland, Northern Rhodesia, and Mozambique. Although the migrants benefited from transportation and food handouts provided by the Rhodesia Labor Bureau, which brought them into the colony, many such migrants left their jobs and the colony (often without notice) as soon as they found an opportunity to proceed to South Africa.[31] In an attempt to stop "foreign natives" from leaving the colony willy-nilly, section 3(1) of the 1902 ordinance provided for the issuance of registration certificates as well as traveling passes and passes to seek work to "any native entering the Territory from any country in which no provision exists for the granting of passes." It also stipulated that "on leaving the territory such native shall deliver up to the Pass Officer, who issues him a travelling pass for that purpose, his certificate of registration."[32] Regarding migrants who entered Southern Rhodesia in possession of identity documents or passes from other countries, the ordinance required such documents to be endorsed, without delay, by the magistrate or other official who would then issue traveling passes or passes to seek work to the concerned individuals. In so doing, Southern Rhodesian officials made it clear that they preferred to shut the colony's southern border to Africans intending to move to the Transvaal while leaving the northern and eastern borders with Northern Rhodesia and Portuguese East Africa open to let in migrant workers.

In further attempts to tighten the control of Africans' mobility, the 1902 ordinance made it mandatory for employers to keep passes of their African workers for the duration of the service contract. At the expiry of employment contracts, employers had to endorse the pass by signing it before returning it to its holder. If a discharged worker wanted to look for another job, he had to take his signed-off pass to the nearest pass office and obtain a traveling pass and a pass to seek work. Failure to observe any stipulations of the pass law attracted various amounts of fines and prison terms for African workers and employers alike. In this respect, section 26(1) of the ordinance states that "any native who, while under contract of service to one employer, shall knowingly enter the service of another employer, shall on conviction, be liable to a fine not exceeding ten pounds, and in default of payment to imprisonment, with or without hard labour, for a term not exceeding three months."[33] Pertaining to employers, the ordinance imposed a fine of

up to £50 or prison terms not exceeding six months in cases involving a misde-
meanor such as knowingly employing an African bound by a contract of service to another employer, withholding a pass or certificate of registration of any
person entitled to it, or destroying or tampering with any pass or certificate of
service belonging to an African.[34]

Over the next few years, the Legislative Council amended the ordinance
to address some inadequacies that had emerged. For example, through the 1905
Natives Pass Amendment Ordinance, Southern Rhodesia made it a punishable
offence for Africans to erase, alter, or destroy a pass.[35] A year later the Natives
Pass Further Amendment Ordinance (1906) was issued, and a 1909 review of the
pass laws revealed that a large section of the white community desired to see a
much tighter native pass system. Although several native commissioners urged
the government to require employers to closely monitor African workers to avoid
desertions that had become a major issue of concern, one went further, arguing
that "some system of finger prints must be enforced if it is desired to really possess an effective Pass Law."[36] In calling for such measures, the colonists wanted
to ensure better state control of Africans' mobility within the colony as well as
movements from Southern Rhodesia to South Africa. Given that Southern Rhodesian officials were, at the time, considering the use of fingerprints to weed out
"undesirable" and "prohibited" immigrants from India, such a recommendation
probably resonated with the majority of British settlers in the colony.[37]

Along with enforcing the pass laws in the colony, the BSAC administration
instructed railway staff to refuse tickets to Africans traveling to South Africa
without permission to leave the territory. Although this requirement may sound
familiar and logical in today's world, where international transporters are
required to check travelers' identity documents before boarding a plane, bus,
train, or ship, such a policy presented several challenges for people who were not
used to carrying identity documents all the time. Furthermore, Southern Rhodesian officials established rudimentary checkpoints at places such as Liebig's
Drift and Main Drift along the Limpopo River and occasionally deployed police
patrol units that apprehended people trying to cross the border without passes.[38]
In implementing such measures, colonial officials in Southern Rhodesia sought
to assert the state's position as the "monopoly of the legitimate means of movement" and to impose a new kind of (dis)order based on the strict control of the
colonized people's mobility.[39] As was the case at the border between Rwanda and
the Democratic Republic of the Congo, the imposition of state-centered instruments of migration control changed the meaning of cross-Limpopo mobility.[40]
Furthermore, state-based controls of Africans' movements had the effect of classifying cross-Limpopo mobility into some movements that were *legalized* and
others that were *illegalized*.

It Takes Two to Tango: The Transvaal's Open Border Policy

In contrast to their northern neighbors who zealously embraced the colonial border and fervently sought to enforce it, the Transvaal authorities did very little to control cross-Limpopo mobility before the formation of the Union of South Africa. Owing to the demand for cheap labor at the Witwatersrand mines, which greatly increased during the 1890s and after the South African war of 1899–1902, the Transvaal Parliament (the Volksraad) did not seek to prohibit the influx of Africans from the Zimbabwean plateau and other areas north of the Limpopo River. Instead, it supported several initiatives that the Transvaal Chamber of Mines[41] put in place with the view to meeting the Witwatersrand (Rand) mines' demands for workers. In this respect, the Kruger administration signed a labor agreement with the Portuguese colonial officials in Mozambique in 1896. Through this agreement, which came to be known as the First Mozambican Convention, the Rand mines received permission to recruit workers from Mozambique's southern districts, which were believed to be in the same climatic region as the Transvaal.[42] In return, the Transvaal officials pledged to help the Portuguese officials in Mozambique by making sure that migrants paid their annual taxes when they were due and returned home at the expiry of their contracts. In that respect, the agreement put in place a framework similar to the Bracero Program, an arrangement that allowed the United States to import temporary workers from Mexico between 1942 and 1964.[43]

The Transvaal officials also supported the mining companies when they set up the Rand Native Labour Association (RNLA) in 1897 to coordinate their labor mobilization efforts. This organization followed the establishment of the chamber's Native Labor Department in 1893, which laid the groundwork for a regional labor recruitment strategy. In 1900, the chamber transformed the RNLA and renamed it the Witwatersrand Native Labour Association (WNLA) with the intention of improving the methods of labor recruitment and reducing "indiscriminate competition, touting and traffic in Natives which [had] in the past existed amongst Mining Companies" on the Witwatersrand.[44] Over the years, the WNLA would become a major player in the politics of labor and mobility across the Zimbabwe–South Africa border and in Southern Africa more generally.

With the Transvaal government backing the efforts to mobilize regional labor for the Rand mines on one hand and the Southern Rhodesian government supporting the Rhodesia Chamber of Mines' competing interests on the other, it became difficult for the two territories to come up with a joint strategy of controlling cross-Limpopo mobility. In an attempt to minimize competition over the Mozambican labor, which had become crucial for the success of mining businesses in both territories, the two chambers of mines signed a memorandum of understanding in 1900. In part, the agreement required the Rhodesia Native

Labour Bureau (RNLB), which acted on behalf of the Rhodesia Chamber of Mines, to withdraw its labor recruiters from Mozambique and employ only Africans from that territory through the help of the WNLA. In return, the Transvaal Chamber of Mines agreed to deliver to their Rhodesian counterparts 12.5 percent of labor recruited in Mozambique and to stop WNLA agents from recruiting in Southern Rhodesia, Northern Rhodesia, and Nyasaland.[45] Unlike the 1896 labor agreement between the Transvaal government and Portuguese officials in Mozambique, this deal did not involve government representatives from either territory. It also did not last long.

In theory, the arrangement that the Transvaal Chamber of Mines signed with its Southern Rhodesia counterpart lasted for just about a year, but in practice it suffered a stillbirth because neither party took it seriously. The RNLB continued to recruit from Mozambique while the WNLA sent its agents to recruit in the southern districts of Southern Rhodesia as well as in Northern Rhodesia and Nyasaland. In a further attempt to strike a deal, the Transvaal Chamber of Mines made a proposal for the establishment of a joint agency to recruit labor from north of the Zambezi River and distribute it to mining companies in both territories, but that plan also did not materialize.[46] Competition for regional labor supplies prevented government officials and business owners in Southern Rhodesia from working with their counterparts in the Transvaal to come up with a durable agreement that could have helped control people's movements across the Limpopo River boundary.

In another development that shows the two territories had different perceptions about the border, the Transvaal officials asked their Southern Rhodesian counterparts not to obstruct the mobility of Africans from other territories who passed through the Zimbabwean plateau on their way to South Africa. In making the request, which coincided with debates surrounding the 1902 Natives Pass Ordinance in Southern Rhodesia, the Transvaal authorities did not want their neighbors to require people in transit to obtain traveling passes if they possessed passes from their territories of origin. In line with that position, the Transvaal government backed the Rand mines' calls for the RNLB to stop recruiting in southern Mozambique. As such, the prime minister's office released a statement stressing that as long as the Southern Rhodesian administration denied the Transvaal companies the permission to recruit from the Zimbabwe plateau, the Transvaal government would not support the RNLB's interests in Mozambique. The Transvaal officials further argued that "the introduction of a competing labour agency in the districts south of Latitude 22° was never contemplated, and would be detrimental to the interests of the Transvaal Mines."[47]

Despite the competition and antagonism between the two territories, the WNLA made further attempts to find a working arrangement on the issue by asking the Salisbury Municipality for space to build a compound to accommodate migrant workers from Mozambique, who passed by Southern Rhodesia on their way to the Rand. The news about this proposal triggered some negative responses from various sectors of the white settler community in Southern Rhodesia. On August 17, 1907, for example, representatives of the Rhodesia Chamber of Mines, the Individual Workers and Distributors Association, the Rhodesian Landowners and Farmers Association, the Rhodesia Agricultural Union, and the RNLB met with some members of the Legislative Council under the auspices of what came to be known as the Native Labor Conference to chart the way forward. Among other things, the conference resolved to urge the Southern Rhodesian administration to turn down the WNLA's request "to bring gangs of natives from territories beyond the Zambesi through Rhodesia to the Rand," arguing that the government should prohibit the WNLA's recruits from passing through the Zimbabwean plateau.[48]

In a letter to the editor of the *Rhodesia Herald*, another resident of Salisbury encouraged the municipality to turn down the request on the ground that Southern Rhodesian mine owners and farmers were concerned that the arrangement would encourage local "natives" to seek employment in South Africa. The concerned resident rhetorically asked, "Has our Rhodesian Administration given any definite assurance as to their intention to restrict by all means in their power the migration of boys from Rhodesian territory to the Rand?"[49] As reflected in this individual's letter, as well as in the Native Labor Conference's resolutions, access to regional labor supplies was one of the major factors that shaped relations between the Transvaal and Southern Rhodesia from the onset of British colonial rule in the latter. Inevitably, this issue significantly influenced the two territories' border enforcement strategies as well as travelers' experiences of crossing what once was merely a river in the Venda territory.

When negotiations for the amalgamation of the Transvaal, the Cape Colony, Natal, and the Orange Free State into the Union of South Africa reached an advanced stage—a few years before the BSAC's permit to run the affairs of Zimbabwe on behalf of Britain was scheduled to expire in 1914—the Southern Rhodesian Legislative Council extensively debated the idea of merging the colony into a united South Africa. During those debates, which went on for several months between 1908 and 1909, the labor question emerged as a key point of disagreement. As one legislator pointed out, the people who opposed the idea of joining the Union of South Africa feared that "the native labour of Rhodesia might be induced to go out of this country south, which would mean the ruin of both the mining and the farming industries here."[50] Contrary to this position, supporters of the merge with South Africa argued that the move would actually reduce competition for labor between the two territories and ultimately benefit Southern Rhodesian companies, which had fewer financial resources than their counterparts in the Transvaal. On this issue, Herbert T. Longden, who represented

Midlands District, said "a mine in Rhodesia would have the same privileges in regard to recruiting and distributing labour as a mine on the Rand. . . . The danger threatening their labour supply would come, not if they entered the Union, but if they remained outside."[51] Stressing the same point, Western District representative Robert A. Fletcher argued that if Southern Rhodesia joined South Africa, employers "would have every right to go to the Union Parliament and ask for the protection of their native labour, as being a part of South Africa."[52] When a territory-wide referendum on this issue eventually took place in 1922, the majority of Rhodesians voted for the "responsible government" as opposed to merging with South Africa. This type of dominion status allowed the settlers to run much of their own affairs, with the British government playing a supervisory role, especially in matters concerning the administration of Africans.

Although it is difficult to speculate on what could have happened if Southern Rhodesia joined the Union of South Africa in 1910, what is clear is that competition for African labor prevented the two neighboring territories from adopting joint strategies for managing cross-Limpopo mobility. Yielding to pressure from mining companies on opposite sides of the border, policy makers in Southern Rhodesia and the Transvaal shared opposing views of the border and its significance to nation-state building. Whereas Southern Rhodesian officials saw the control of Africans' mobility across the Limpopo as a necessary measure in preventing loss of labor and in safeguarding the colony's territorial sovereignty, their counterparts in the Transvaal viewed the same measures as unwarranted obstruction of the free movement of people in the region. Because the Rand mines were richer and better positioned to pay higher wages, the Transvaal officials preferred to not obstruct migrant workers' movements across the Limpopo. On their part, Africans from communities astride the border and others from areas far from it welcomed the lack of cooperation and coordination between policy makers in these territories as an opportunity to continue traveling back and forth across the Limpopo. All they needed to do was to figure out strategies for evading Southern Rhodesia's pass laws and other measures of migration control.

Through the Cracks: The Rise of Border Jumping from Zimbabwe to South Africa

In describing the European partition of Africa as a "political surgery" that split cultural communities into two or more competing entities, Anthony I. Asiwaju has argued that despite being so divided, "partitioned Africans have tended in their normal activities to ignore the boundaries as dividing lines and to carry on social relations across them more or less as in the days before Partition."[53] This observation brings out two ideas that feature in most discussions of "illegal" border crossings in Africa. The first is that people from communities that were divided by colonial borders challenged the legitimacy of colonial states by continuing with activities that straddled the newly imposed boundaries. This argument, which echoes broader ideas about resistance to colonial conquest in Africa, resonates with James C. Scott's conceptualization of peasant struggles in Malaysian history, in which he deployed the notion of "weapons of the weak."[54] Put differently, this idea suggests that the continuation of prohibited (precolonial) patterns of mobility and other activities that crossed colonial boundaries was a form of subaltern agency or activism against colonial rule. The second point that Asiwaju's observation brings out is that it was easy for Africans to ignore colonial borders because they were largely porous, unguarded, and sometimes not even marked on the ground.[55]

Both ideas help greatly in understanding how border jumping across the Zimbabwe–South Africa border emerged in the 1890s. Given that the conquest of the Zimbabwean plateau came on the backdrop of centuries of cross-Limpopo mobility, the imposition of the colonial boundary and the beginning of state-based controls of mobility produced new kinds of struggles and illegalized activities in the region. Although the Venda and other communities in Beitbridge did not wage a military struggle against the colonists as the Ndebele did in 1893, they sought ways of continuing with cross-Limpopo mobility because such movements were crucial in maintaining their cultures and means of livelihood. As Tshabeni Ndou pointed out in an interview I had with him, the Venda people "continued to view the Limpopo as a river within their territory because they continued to water their cattle there and to cross it regularly using footpaths and crossing points that had been in use for generations."[56] This was possible because Southern Rhodesian authorities did not have enough personnel and financial resources to monitor movements across the entire length of the boundary. Although people traveling in horse- and ox-drawn carts (mostly white settlers) crossed the border at the rudimentary checkpoints that the BSAC administration had established, many Africans traveled on foot and crossed at various points, using what Alan H. Jeeves and Jonathan Crush call "secret foot paths" for the larger part of the year when the Limpopo was dry.[57]

Furthermore, there were no native commissioners' offices in Beitbridge district until the 1930s. As such, expecting people who resided only a kilometer or so away from the Limpopo to travel several kilometers to obtain passes every time they wanted to cross the river created the incentive for noncompliance. Commenting on a similar scenario in the West African context, Paul Nugent has argued that the colonists' efforts to control precolonial trading activities following the demarcation of the Gold Coast–Togo boundary in the 1880s "caused intense annoyance on the part of traders and chiefs alike."[58] In addition to the desire to keep preexisting ties with relatives across the Limpopo, some border people moved to the Transvaal hoping to work and raise money to pay taxes in Southern Rhodesia, but others crossed the border to escape taxation. With their knowledge of the landscape, it was relatively easy for the Venda people to evade official measures of controlling mobility across the border.[59]

Away from the border districts, pass laws were a huge inconvenience to people who wanted to maintain sociocultural ties with kith and kin across the boundaries of "native" districts. Commenting on this issue, the native commissioner for Umtali district, along Southern Rhodesia's eastern border with Mozambique, wrote, "The natives living in Inyanga district are under chief Umtasa and are of the same tribe as those in Umtali district, and yet to visit one another they must travel 40 miles to Inyanga to take out a pass, this means that a native living on the Nyatande River would, by the time he reached his home from Umtali have travelled some 120 miles, whereas under ordinary circumstances it should have been a journey of 40 miles only."[60] In this respect, Southern Rhodesia's pass laws, together with cash taxation, land alienation, low wages, and poor work conditions at the emerging mines and farms, made life difficult for the colonized people.

Instead of attending to African people's complaints about various aspects of the colonial system, the administration focused on finding ways to tighten pass laws and punish offenders. Developments such as the doubling of hut tax between 1903 and 1907—a period when wages and direct expenditure toward the provision of accommodation, medical facilities, and food in the mining industry significantly declined—did not help the officials' efforts to enforce pass laws. Commenting on the state of affairs in the mining industry in 1907, one health inspector argued that the conditions under which African workers lived in most mine compounds were "gloomy and comfortless," noting, "a damp floor is not the healthiest resting place for a man who has done a good day's work . . . but it is the only bed the majority get as a rule. . . . A few sleep on rough structures erected by themselves."[61] Whereas some people complied with the new order of things, others devised subtle and not-so-subtle strategies to challenge state-centered efforts to control mobility within the colony and across the Limpopo River.

As Southern Rhodesia's Chief Secretary observed in 1901, some people who obtained "town passes" under the auspices of the 1895 Natives Registration Regulations loaned or sold them when they did not need to travel.[62] Despite lacking previous experiences with identity documents of the kind that the colonists introduced, Africans took advantage of the fact that the concerned passes did not include the photos or fingerprints of the individuals to whom they were originally issued. As such, being able to exchange passes allowed people who did not have permission to enter certain spaces to do so clandestinely. It also helped those who did not particularly like the working conditions in one place or another to simply walk away without their employer's permission. In this respect, desertion emerged as the most common strategy that African workers used to reclaim freedom of movement, which the colonists intended to take away from them. By engaging in such activities, the colonized people's objective was not to do away with colonial rule (although they might have wanted to) but to create alternative spaces for themselves as the colonized people.

With the introduction of Southern Rhodesia's 1902 Natives Pass Ordinance, border jumping gathered momentum within the territory (across district boundaries) and across the border with the Transvaal. Within the first few years of the implementation of this ordinance, Southern Rhodesia's attorney general revealed that the number of Africans imprisoned for contravening the pass laws had risen dramatically. While pushing for the amendment of the Natives Pass Ordinance in 1905, the attorney general said that "a number of boys after getting into difficulty, had mutilated their passes, and had torn or erased many important particulars, such as description of previous wages."[63] Because the pass system tied Africans to specific areas in the colony, some people destroyed or discarded their original passes as soon as they entered a new area and then applied for new ones using different names. This strategy was particularly common among migrant workers from Malawi, Zambia, and Mozambique who destroyed the documents that identified them as "foreign natives" and proceeded to obtain new ones purporting to be locals. Being in possession of documents that identified them as "Rhodesian natives" provided them with better chances of obtaining passes to visit the border districts where they worked while waiting for opportunities to sneak out and proceed to South Africa.[64]

In a development that shows how the increase in border jumping had become an issue of concern to colonial authorities, the representative for Southern Rhodesia's Western District (Gordon Forbes) brought this issue up for discussion in the Legislative Council in 1907. He asked if the administration knew that "numbers of natives have left Victoria District for the Transvaal not in possession of proper passes" and demanded to know "what, if any, steps have been taken to enforce compliance with the law on part of such natives, and to prevent such exodus in future." In response to his question, the treasurer said, "It is known that a certain number do leave the territory. . . . It has not been found possible to establish stations in the low country along the Limpopo, in the south-east of the territory, from which it is believed that the bulk of these natives proceed."[65] The 1909 review of the pass system, which we discussed earlier, also revealed that the number of Africans who left the territory without permits was on the increase. However, Southern Rhodesian officials' efforts to address this situation stirred the contestations that promoted border jumping from Zimbabwe to South Africa.

Border Enforcement and the Rise of Human Smugglers along the Limpopo

With the beginning of state-centered controls of people's movements across the Limpopo River, human smuggling also emerged as a salient feature of the "informal" economy of the Zimbabwe–South Africa border. Although other factors might have contributed to the rise of this phenomenon, Southern Rhodesian authorities' imposition of restrictions on labor recruitment using the Natives Employment Ordinance of 1899 was probably the major producer of human smugglers. This ordinance not only made a distinction between recruiting for the local and foreign markets but also created the incentive for unlicensed recruiting by requiring labor agents to pay more than twice as much for permits to recruit workers for other territories as they would for permits to recruit for local employment. This requirement inadvertently encouraged some labor agents to recruit workers in Southern Rhodesia and sent them to the Transvaal without obtaining the necessary permissions and licenses. As the chief secretary of the BSAC administration noted while supporting the proposed amendments of the Native Employment Ordinance in 1907, "the government was concerned about labour agents who came up from the Transvaal and recruited labour on the Southern Rhodesia side of the border, and recruited Portuguese natives coming across into the Southern Rhodesia territory without a license."[66] Although some of these agents were independent and recruited workers on behalf of different organizations and employers, others were employees of the WNLA. It was also common for recruiters who were licensed to operate in Southern Rhodesia to transport migrant workers to the Transvaal without following official channels, thereby breaching the terms and conditions of their licenses. As such, the first decade of the twentieth century saw a proliferation of unlicensed recruiting and human smuggling across the Limpopo River.[67] As the contestation over the control of cross-Limpopo mobility evolved over the period that I cover in this book, this phenomenon also evolved, leading to the rise of the *maguma-guma* (human smugglers) in the mid-1990s.

People from communities astride the border did not need much assistance with crossing the Limpopo and finding work in the Transvaal; however, long-distance migrants who had very little knowledge about the Limpopo Valley relied on labor recruiters. Given that Beitbridge district, on the Zimbabwean side of the border, was barely served by any form of public transport before the construction of the cross-Limpopo bridge that became operational in the early 1930s, such people had two ways of getting to the Transvaal. One was to use the train that plied the Bulawayo-Mafeking (Botswana) route, disembarking at the Southern Rhodesia–Botswana border and then walking to the Limpopo River. The other was to walk from various departure points to the Transvaal, following footpaths and routes that led to the Limpopo River. Regardless of the method they used, such people often arrived in the border area without much knowledge about how to cross the Limpopo and where to go after crossing it. It was mostly people in this situation who ended up engaging labor recruiters roaming around areas adjacent to the Limpopo River.[68]

By saying that migrants sought the assistance of smugglers who helped them to dodge the Southern Rhodesian authorities' measures of controlling cross-Limpopo mobility, I am by no means suggesting that the interactions between these two groups always happened in a pleasant and business-like environment. Labor recruiters often "used all sorts of tricks and ploys," to force work-seeking migrants to sign up with them.[69] One strategy they used was to establish makeshift camps in the border zone, from which they deployed African "touts" and "runners" along the routes that migrants used as they traveled between the two territories. In addition to intercepting migrants already en route to the Transvaal, labor recruiters sometimes paid bribes to village leaders to gain access into the African communities where they met potential clients. On entering African communities, recruiters often used cash advances, clothes, and food handouts to lure potential workers to sign up for work contracts and leave their villages.[70] Given the challenges that cash taxation, land alienation, and other colonial policies caused among the African communities in Southern Rhodesia, it is not surprising that some people embraced labor recruiters, who they regarded as helpers rather than the exploiters that they were.

As the demand for labor in the Transvaal grew rapidly in the first decade of the twentieth century—when Southern Rhodesian authorities increased controls of cross-Limpopo mobility—the triangular space at the intersection of the Southern Rhodesia–Mozambique–Transvaal borders became a hive of activities associated with labor recruitment and smuggling. This area, then known as the Pafuri Triangle, was in a remote and rugged terrain infested with the tsetse fly and malarial mosquitoes. Emphasizing how difficult it was to get to Pafuri, Thomas V. Bulpin says, "The journey to this spot was as arduous as it was perilous, passing through a land tormented by the devils of heat and thirst where constant danger lurked around every corner, and only the most adventuresome or foolish attempted it."[71] Given that Southern Rhodesia did not have any administrative post in the Beitbridge area, the nearest place where state officials were located was the police station at Sibasa in the northern Transvaal, more than a hundred miles away.

Because the Transvaal government was not much invested in the control of cross-Limpopo mobility, the Sibasa police station served little purpose. As such, there was barely any presence of law enforcement agents at Pafuri during much of the first decade of the twentieth century. Taking advantage of the general absence of state functionaries in the Pafuri Triangle, numerous individuals with criminal records in the Transvaal sought to escape the law by camping in this place. Consequently, the Pafuri Triangle also became known as "Crooks' Corner."[72]

While some fugitives at Pafuri survived on hunting elephants and other wild animals in the Limpopo Valley, others joined the rank and file of unlicensed recruiters who also camped at Crooks' Corner. As Martin J. Murray put it, most of the campers at Crooks' Corner were "unscrupulous fortune-hunters specialising in smuggling a particular kind of contraband: African labour."[73] Being at the intersection of three different territories, this location also made it easier for the residents of Pafuri to play hide and seek with the police whenever the latter visited the area in pursuit of one individual or another. Boasting about how they used the beacon at the intersection of the three territories' borders to avoid arrest, a former labor recruiter, who spent several years at Crooks' Corner, said, "Whoever comes for you, you can always be on the other side in someone else's territory; and if they all come at once, you can always sit on the beacon top and let them fight over who is to pinch you."[74] Migrants originating from areas far from the border, such as Nyasaland, Northern Rhodesia, and other parts of Southern Rhodesia, also went to Crooks' Corner, where they linked up with labor recruiters ready to take them to potential employers in the Transvaal. It was also common for recruiters at Crooks' Corner to dispatch touts to communities adjacent the Limpopo River to scout for potential workers. That the WNLA stationed some of its labor agents at Crooks' Corner shows not only the extent to which this place had become an important part of the region's market-oriented economies but also the ways in which border jumping blurred the distinction between formal- and informal-sector activities in Zimbabwe and South Africa.

Sometime in 1910 two European adventurers, Alec Thompson and William Pye, built a store "atop a low, 500-feet high ridge, which formed a sort of topographical backbone to the wild wedge of land" between the three territories.[75] In addition to selling food, clothes, malaria drugs (mostly quinine), and whisky, Pye and Thompson, like the rest of the campers at this place, also functioned as labor recruiters. They often engaged work-seekers who arrived at the store in starving conditions and passed them along to the Transvaal mine owners. In that respect, the pair used their store as a clearinghouse or auction floor for work-seeking migrants who ate, rested, obtained new clothes, and signed engagement contracts at Crooks' Corner before proceeding to different places in the Transvaal and beyond.[76] This effectively made the Pafuri Triangle the headquarters of labor pirates who promoted border jumping from Zimbabwe to South Africa in the early twentieth century.

The significance of Crooks' Corner in this history is not simply that it quickly became the most known place where border jumpers met human smugglers. This place also became the center of migration-related violence within a few years of the British colonization of Zimbabwe. As labor recruiters sought to maximize returns in this environment, where lawlessness prevailed, some of them deployed violent methods. This often involved the use of guns to intercept border jumpers and force them to sign contracts that directed them to specific employers. It was also common for recruiters to fight over and rob each other of the migrants they would have mobilized. Referring to recruiters' violent behavior, Bulpin wrote,

"The bushrangers were as tough a crowd as any bully bosun. They asked no quarter from life, and gave none."[77]

By the time the Transvaal merged with the Orange Free State, Natal, and the Cape Colony, forming the Union of South Africa in May 1910, border jumping had emerged a defining feature of the Transvaal–Southern Rhodesia border. What previously was simply a river in a frontier zone had become a geopolitical and juridical boundary. As was the case with the US–Mexico border, which split culturally homogenous groups into two sovereign states, the South Africa–Zimbabwe border tore communities asunder.[78] Although official efforts to enforce the colonial boundary by controlling cross-Limpopo migrations established a new kind of order in the region, they also produced tensions between state functionaries and people who desired to retain their freedom of movement. Rather than complying with colonial orders relating to registration certificates and passes, many inhabitants of the border districts and people from other parts of the region traveled to and from South Africa without official permission. Networks of recruiters who engaged migrant workers and helped them to cross the border clandestinely also emerged. In other words, the foundation had been set for border jumping to grow and evolve as the states on either side of the border developed.

Notes

1. David Newbury, "From 'Frontier' to 'Boundary': Some Historical Roots of Peasant Strategies of Survival in Zaire," in *The Crisis in Zaire: Myths and Realities*, ed. Georges Nzongola-Ntalaja (Trenton, NJ: Africa World, 1986).

2. Newbury, "From 'Frontier' to 'Boundary,'" 92.

3. Gail S. Schoettler, "The Sotho, Shona and Venda: A Study in Cultural Continuity," *African Historical Studies* 4, no. 1 (1971): 1–18; Edward Lahiff, *An Apartheid Oasis? Agriculture and Rural Livelihoods in Venda* (London: Cass, 2000); David N. Beach, *A Zimbabwean Past* (Gweru: Mambo, 1994); Hugh A. Stayt, *The Bavenda* (1931; London: Oxford University Press, 1931).

4. Tshabeni Ndou, interview with author in Beitbridge Town, May 17, 2010. See Nicholaas J. van Warmelo, *Contributions towards Venda History, Religion and Tribal Ritual* (Pretoria: University of South Africa, 1932).

5. Nkhumeleni M. N. Ralushai, "Further Traditions Concerning Luvhimbi and the Mbedzi," *Rhodesian History* 9 (1978): 1–12; Nemudzivhadi, "Attempts by Makhado"; Nicholaas J. Van Warmelo, *Anthropology of Southern Africa in Periodicals to 1950: An Analysis and Index* (Johannesburg: Witwatersrand University Press, 1977), vol. 1; Nkhumeleni M. N. Ralushai and J. R. Gray, "Ruins and Traditions of the Ngona and Mbedzi among the Venda of the Northern Transvaal," *Rhodesian History* 8 (1977): 1–11.

6. JoAnn McGregor, *Crossing the Zambezi: The Politics of Landscape on a Central African Frontier* (Suffolk: Currey, 2009).

7. David Siyasongwe, interview with author in Malabe Village, Beitbridge, May 31, 2010.

8. Nemudzivhadi, "Attempts by Makhado," 2. See Robson Mutandi, "Locally-Evolved Knowledge in Livestock and Range Management Systems in Southern Zimbabwe's Dry Lands: A Study of Pastoral Communities in Beitbridge District" (PhD diss., University of Waterloo, 1997).

9. Stefanus J. Du Toit, *Rhodesia: Past and Present* (London: Heinemann, 1897), 78. See Hermann B. Giliomee, *The Afrikaners: Biography of a People* (Charlottesville: University of Virginia Press, 2003); T. Dunbar Moodie, *The Rise of Afrikanerdom: Power, Apartheid, and the Afrikaner Civil Religion* (Berkeley: University of California Press, 1975).

10. For more on this topic, see Francis Wilson, *Labour in the South African Gold Mines, 1911–1969* (Cambridge: Cambridge University Press, 1972); MacDonald, "Colonial Trespassers."

11. Harald Von Sicard, "The Origin of Some of the Tribes in the Belingwe Reserve," *NADA*, (1952): 43–64.

12. Mlambo, "History of Zimbabwean Migration." See van Onselen, *Chibaro*; Paton, *Labour Export Policy.*

13. Ian Phimister, *An Economic and Social History of Zimbabwe 1890–1948: Capital Accumulation and Class Struggle* (London: Longman, 1988), 16. See Robert Blake, *A History of Rhodesia* (New York: Knopf, 1977).

14. Tsuneo Yoshikuni, *African Urban Experiences in Colonial Zimbabwe: A Social History of Harare before 1925* (Harare: Weaver, 2007); Percy F. Hone, *Southern Rhodesia* (London: Bell, 1909); Arthur Keppel-Jones, *Rhodes and Rhodesia: The White Conquest of Zimbabwe, 1884–1902* (Kingston: McGill-Queen's University Press, 1983).

15. Vazira Fazila-Yacoobali Zamindar, *The Long Partition and the Making of Modern South East Asia: Refugees, Boundaries, Histories* (New York: Columbia University Press, 2010).

16. For more on the effects of land alienation in colonial Zimbabwe, see Terence O. Ranger, *Voices from the Rocks: Nature, Culture and History in the Matopos Hills of Zimbabwe* (Oxford: Currey, 1999); Lawrence Tshuma, *A Matter of [In]Justice: Law, State and the Agrarian Question in Zimbabwe* (Harare: SAPES Trust, 1997); Jocelyn Alexander, *The Unsettled Land: State-Making and the Politics of Land in Zimbabwe, 1893–2003* (Oxford: Currey, 2006); Donald S. Moore, *Suffering for Territory: Race, Place, and Power in Zimbabwe* (Harare: Weaver, 2005).

17. National Archives of Zimbabwe (NAZ), N1/2/2, Native Commissioner Hartley to Chief Native Commissioner, Salisbury, November 30, 1895. Native commissioners were colonial officials in charge of native districts made up of one or more native reserves.

18. Harry C. Thomson, *Rhodesia and its Government* (London: Smith, Elder, 1898), 82. Speaking on the same issue, one of Thompson's informants said, if "a boy engages to serve me for a certain time, and I give him food, and [then] he bolts before his time is up, naturally I can have him flogged."

19. Ali M. H. Kalsheker, "The 1908 Asiatics Ordinance in Perspective" (Henderson Seminar Paper, University of Rhodesia, 1974); Hasu H. Patel, *Indians in Uganda and Rhodesia: Some Comparative Perspectives on a Minority in Africa* (Denver: Center on International Race Relations, 1973). See Sally A. Peberdy, *Selecting Immigrants: National Identity and South Africa's Immigration Policies, 1910–2008* (Johannesburg: Wits University Press, 2009); Audie Klotz, *Migration and National Identity in South Africa, 1860–2010* (New York: Cambridge University Press, 2013).

20. NAZ, A11/2/8/14, Recruiting British Central Africa, 1901–1908. See W. E. Fairbridge, "Labour for the Mines," *Rhodesia Herald*, August 4, 1900; "Black Labour Crises," *Rhodesia Herald*, August 25, 1900; van Onselen, *Chibaro*; Wilson, *Labour in the South African Gold Mines.*

21. Mlambo, "History of Zimbabwean Migration"; Paton, *Labour Export Policy*; Crush, "Migrations Past."

22. NAZ, SRG 2, Southern Rhodesia: Legislative Council Debates, June 7, 1899. This was among the first laws that Southern Rhodesia's Legislative Council introduced following its establishment in April of the same year.

23. See *Rhodesia Herald*, "Native Labour Conference," December 20, 1907; NAZ, A3/18/31/6, Chief Native Commissioner to Administrator, December 1, 1909, and Native Commissioner Gutu to Superintendent of Natives, Victoria, December 4, 1909.

24. NAZ, A3/18/30/26, Southern Rhodesia, Native Employment Ordinance, 1899.

25. NAZ, SRG 2, Southern Rhodesia: Legislative Council Debates, November 7, 1902.

26. NAZ, A3/18/31/6, Southern Rhodesia, Natives Pass Ordinance, no. 10, 1902.

27. NAZ, A3/18/31/6, Southern Rhodesia, Natives Pass Ordinance, no. 10.

28. NAZ, A3/18/31/6, Southern Rhodesia, Natives Pass Ordinance, no. 10.

29. NAZ, A3/18/31/6, Southern Rhodesia, Natives Pass Ordinance, no. 10.

30. Terence O. Ranger, *The Invention of Tribalism in Zimbabwe* (Gweru: Mambo, 1985); Leroy Vail, ed., *The Creation of Tribalism in Southern Africa* (Berkeley: University of California Press, 1989); Msindo, *Ethnicity in Zimbabwe.*

31. NAZ, SRG 2, Southern Rhodesia: Legislative Council Debates, November 7, 1902.

32. NAZ, A3/18/31/6, Southern Rhodesia, Natives Pass Ordinance no. 10.

33. NAZ, A3/18/31/6, Southern Rhodesia, Natives Pass Ordinance no. 10.

34. NAZ, A3/18/31/6, Southern Rhodesia, Natives Pass Ordinance no. 10.

35. NAZ, A3/18/31/6, Southern Rhodesia, Natives Pass Amendment Ordinance, 1905.

36. NAZ, A3/18/31/6, Posselt to Chief Native Commissioner, January 2, 1909.

37. For more information about the exclusion of Indians in early colonial Zimbabwe, see Floyd Dotson and Lillian O. Dotson, *The Indian Minority of Zambia, Rhodesia and Malawi* (New Haven, CT: Yale University Press, 1968); Patel, *Indians in Uganda*; Busani Mpofu, "'Undesirable Indians,' Residential Segregation and the Ill-Fated Rise of the White 'Housing Covenanters' in Bulawayo, Colonial Zimbabwe, 1930–1973," *South African Historical Journal* 63, no. 4 (2011): 553–80; and Francis Musoni, "Contested Foreignness: Indian Migrants and the Politics of Exclusion in Early Colonial Zimbabwe," *African and Asian Studies* 16, no. 4 (2017): 312–35.

38. W. Ranke, "Down the Limpopo," *South African Geographical Journal* 15, no. 1 (1932): 35–44; Julius Jeppe, "South African Coal Estates (Witbank) Limited," *Sun and Agricultural Journal of South Africa* (December 1926).

39. John Torpey, *The Invention of the Passport: Surveillance, Citizenship and the State* (Cambridge: Cambridge University Press, 2000), 1. For further discussions of the use of legal instruments to changes the order of things in colonial Africa, see Kristin Mann and Richard Roberts, eds., *Law in Colonial Africa* (London: Currey, 1991).

40. Newbury, "From 'Frontier' to 'Boundary.'"

41. This organization has changed names several times. When it was first formed on December 7, 1887, it was called the Chamber of Mines of Johannesburg. On October 5, 1889, it was relaunched as the Witwatersrand Chamber of Mines before it became known as the

Chamber of Mines of the South African Republic between 1897 and 1901. From 1902 to 1952 it was known as the Transvaal Chamber of Mines, then it became the Transvaal and Orange Free State Chamber of Mines from 1953 to 1967. In 1968 it was renamed the Chamber of Mines of South Africa, and remained so until May 2018 when it adopted its current name: the Minerals Council South Africa. See https://www.mineralscouncil.org.za/about/history.

42. National Archives of South Africa (NASA), AMPT PUBS, vol. 45, file CD1894, Reports of the Transvaal Labour Commission 1904. See also, Patrick Harries, "Capital, State, and Labour on the 19th Century Witwatersrand: A Reassessment," *South African Historical Journal* 18, no. 1 (1986): 25–45.

43. Kitty Calavita, *Inside the State: The Bracero Program, Immigration, and the INS* (New York: Routledge, 1992); Aristide Zolberg, *A Nation by Design: Immigration Policy in the Fashioning of America* (New York: Russell Sage, 2006) Mae M. Ngai, *Impossible Subjects: Illegal Aliens and the Making of Modern America* (Princeton, NJ: Princeton University Press, 2004).

44. The Employment Bureau of Southern Africa (TEBA) Documents, University of Johannesburg Library, WNLA Circular Letters vol 2: The Secretary of the Transvaal Chamber of Mines Circular to the Chairman and Directors of Mining Companies, May 18, 1901. In addition to the WNLA, whose mandate was to recruit foreign (non–South African) workers for the Transvaal mines, the Transvaal Chamber of Mines formed the Native Recruiting Corporation in 1912, to recruit mine workers from within South Africa.

45. NASA, PM, vol. 32, file 73/14/1907, Labor: PEA for Rhodesia.

46. NAZ, SRG 2, Southern Rhodesia: Legislative Council Debates, July 2, 1903.

47. NASA, PM, vol. 32, file 73/14/1907, Labor: PEA for Rhodesia; NAZ, SRG 2, Southern Rhodesia: Legislative Council Debates, November 11, 1902. By that time, it was believed that more people from areas north of latitude 22° south died from diseases on the Rand mines than those from the south of the concerned line.

48. *Rhodesia Herald*, "Native Labour Conference."

49. L.K.R., "WNLA in Rhodesia" *Rhodesia Herald*, December 6, 1907.

50. NAZ, SRG 2, Southern Rhodesia: Legislative Council Debates, May 25, 1909.

51. NAZ, SRG 2, Southern Rhodesia: Legislative Council Debates, May 19, 1909.

52. NAZ, SRG 2, Southern Rhodesia: Legislative Council Debates, May 25, 1909.

53. Asiwaju, "Conceptual Framework," 3.

54. James C. Scott, *Weapons of the Weak: Everyday Forms of Peasant Resistance* (New Haven: Yale University Press, 1985); "Everyday Forms of Peasant Resistance," *Journal of Peasant Studies* 13, no. 2 (1986): 5–35; and *The Moral Economy of the Peasant: Rebellion and Subsistence in Southeast Asia* (New Haven: Yale University Press, 1976).

55. Griffiths, "Permeable Boundaries." See also Mechlinski, "Towards an Approach to Borders."

56. Tshabeni Ndou, interview.

57. Alan H. Jeeves, and Jonathan Crush, "Introduction," in *White Farmers, Black Labor: The State and Agrarian Change in Southern Africa, 1910–50,* ed. Alan H. Jeeves and Jonathan Crush. Portsmouth, NH: Heinemann, 1997. See also NAZ, SRG 2, Southern Rhodesia: Legislative Council Debates, July 17, 1901.

58. Nugent, *Smugglers, Secessionists,* 23.

59. Tshabeni Ndou, interview. See, also SRG2, Southern Rhodesia Legislative Council Debates, June 8, 1910.

60. NAZ, A3/18/31/6, Native Commissioner Umtali to Secretary, Department of Administrator, February 11, 1910.

61. NAZ, NB/6/1/20, Compound Inspector, Selukwe Division, Report of the Year ended December 31, 1907.

62. NAZ, SRG 2, Southern Rhodesia: Legislative Council Debates, July 16, 1901.

63. NAZ, SRG 2, Southern Rhodesia: Legislative Council Debates, April 28, 1905.

64. NAZ, SRG 2, Southern Rhodesia: Legislative Council Debates, April 28, 1905.

65. NAZ, SRG 2, Southern Rhodesia: Legislative Council Debates, December 18, 1907.

66. NAZ, SRG 2, Southern Rhodesia: Legislative Council Debates, May 7, 1907.

67. NAZ, SRG 2, *Southern Rhodesia: Legislative Council Debates*, July 17, 1901; November 11, 1902; April 28, 1905; May 15, 1906; May 7, 1907. See also NASA, AMPT PUBS, vol. 45, file CD 1894, Report of the Transvaal Labour Commission 1904.

68. NAZ, AOH/46, Amon Makufa Mlambo, interview with Dawson Munjeri, Rhodesdale Estate, December 13, 1978; NAZ, S1226, British South Africa Police, Mtetengwe to Superintendent CID, Bulawayo, January 4, 1926. See also, Clapperton C. Mavhunga, "Navigating Boundaries of Urban/Rural Migration in Southern Zimbabwe, 1890s to 1920s," in *An African Agency and European Colonialism: Latitudes of Negotiation and Containment: Essays in Honor of A.S. Kanya-Forstner*, ed. Femi J. Kolapo and Kwabena O. Akurang-Parr (Lanham, MD: University of America Press, 2007).

69. Martin J. Murray, "'Blackbirding' at 'Crooks' Corner': Illicit Labour Recruiting in Northeastern Transvaal, 1910–1940," *Journal of Southern African Studies* 21, 3 (1995): 374.

70. NAZ, N3/22/4 Vol 2, A Draft Dispatch by Chief Native Commissioner for Submission to the South African High Commissioner, February 7, 1916. See also, Clapperton C. Mavhunga, "The Mobile Workshop: Mobility, Technology and Human-Animal Interaction in Gonarezhou (National Park), 1850– Present," (PhD diss., University of Michigan, 2008); Clapperton C. Mavhunga, *Transient Workspaces: Technologies of Everyday Innovation in Zimbabwe* (Cambridge, MA: MIT Press, 2014).

71. Thomas V. Bulpin, *The Ivory Trail* (Cape Town: Timmins, 1954): 31. See, also NAZ, N3/22/4 Vol 2, Native Commissioner Zoutpansberg to Director of Native Labor, Johannesburg, October 26, 1915.

72. See Bulpin, *Ivory Trail*; Murray, "'Blackbirding' at 'Crooks' Corner'"; Mavhunga, "Navigating Boundaries."

73. Murray, "'Blackbirding' at 'Crooks' Corner,'" 374.

74. Bulpin, *Ivory Trail*, 29

75. Bulpin, *Ivory Trail*, 14.

76. NAZ, S1226, Assistant Commissioner, CID, BSAP, Bulawayo, to Senior Immigration Officer Beitbridge, December 3, 1941. See also, Bulpin, *Ivory Trail*.

77. Bulpin, *Ivory Trail*, 159. See also, Alan H. Jeeves, "Over-Reach: The South African Gold Mines and the Struggle for the Labour of Zambesia," *Canadian Journal of African Studies* 17, no. 3 (1983): 393–412; NAZ, N3/22/4 vol.2, Chief Native Commissioner, Rhodesia to South African High Commissioner, February 7, 1916.

78. For a discussion of the Latino/Chicano communities' perceptions and experiences with the US–Mexico border, see Cisneros, *Border Crossed Us*.

2 Promoting Illegality

South Africa's Ban on "Tropical Natives"

THE PROCESS OF synchronizing the economic, political, and administrative structures of the Transvaal, the Orange Free State, Natal, and the Cape Colony unfolded after they became provinces of the same country in May 1910, and the Southern African region witnessed the beginning of a new phase in the history of cross-Limpopo mobility. Whereas previously the Transvaal authorities showed no interest in enforcing the Limpopo River as a geopolitical boundary, it did not take long before the new government of a united South Africa became involved in the control of migration from Southern Rhodesia. On November 8, 1910, Henry William Sampson, an opposition member of parliament (MP) in the Union of South Africa's House of Assembly, asked whether the government was aware of reports showing that some thirty thousand migrant workers had perished in the Witwatersrand mines between 1904 and 1909. Emphasizing that all but five thousand deaths were caused by unhealthy working conditions in the mines, Sampson proceeded to ask about the steps, if any, that the new government intended to take to avoid further waste of human life in the Transvaal's mining industry.[1] In response to Sampson's question, Henry Burton, who was the minister for native affairs, said the government was aware that the conditions under which miners worked needed improvement and was working on regulations to ensure the improvement of mine workers' health. He further noted that the government was also planning to appoint a medical inspector to oversee mine workers' health provisions and had commissioned research for the development of a dust-laying device that would help prevent miners' phthisis, a condition that government officials believed was the major cause of mine workers' deaths.[2]

When this issue came up during another debate in Parliament, about four months later, Burton revealed that the government had called the attention of the mining companies to what he referred to as an "awful death rate" and had implored them to do everything they could "to ascertain what really was the cause of it."[3] However, he made it clear that the government had no immediate plans for controlling the importation of foreign workers and assured the House of Assembly that the WNLA was making every effort to reduce the death rate of mine workers. Contributing to the same debate, Frances Drummond

Chaplin—another opposition MP—stated that pneumonia was the major killer of mine workers from "northern territories" and went further to propose that if the government did not have the means to reduce the mortality of this category of workers in the shortest possible time, Parliament should consider stopping their importation. Chaplin's proposal garnered the support of several other opposition MPs. Among them was Frederic Hugh Creswell, who argued that the ruling party was reluctant to act on the issue because it relied heavily on the advice and support of the Transvaal Chamber of Mines. Creswell strongly criticized the recruitment and employment of unskilled African workers in the Witwatersrand mining industry, describing it as a "slave system," adding, "He who sups with the devil must have a long spoon."[4] In characterizing the Chamber of Mines as a "devil," Creswell expressed a common sentiment among a section of South African society that desired to see major improvements in the working conditions in the mining industry.

On May 14, 1912, Creswell formally moved a motion for Parliament to reduce the mortality of mine workers by "prohibiting the entry into the Union of natives recruited in territories situated north of 22nd degree of south latitude."[5] Although the majority of MPs opposed the motion when it was raised, the ruling party gave into the opposition's demands after another year of "fighting" over the issue. On May 8, 1913, Jacobus Wilhelmus Sauer, who succeeded Burton as minister for native affairs, announced that the South African government had decided to ban the employment of migrants from areas north of latitude 22° south. As he put it, "every motive required that the recruiting of tropical natives should be stopped, because the mortality was of a character that, should it continue at that rate, it would be little less than murder."[6] While announcing the ban, Sauer expressed concern that instead of heeding the government's recommendations for reducing the risks of death among the so-called tropical natives, mining companies had chosen to provide misleading information and to underestimate the rate at which migrant workers died.

Although scholars such as Randall Packard view South Africa's ban on "tropical workers" as an example of how the colonists used medical (and sometimes pseudomedical) sciences as governmental technologies in Africa, I am more interested in the ban's contribution to the historical evolution of border jumping in this region.[7] This chapter shows that rather than helping to stop "illegal migration" across the Southern Rhodesia–South Africa border, the introduction of the ban was like pouring gasoline onto a burning fire. During the twenty years that the ban was officially in force, contestations over its legality and utility grew and compromised its effectiveness as a border enforcement strategy. This effect fueled border jumping as large numbers of work seekers from Zimbabwe and other restricted areas entered South Africa, largely through unofficial and illegalized channels. In this respect, the Union of South Africa boosted and extended the life of a phenomenon that the BSAC administration had created through its efforts to control cross-Limpopo mobility.

Politicizing Migration: South Africa's Controversial Ban on "Tropical Workers"

Given that the announcement of the ban on northern migrants came almost three years after the South African Parliament first debated the issue of mine workers' mortality, one might have expected the minister to outline a clear framework to guide its implementation. However, Sauer did not do that. In spite of the opposition MPs' demands, the minister refused to identify the law and explain the enforcement strategy that the government intended to use to achieve the ban's objectives. On May 14, 1913—barely a week after the announcement of the ban—Creswell asked Sauer to say how he was going to ensure that the WNLA would adhere to the ban. In addition to raising this question, the MP argued that the country's northern borders were wide and porous, that people from areas north of latitude 22° south did not look different from other Africans, and that it was possible for such persons to move into areas south of latitude 22° south so they could be "legally" engaged for work on the Rand. Rather than allowing Sauer to answer Creswell's question, Henry Burton (who was now minister of railways and harbors) intervened, saying the question was "a little ungracious," and argued that mine owners understood the government's position and were committed to making sure that "there would be no more recruiting of this sort."[8] While it is probable that Sauer and other cabinet ministers did not think about strategies for enforcing the ban before making the announcement, it is also likely that they recognized the challenges but did not have a clear strategy for tackling them. To people like Creswell, however, Sauer's failure to provide such important information suggested that cabinet ministers were hesitant to act against the will of the Transvaal Chamber of Mines. On this point, the MP remarked that "when interests conflicted, the Government did not seem to care very much about scrupulously working up to their own pledges."[9]

After some further pushing by Creswell and other opposition MPs, on May 23, 1913, the minister revealed that the government planned to use the Immigrants Regulation Act, which would take effect August 1, 1913, as the legal basis for implementing the ban. Among other things, the Immigrants Regulation Act stipulated that any person wishing to enter the Union of South Africa may be required to submit to a medical examination or go through any other examination deemed necessary by the minister of immigration and Asiatic affairs.[10] In line with this legislation, Sauer announced, "Natives domiciled north of Latitude 22 degrees south who entered the Union subsequent to August 1st 1913 can be declared prohibited immigrants if they are unable to read and write any European language to the satisfaction of an immigration officer, or fall under any other of the classes of individuals referred to in section 4 of the Immigrants Regulation Act. Once declared a PI [prohibited immigrant] a tropical native must either leave the Union or obtain from the Minister a temporary permit."[11] As was the case with the initial announcement of the ban, the decision to use the Immigrants Regulation Act stirred a lot of controversies and contestations in the region. Instead of addressing the fundamental issues that Creswell pointed out, the South African government chose to move ahead with the implementation of the ban.

Early in June 1913, the director of native labor in Johannesburg wrote letters to the Transvaal Chamber of Mines, the South Africa Immigration Department, and the Portuguese curator in Johannesburg, informing them of the country's impending ban on "tropical natives." The governor general of South Africa wrote a similar letter to the governor general of Mozambique.[12] The inclusion of Portuguese colonial officials in this correspondence was done in respect of the 1896 Labor Agreement, which the Transvaal government had signed with Mozambique. Furthermore, the director instructed all pass officers "to carefully interrogate all natives presented for registration for employment . . . with a view to ascertaining whether they are prohibited immigrants under the Immigrants Regulation Act No. 22 of 1913" and continued, "If you consider that any native is a prohibited immigrant will you kindly detain him and immediately send in a report to me."[13] Within the first year of implementing the ban, South African authorities turned down several labor agents' requests for the registration of migrant workers from the northern territories. In so doing, the government created an atmosphere of serious commitment to the enforcement of the ban.

Nevertheless, it did not take long before controversies and contestations surrounding the ban began to affect its implementation. The deployment of the Immigrants Regulation Act of 1913 to enforce the ban triggered some questions, mainly because South African lawmakers did not formulate this law to address the mortality of African migrant workers in the country. Instead, the law's primary purpose was to curtail the immigration of people from India and other Asian countries who had become major targets of racist and xenophobic sentiments among white people in Natal, Transvaal, and other parts of South Africa. When the Immigrant Regulation Bill was first mooted, the Union authorities' objective was to come up with a law that restricted, as much as possible, the entry, settlement, and movements of Indians in South Africa. However, South Africa's status as a dominion state of the British Empire prevented the enactment of an explicitly anti-Indian legislation. After the Indian government and the Indian community in Transvaal protested against what they perceived as a racist law in the making, the British government advised South African officials to follow the example of Australia, which took "a wider view to the question of immigrants restriction."[14]

Earlier in 1908, an attempt to come up with a similar law hit a wall in Southern Rhodesia. The BSAC administration had proposed what it called an "Asiatic Ordinance," which sought to "restrict the immigration of Asiatics into this territory, and to provide for the registration of such Asiatics as are already resident therein."[15] The Rhodesian bill required every Asian above sixteen years of age, including guardians of minors, to have fingerprints recorded and to possess, at all times, a registration certificate issued by the Registrar of Asiatics. According to the bill, failure to comply with these requirements would lead to arrest, imprisonment, or expulsion from the colony. Although Southern Rhodesia's Legislative Council passed the ordinance on June 22, 1908, the colonial secretary vetoed it following an empire-wide campaign against what was overtly an anti-Indian law.[16] In a bid to avoid tension with the British and Indian governments, the South African Parliament came up with a more broadly defined bill that seemingly applied to all foreigners seeking to enter and work in the Union. That bill became the Immigrants Regulation Act No. 22 of 1913.

Most questions about the Immigrants Regulation Act and its suitability as the legal framework for the ban were concerned with section 4(1), which listed three major categories of persons that South African officials could deport or bar from entering the country. The first category pertained to people whom the minister of immigration and Asiatic affairs found unsuited, on economic grounds or on account of standards or habit of life, to the requirements of the Union or any of its provinces. The second category referred to individuals unable, by reason of deficient education, to read and write any European language to the satisfaction of immigration officers. Third, the minister of immigration and Asiatic affairs could declare as a prohibited immigrant "any person who is likely, if he entered the Union, to become a public charge by reasons of infirmity of mind or body, or because he is not in possession for his own use of sufficient means to support himself and such of his dependencies as he shall bring with him into the Union."[17] Given that the majority of African migrants went to South Africa in search of employment, they did not possess adequate financial resources to support themselves. Also, the majority could not read or write any European language. As such, a strict application of this law meant that very few Africans, whether "tropical" or not, would qualify to enter South Africa.

It was also not clear how the ban affected "tropical natives" from Mozambique given that section 5 of the Immigrants Regulation Act stipulated that persons domiciled in neighboring territories having a treaty with the Union of South Africa would not be prohibited from entering the country. Mozambique presented a challenge not only because the Union government inherited the 1896 Labor Agreement between Portuguese colonial officials and the Transvaal authorities but also because the larger part of the country fell into the restricted area. What added to the confusion about migrants from Mozambique was that, at one point, the secretary for native affairs wrote that he did not think the South African government would invoke the Immigrants Regulation Act "to any great extent in regard to Portuguese Tropical Natives."[18] Despite the fact that the governor general of Mozambique embraced the idea of the ban and pledged to stop people from the northern parts of the country from seeking employment in South Africa, this message gave the impression that South African officials were not going to apply the ban in dealing with migrants from Mozambique.

In an effort to address the confusion surrounding the Immigrants Regulation Act and its applicability in enforcing the ban, the secretary for justice pointed out that there was no obligation for the government or any of its officials to treat anyone as a prohibited immigrant under this law. As he put it, the "government may choose not to apply the test under section four (1) (b) or express an opinion under section four (1) (a): and if it fails to apply the test or express the opinion the person is not a prohibited immigrant until it does so."[19] What this statement implied was that immigration officials were not obliged to administer literacy tests or to require medical exams or proof of financial resources from every person seeking to enter the country. It also meant that migrants from Africa's tropical regions could enter the country and obtain work anywhere they wished as long as they were not declared prohibited immigrants. By extension, labor agents could also recruit such persons and pass them on to the Witwatersrand mines without any sanctions. This also gave the impression that the South African government did not intend to entirely stop the recruitment of migrant workers from the northern territories. Rather than addressing the confusion surrounding the interpretation of the law, the Justice Department's statement exposed the loopholes created by the government's decision to use this piece of legislation to enforce the ban on "tropical" migrants.

There was also confusion about whether the ban applied to the employment of northern migrants only by the Witwatersrand gold mines or by businesses in other parts of the country as well. Although Sauer did not address this point when he announced the ban, it soon emerged that various government officials believed the prohibition was applicable only to the Transvaal gold mines. Evidence of this interpretation appeared in November 1913 when the director of native labor stated that if colonial officials in Mozambique did not want to bear the costs of repatriating Mozambicans who were prohibited from working in South Africa, such persons "shall be allowed to obtain employment in the Transvaal, provided that they shall not be employed on any Mines or Works."[20] The secretary for native affairs expressed a similar understanding in his response to one Hendrick Mentz's request for permission to recruit "tropical" migrants for the Rand mines. Communicating the minister's decision to not grant Mentz's request, the secretary pointed out that "tropical natives" would not be attested for work in the Witwatersrand gold mines, but "Government will not offer objection to their employment on the Tin Mines in the Waterberg District."[21] Despite issuing these statements, which suggest that South African government officials had a clear position on this issue, the two clashed in May 1914 when the secretary for native affairs questioned the director's decision to approve the employment of more than three hundred "tropical natives" at the Hlobane Colliery in Natal. In justifying his decision, the director argued that the controversial policy allowed him to exercise discretion in giving permissions for "tropical" migrants to work in certain areas outside the Witwatersrand where the climatic conditions were regarded to be more favorable to them and where he was satisfied that adequate medical attention was available.[22] This did not help to cover up the contradictions and inconsistencies that shrouded government officials' handling of the ban, however.

In 1916, when the Southern Rhodesian authorities raised concerns about the continued employment of Zimbabweans at the Natal coal mines, the director of native labor argued that the laws, which governed the employment of "tropical" migrants in the Transvaal, were not in force in Natal and other provinces of the Union.[23] However, when Southern Rhodesia's chief native commissioner asked the same question two years later, the same official said, "This Regulation applies to the whole of the Union."[24] Although it is not unusual for people (not least government officials) to change their minds about certain issues or contradict themselves, this statement added to the confusion and contestations surrounding South Africa's ban on "tropical natives." Commenting on this scenario, a Native Affairs Department official at the country's border with Southern Rhodesia complained that "various instructions on the subject [of tropical natives] have from time to time been issued with the result that the position has become rather confusing both to myself and to those authorized to employ such natives."[25] Unfortunately, this confusion compromised the effective application of the ban and created loopholes, which South African employers and recruiters intelligently took advantage of to continue to bring work seekers from restricted areas into the country.

In addition to the questions of interpretation, which officials in various state departments grappled with, it was also difficult to know whether certain individuals came from north or south of the concerned line. The South African government did not provide maps showing the areas where recruitment was prohibited or allowed. Consequently, immigration officials, Native Affairs Department officials, the police, and other state functionaries had to rely on the railway maps, which proved to be useless because of a lack of detail about the position of latitude 22° south.[26] After several requests for the maps failed to yield anything beyond the latitude maps for northern Transvaal, the secretary for native affairs asked the governments of Southern Rhodesia and Mozambique to provide lists of chiefs whose territories were located to the south of latitude 22° south, but that also did not help. As the sub-native commissioner of the Louis Trichardt district observed in August 1915, the latitude 22° south cut through territories belonging to different chiefs in both Southern Rhodesia and Mozambique.[27] This was not surprising given that the concerned line was simply a line on the world map, which did not have any meaningful significance in the lives of the African people in this region and elsewhere. Many chiefs had portions of their followers on both sides of the line. In some cases, the chiefs' names, which appeared in official records, differed from those that their people used in everyday interactions. In addition, South African officials did not know some of the place names identified by migrants as their villages and areas of origin.

The manner in which South African officials tried to control the activities of labor agents in the country's northern border districts also affected the enforcement of the ban. Acknowledging that it was not going to be possible to completely stop "tropical natives" from entering the country, the director of native labor and the secretary for native affairs allowed licensed labor agents to register "tropical natives" recruited *within* the borders of South Africa, mainly in the northern districts of Louis Trichardt and Pietersburg. By taking that position, these officials probably avoided the expenses of having to repatriate "prohibited migrants"; however, they also poked some holes in the entire justification for the ban and encouraged recruiters to sneak through them. It did not take long for evidence to surface showing that labor agents actively recruited from areas to the north of latitude 22° south and deployed a wide array of strategies to bring their clients into the country. Apart from what labor recruiters and migrants had to say, officials did not have any other means of knowing for sure where recruitment took place.

As the government struggled to enforce the ban, the demand for labor continued to surge, intensifying competition and violence among labor agents, who "clandestinely" supplied "tropical" migrants to the Transvaal gold mines and other places. This was particularly so in Crooks' Corner, where agents affiliated with the Native Recruiting Corporation (NRC)—formed by the Transvaal Chamber of Mines in 1912 to recruit mine workers from within South Africa—and another recruiting company called the Robinson Group faced tough competition from various unlicensed recruiters.[28] In an attempt to curb violence in the border zone, the Native Affairs Department slightly shifted the focus of the ban. Whereas on May 8, 1913, the minister emphasized that the high mortality rate among "tropical" migrants was the reason for the ban, the director of native labor had this to say five years later: "The policy of the Union as understood by me since 1913 and as understood by executive officers of the NAD [Native Affairs Department] has been to eliminate the profit which could be made by the people who engaged in the recruitment of Tropical Natives. By the elimination of the incentive it was hoped to do away with the illicit practices that took place on our borders and which had for their objective the introduction of Tropical Natives in order that certain people might make money out of them."[29]

In line with the new focus, the prime minister's office issued Government Notice No. 1693 dated December 24, 1918, which made it a punishable offence, under the Native Labor Regulation Act of 1911, for labor agents to recruit "tropical" migrants. In a follow-up circular to various government officials in northern Transvaal, the director of native labor stressed that "the recruitment of natives domiciled in North and South Rhodesia by Labour Agents is *definitely prohibited* . . . but it will be observed that this prohibition has not been extended to holders of employers' recruiting licenses, so that the employment of such labour as *voluntarily filters through is permissive* on approved local mines but cannot be extended to the Witwatersrand Gold Mines."[30] Apart from bringing back the debate about whether or not the ban applied to Rand mines only, the new position further complicated the enforcement of the ban.

In seeking to prohibit the recruitment of migrant workers from northern territories by labor agents while permitting employers to engage the same class of migrants who entered the country on their own, the government encouraged unauthorized recruiting. To begin with, it was not easy for pass officers and other state officials to distinguish between migrant workers recruited on the other side of the border and those who entered South Africa on their own. It was also common for South African employers to collude with independent recruiters (licensed and unlicensed) who charged fees for migrant workers they brought into the country. When employers' agents (not licensed labor recruiters) took recruits for attestation with the Native Affairs Department authorities—in line with Government Notice no. 1693 discussed above—they often argued that such workers came into the country without any assistance from recruiters. It was only on the rare occasions when officials interviewed the migrant workers they apprehended that they got to know how foreigners reached various destinations in South Africa.[31]

Regardless of the several loopholes in the modified ban, the government's decision to clamp down on the activities of labor recruiters triggered extensive debate about the labor supply situation in South Africa. To some extent, the timing of the policy shift, which coincided with the 1918 outbreak of so-called Spanish influenza, encouraged the contestations that ensued. Although leaders of the WNLA and the NRC argued that the country was facing an acute shortage of labor because the epidemic killed thousands of people, several groups representing local Africans' interests claimed there was no shortage of labor in South Africa. In addition to demanding higher wages for South African workers, various "native associations," such as the Transkei Territories General Council, argued that mining companies fabricated labor statistics to put pressure on government to legalize the recruitment of "tropical natives" whom they paid less than locals. In one of the letters written by people opposed to the increased employment of foreign Africans, one J. A. Starke argued that the gold mines were constantly pressing for the introduction of workers from north of latitude 22° south "to obtain cheaper labour," adding, "this idea of cheaper labour is really the object the Mines have in view, although for some cause or other they are not advancing it now as the actual reason, but on the contrary are pleading shortage of labour."[32]

As debates about the ban raged on, the Native Affairs Department officials turned down several recruiters' requests for permission to engage "tropical" migrants. However, many employers had their applications approved. As was the case prior to Government Notice no. 1693 of December 1918, government officials approved the employment of "tropical" migrants who "filtered" through the country's northern borders. Rather than maintaining a total ban, the director of native labor emphasized the need to avoid sending "tropical natives" to the high veld of the Transvaal during Southern Africa's winter months of April to August. In line with the new stance, government officials also urged employers (mostly farmers) to provide warm clothes to "tropical" migrants as a condition for the renewal of employment permits. On this issue, the director of native labor wrote to several employers and recruiters, informing them that "tropical" migrants would not be registered in winter unless they were in "possession of at least two blankets, a jersey and a pair of trousers or other equivalent clothing."[33] In the same spirit, immigration officials allowed "tropical natives" in possession of employment contracts to enter the country under relaxed terms. Those who wanted to enter the country for business or visiting purposes would only have to provide proof of their intent to return to their home areas at the end of their visits. In this respect, the chief pass officer encouraged the Native Affairs Department officials to give employment permits to "illegal" migrants from Southern Rhodesia, arguing, "as they have managed to evade stoppage on the border, they must either obtain work, starve, or live on the community by some means."[34]

Notwithstanding the challenges that affected the enforcement of the ban from the onset, another wave of contestations set in after a magistrate in Louis Trichardt ruled on December 19, 1923, that Paragraph 10 of Government Notice No. 1693 of December 24, 1918, which banned labor agents from recruiting "tropical" migrants, contradicted the 1911 Native Labor Regulation Act, and was therefore ultra vires. The judgment came after one W. P. de Villiers challenged his conviction for allegedly contravening section 4 of the Native Labor Regulation Act as read with the concerned government notice. In making that decision in what became known as the case of *Rex v. de Villiers*, the Louis Trichardt court found that the 1911 Native Labor Regulation Act was more appropriate to regulate the recruitment of "natives" for employment in South Africa than the 1913 Immigrants Regulation Act. Unlike the latter, which was formulated with Indian migrants in mind and never mentioned the word *natives*, the Native Labor Regulation Act defined these people simply as members of "aboriginal tribes or races of Africa." Consequently, the court argued that this definition did not distinguish between "local" and "foreign" Africans, adding that section 23 (1) of the act actually "contemplate[d] that recruiting of natives will take place outside the Union."[35] Furthermore, the court argued that if the law were intended to prohibit the recruitment of Africans outside the Union, why was there "no provision similar to the one which expressly gives the Governor-General the power to prohibit the recruiting of 'natives' within the Union for employment outside the Union?"[36] The enforcement of South Africa's ban on "tropical" migrants could not be more complicated than it became after this court case.

In a development that revealed more contradictions among South African government officials involved with the implementation of the ban, the secretary for native affairs dismissed the judgment as a nonbinding interpretation of the law and urged officials in his department to continue with the restrictions as before. Expressing similar sentiments, the Transvaal and Pietersburg divisions of the South Africa police department argued that the judgment should be revisited because it rendered law enforcement agents powerless in dealing with border jumpers from areas north of latitude 22° south. In particular, the district commander for Pietersburg wrote that "the WNLA have an office in Louis Trichardt and while this judgment stands good, thousands of natives will be imported into the Union from Rhodesia."[37] However, the Justice Department upheld the ruling. In his support of the Louis Trichardt magistrate's findings, the attorney general warned that "authority is given in section 23(1)(a) of Act No. 15 of 1911 to make regulations, not inconsistent with the Act, in regard to 'the conditions upon which any license or permit may be issued.' . . . A license to recruit 'natives' may have conditions imposed by regulations, but limiting the subject matter of the license is not imposing a condition and to give to the term 'native' in the license a meaning different from that given to it in the Act is to do what is inconsistent with the Act."[38]

From this judgment and debates around it, the South African government seems to have been better off using the Native Labor Regulation Act of 1911 rather than the Immigrants Regulation Act of 1913 to enforce the ban on "tropical" migrants. However, it is not clear if the use of that piece of legislation would have prevented the contestations that engulfed the country's attempt to restrict the importation of foreign African workers and stoked border jumping in the region.

Following the court's ruling in the case of *Rex v. de Villiers*, it became practically difficult to regulate the entry and employment of "tropical natives" in South Africa. Although the ban was still in place, immigration officers, the police, and Native Affairs Department officials received contradictory instructions on how to handle migrants from Southern Rhodesia, Nyasaland, and Mozambique who went to South Africa with or without the assistance of labor agents. In a move that infuriated senior police officers, the public prosecutor at Louis Trichardt Magistrates Court declined to prosecute several labor agents arrested for recruiting "tropical natives," citing the judgment in the case of *Rex v. de Villiers*. Complaining about this scenario, the sub–native commissioner of Louis Trichardt wrote, "I have now arrived at a dead end and am unable to proceed against any Labour Agent who may recruit Rhodesian Native Labour."[39] Although pass officers gave permission to some "tropical" migrants to find work, they had others arrested and jailed for entering the country without permits. However, instead of deporting the migrants they arrested, South African officials often issued passes to these migrants after they paid fines or served their jail terms. In the confusion that ensued, border jumping across the Southern Rhodesia–South Africa border reached considerably higher proportions. As the director of natives pointed out in March 1926, large numbers of migrants were entering South Africa clandestinely from Southern Rhodesia and Nyasaland.[40]

Contesting the Ban: South African Employers' Responses

As the foregoing discussion shows, lack of diligent planning by the South African government resulted in multiple inconsistencies in the implementation of the ban on "tropical natives." However, that was not the only factor that affected the enforcement of the ban. South African employers—especially mine owners and farmers—also challenged the ban in various ways, making its implementation bumpy. This was particularly so because the post-1910 period witnessed rising demand for labor in various sectors of the South African economy. Whereas the mining industry continued to grow after a brief slow down during the 1899–1902 South African war, the agriculture sector experienced more rapid expansion. Benefiting from the loans, marketing opportunities, and other forms of support that the government provided in a bid to boost food production to feed the country's growing population, areas such as Bethal in northern Transvaal became major farming districts.[41] Because these two major sectors relied on migrant workers, whom they considered less expensive and more dependable than locals, South African employers did not passively accept the ban. Instead, they deployed a combination of diplomatic engagements with the government and adaptive resistance characterized by subtle encouragement of clandestine entry by tropical workers.

To better understand how the Transvaal mine owners responded, it is important not to forget that negotiations between them and the Union government began soon after the first parliamentary debate over the death rate of migrant workers employed at the Rand mines. As opposition MPs and other sections of South African society called for the banning of "tropical" migrants, the

Transvaal Chamber of Mines began negotiations with the government. These talks resulted in the establishment of the South African Institute for Medical Research (SAIMR) in 1912. The South African government and the WNLA agreed to jointly fund and administer the SAIMR, the mission of which was to develop laboratory facilities and medical research focusing on industrial diseases. As part of the agreement, the initial research agendas of the SAIMR staff focused on pneumoconiosis, nutrition, and infectious, protozoan, and helminthic diseases, which were believed to be the main health challenges facing the mining industry.[42] As such, when the ban was announced, the Transvaal Chamber of Mines and its recruiting company (the WNLA) did not directly contest the government's position. Instead, they decided to continue investing in medical research while lobbying for the lifting of the ban.

On May 20, 1913—barely two weeks after the announcement of the ban—the WNLA sent a report to the director of native labor providing details of the mortality rates among "tropical natives" employed in different mines during the year ending December 31, 1912, and for the first four months of 1913. In sending the report, which also outlined some measures that mining companies had started implementing in a bid to reduce migrant worker mortality—such as conducting medical exams on all "tropical" migrants and imposing a four-week acclimatization period before deployment underground—the WNLA's objective was to convince the government that it was committed to finding the solution to this problem.[43] However, just as government officials were sending out information about the ban, the secretary of the WNLA wrote another letter to the director of native labor asking him to provide information about the law or regulation under which the proposed prohibition was going to be enforced.[44] Given that the ban was triggered by reports of high mortality rates among mine workers, the WNLA management and general members the Transvaal Chamber of Mines likely followed parliamentary debates on this issue closely. It is also likely that the WNLA secretary was aware of the minister of native affairs' statement of May 23, 1913, specifying that the government was going to use the Immigrants Regulation Act to enforce the ban. Perhaps what remained unclear to the WNLA and other employers at the time were the exact clauses of the act that the government was going to use for this purpose. It is also likely that the WNLA sent this letter to stay closely engaged with, and possibly ahead of, government officials to position itself to change the course of events.

It is also interesting to note that within the first month of the implementation of the ban, the WNLA secretary argued that the mortality of "tropical" migrants was on a downward trend because mining companies complied with the government's recommendations on systematic inoculation of "tropical natives" and the repatriation of those found unfit for employment by the mines. Noting that the mortality rate for August 1913 was 17.16 per 1000 per annum, the

WNLA claimed that this mortality rate was the lowest on record. To substantiate its argument, the WNLA produced a detailed analysis of the mortality rates for each of its affiliate mining companies for the period from January to August 1913.[45] The reason for compiling such a detailed analysis was to show the government that the association was leaving no stone unturned in its bid to address the cause of death among "tropical" migrants. The WNLA also wanted to show that the situation was already improving.

Over the following four years, the WNLA took several steps to show that mining companies were addressing government concerns about "tropical" migrants' health. Having already built a hospital at the WNLA compound in Johannesburg, the association hired Allen Percival Watkins, a physician with extensive experience working in Africa's tropical areas, to fill the position of assistant medical officer. Watkins and A. I. Girdwood, the WNLA's chief medical officer, made several recommendations for the improvement of "tropical" migrants' health in the mines. Regarding housing, for example, they suggested that mining companies accommodate "tropical" migrants "in Compound rooms built on the cubic system with individual bunks for each native with plenty of cubic space."[46] Over and above the medical officers' recommendations, the WNLA encouraged mining companies to construct on-site clinics, which it referred to as "native hospitals," and changing houses to be used by "tropical" migrants. The association also instructed mining companies to make sure the concerned migrants were properly dressed when they moved from the changing houses to their rooms. In a development that projected the Chamber of Mines as committed to addressing the situation, the WNLA threatened to stop allocating migrant workers to mines with consistently high mortality rates.

In 1917, the Transvaal Chamber of Mines intensified its efforts to regain the permission to recruit from restricted areas by making a proposal for the government to allow the WNLA to recruit approximately 2,000 migrants from Malawi and Mozambique to be inoculated with a pneumonia vaccine developed by Dr. Spencer Lister, who was a research bacteriologist at the SAIMR. In making the proposal, the Chamber of Mines stressed that the antipneumococcal vaccine called *prophylactic*, which functioned both as a preventative and curative measure, had proved to be so effective that pneumonia was almost nonexistent at mines where it had been used. The chamber also emphasized that its request was for a limited and controlled lifting of the ban to allow for a medical experiment with no more than 2,000 migrants.[47] It was very strategic that the chamber made its request at the time that the country faced shortages of labor due to the recruitment of local Africans to fight in World War I. As noted already, debates surrounding the WNLA's request also coincided with the outbreak of the 1918 influenza epidemic, which affected large parts of the world, including South Africa.

After extensive debates over this issue, the prime minister agreed to lift the ban temporarily to allow an experiment with the pneumonia vaccine to proceed. The Justice Department gave a nod to the proposal as permissible under the Immigrants Regulation Act. Although the medical officer in the Government Labor Bureau rejected the proposal as being too risky for the concerned human beings, the director of the SAIMR, the medical officer in the Native Affairs Department, the chairman of the Miners' Phthisis Medical Bureau, and the two medical officers in the WNLA supported the idea. Before he could lift the ban, the prime minister presented the idea in Parliament, where he pointed out that instead of 2,000, the experiment would start with 1,000 "tropical" migrants. As part of his presentation, the prime minister also showed statistics from the WNLA that suggested a major reduction in the mortality rate of "tropical natives." Despite what appears to have been overwhelming support for the proposal, Creswell and other opposition MPs objected and the prime minister withdrew his support for the idea.[48] Although some sections of the mining community criticized the opposition to the proposal as the Labor Party's effort to force mine owners to employ local Africans, the Transvaal Chamber of Mines and the WNLA did not engage in that debate. Instead, they chose to continue engaging with the government's recommendations in a bid to have the ban lifted.

However, outside the organizational framework of the chamber or the WNLA, mining companies devised ways of continuing with the employment of workers from north of latitude 22° south. Individual mines employed "prohibited migrants" who were illegally smuggled by unlicensed recruiters, touts, and runners who operated in the border districts and in areas such as Crooks' Corner. Some mine owners recruited from the restricted regions by giving batches of stamped contract forms to former employees when they went back to Southern Rhodesia, Nyasaland, or Mozambique. The former employees would give the documents to prospective migrants who filled in their names and other identity information, pretending to be employees of the companies. They would then use the fake contract documents to obtain passes as if they were returning to their jobs in South Africa. As the sub–native commissioner for Louis Trichardt pointed out in 1926, this practice was common among some employers in the mining industry.[49] Such practices by mining companies fueled border jumping across the Zimbabwe–South Africa border. The companies adopted a two-pronged approach in a bid to keep labor costs low.

Farmers' responses to the ban were slightly different from those of the mine owners. The prohibition of labor recruitment from areas north of latitude 22° south affected the agricultural sector differently than the mining sector. For example, before the controversial Government Notice No. 1693 of December 24, 1918, farmers did not do much about the ban because it did not adversely affect them. Whereas the government placed an embargo on mining companies' employment of "tropical" migrants, farmers could still employ migrants who "voluntarily filtered" through the cracks of the prohibition. In this context, the Transvaal farmers could easily register "tropical" migrants as long as they satisfied the Native Affairs Department officials at Louis Trichardt and Pietersburg who wanted to know that such workers were recruited within the borders of South Africa. However, after the decision to stop all labor agents from recruiting "tropical" migrants within or outside the Union of South Africa was adopted, government authorities began to require farmers to also apply for permission to employ this class of migrant workers. Before granting permission to farmers interested in employing "tropical natives," the director of labor had to be satisfied that the applicant would provide acceptable accommodation, clothing, food, medical facilities, wages, and leisure time for the employees.[50]

As the merit-based approval system took effect, the Native Affairs Department was swamped with petitions from farmers who felt shortchanged. On December 30, 1921, for example, the Medalie brothers who had farms in Louis Trichardt wrote the director of native labor to protest the cancellation of their license to recruit "tropical" migrants. They specifically asked the director to "write to the Sub-Native Commissioner, Louis Trichardt and cancel the order given with reference to our engagement of Rhodesian natives."[51] Several farmers in and outside the Transvaal area sent similar petitions to the Native Affairs Department in a bid to regain the privilege of recruiting migrants from north of the Limpopo River. In one of the petitions that the Natal Estates Ltd of Mount Edgecombe sent to the secretary for native affairs in July 1921, the company asked for permission to recruit workers from Southern Rhodesia, arguing that climatic and labor conditions at Mount Edgecombe were favorable to the health of "tropical natives." Other farmers such as E. Lazarus, who had become prominent for his maize farms in Bethal district, and "Messrs Spain and Stein" also wrote several letters seeking permission to recruit from Southern Rhodesia.[52]

In addition to petitions by individual farmers or companies, farmers' groups also approached various government offices with similar requests. In October 1919, for example, a group of farmers teamed up with labor agents, contractors, and ordinary residents and sent a petition to the minister of native affairs. Part of the group's petition read as follows:

> The conditions governing Labour Agents' and Employers' recruiting licenses at present in force do not give satisfaction and are regarded as unfair and unjust, and the manner in which they are carried out in practice is illogical.... Before these restrictions were imposed, such natives at the end of their period of labour were permitted to return to their homes by whatever route they liked and how they liked. The result was that they chose the route by which they entered the country.... We urgently submit that freedom of contract should be restored, and that the restrictive conditions should be cancelled and abolished.[53]

Given that the moratorium placed on labor recruiting affected a wide spectrum of South African society, it was possible for such alliances of convenience to be formed. But what makes this petition interesting is that its authors presented themselves as being treated unfairly by officials in the Native Affairs Department. They alleged that the allocation of "tropical" migrants who entered the country on their own was skewed in favor of the WNLA. For this reason, they urged the government to either deport all "tropical natives" who entered the country "clandestinely" or allow them the freedom to choose where they wanted to work.

In the same vein, hundreds of farmers producing fruits, vegetables, tobacco, and cotton in northern Transvaal came together and formed the Low Veld Farmers Association, which also put pressure on government authorities requesting permissions to recruit migrant workers from areas north of latitude 22° south. In September 1924, this organization sent a delegation to the prime minister hoping to convince him to allow them to recruit migrant workers from Southern Rhodesia. In a follow-up letter to the secretary for native affairs, the Low Veld Farmers Association's secretary argued that an acute shortage of labor in the Transvaal compelled the association to send the delegation. He stressed that "farmers wish to take advantage of the early rains for planting cotton, etc., and are held up for want of labour."[54] In response to critics who argued that the Transvaal farmers, like mine owners, preferred to employ foreigners ahead of locals who demanded higher wages and better conditions of work, the Low Veld Farmers Association came up with a creative spin. It invoked the debate over migrant workers' health, arguing that African workers from within the Union of South Africa were unsuitable for the low veld, "as the majority would come from non-malarial areas into an area which is malarial," adding "we have attempted to employ such natives in the past with bad results to the health of such natives."[55] In arguing that workers from south of latitude 22° south were susceptible to malaria in the low veld region, the association deployed the same rhetoric that inspired the ban of the employment of "tropical" migrants on the Transvaal gold mines.

As was the case with mining companies, which combined diplomatic negotiations with government and unauthorized recruiting of workers from restricted areas, farmers obtained "tropical" migrants through "clandestine" means. This channel became more pronounced after the illegalization of all recruiting activities in December 1918 and the imposition of a merit-based approval system. Under this system, farmers applied for permission to receive "tropical" migrants from the Native Affairs Department, not to recruit on their own. In response to the new dispensation, several farmers engaged so-called domestic servants who functioned mostly as labor touts and runners. Because such people were not labor agents, they were not legally bound to be registered or to have recruiters' permits to carry out their recruiting activities. However, they could not recruit openly. Consequently, their main strategy was to offer cash, clothes, and various other kinds of items to induce work-seeking migrants to go to specific farms.[56]

Although this practice was common among farmers who failed to obtain permits to employ "tropical natives," approved employers often went beyond the terms of their permits. For example, after being listed as approved employers, farmers such as Spain and Stein engaged labor touts who targeted slum areas of Johannesburg, which had become major destinations for northern migrants in search of employment.[57]

Endorsing the Ban: Southern Rhodesia's Response

Despite the controversies, inconsistencies, and contestations that engulfed the implementation of South Africa's ban on "tropical natives," mine owners, farmers, and state officials in Southern Rhodesia welcomed it. Because the pre-1910 government of the Transvaal did not do much to control cross-Limpopo mobility, the BSAC administration viewed the ban as an opportunity to strengthen several measures it had introduced since the mid-1890s in an effort to prevent loss of labor to South Africa. In fact, two years before the announcement of the ban, Southern Rhodesia's Legislative Council passed the Native Labor Regulations Ordinance hoping to curb the activities of unlicensed labor recruiters in the border zone, but that proved ineffective given lack of cooperation from their South African counterparts. Interestingly, in the same year that South Africa announced the ban, Southern Rhodesian authorities introduced the Natives Pass Consolidation Ordinance (1913), which repealed the Natives Pass Ordinance of 1902. Although it is not clear that they deliberately timed their law to coincide with the announcement of the ban on northern migrants in South Africa, Southern Rhodesian authorities did not hide the fact that they wanted to capitalize on what appeared to be a new and promising approach by their southern neighbors.

The main purpose of the 1913 ordinance was to consolidate the pass system to have better control of the mobility of Africans, especially those from Nyasaland and Mozambique, who came into the colony as migrant workers. At minimum, Southern Rhodesian authorities and employers wanted a situation in which African migrants from other territories found it easier to enter the colony but very hard to proceed to South Africa.[58] In line with the new piece of legislation, Southern Rhodesian authorities imposed more stringent measures of controlling Africans' mobility within and out of the colony. As a first step in their latest bid to prevent loss of labor, the chief native commissioner invoked section 19 of the Natives Pass Consolidation Ordinance, which says "no native shall, save as is in this Ordinance excepted, leave the Territory unless he be in possession of a pass duly granted for that purpose," and instructed all pass officers to not issue passes to Africans, whether locals or migrants, intending to go to South Africa in search of work.[59] When it emerged that Africans could still obtain passes for the country's southern districts, from which they slipped into South Africa, the same official dispatched a circular to all superintendents of natives, pleading, "Will you please point out to all officials in your divisions that the employment in labour districts in the Union of native inhabitants of areas North of latitude 22° south is prohibited, and as practically the whole of Southern Rhodesia lies within the prohibited area, the issue of [passes to go to South Africa] must cease."[60] In another circular, he pointed out that no passes were to be issued to Africans who desired to go to the Union unless special permission was obtained from the chief immigration officer in Pretoria "for such native or natives to enter the Union."[61]

However, Southern Rhodesian authorities could not convict anyone for going to South Africa without permission. They could cite the ban (and the supposed health risks that migrant workers faced on the Transvaal mines) in rejecting applications for passes to South Africa, but it was not possible for them to use this rationale as a basis for prosecuting offenders in court. In this respect, the minister of mines and public works wrote, "We cannot ourselves debar our natives or natives from the north from crossing the Limpopo River," continuing, "We are helpless to prevent natives from crossing the Limpopo and I presume legislation on these lines would not be desirable."[62] The legal complication emanated from the fact that migrants would not commit the offence of leaving the country without a pass until they crossed the border. Yet, when migrants crossed the border into South Africa, Southern Rhodesian authorities lost jurisdiction over them because they were in a different territory with different laws. It was up to the South African authorities to decide how they wanted to handle such people. Faced with this challenge, Southern Rhodesian authorities devised strategies not simply to support the ban but also to encourage the South African government to enforce it.

Having spent several years "chasing" labor recruiters in the border districts, Southern Rhodesian authorities took advantage of the ban to court their South African counterparts to join the fight against unlicensed recruiting in the region. In this respect, the commissioner of the British South Africa Police made a proposal for a joint patrol unit comprising police officers from Southern Rhodesia, South Africa, and Mozambique that would be deployed in Crooks' Corner. Realizing the importance of having a joint police unit in the border zone, Southern Rhodesia's chief native commissioner weighed in by saying that such an arrangement would make it easier for the police forces of the three territories to pursue illegal recruiters regardless of the boundaries. He also suggested that a mobile magistrate be seconded to police patrols to handle cases that would potentially crop up. In justifying his proposal, the chief native commissioner pointed out that this approach would make the prosecution of convicted recruiters much easier because the police would not have to travel between 200 and 300 miles to the nearest magistrates court. Furthermore, he emphasized the importance of setting up such a structure by saying, "while fully appreciating the steps taken by the Union Government it is feared that until some definite steps are agreed to and co-operation ensured and that so long as these 'Bandits' . . . are allowed to be at large within the vicinity of where the three territories join, they will be a continual source of trouble and menace to the natives on our borders," and stating that "more effectual steps must be taken. This can best be done by concerted and simultaneous action by the police authorities of the territories concerned with hunting down these outlaws."[63] In addition to making these proposals, Southern Rhodesian authorities explored the possibility of establishing a police station in the vicinity of the Pafuri Triangle. However, they could not proceed with that project as proposed because of a lack of resources. In addition, despite the pledge of support from the governor general of Mozambique, South African authorities did not commit to the idea of deploying a joint police unit in Crooks' Corner.

Even with the failure of the joint police operation proposal, Southern Rhodesian authorities continued to engage their South African counterparts, encouraging them to enforce the ban. In this endeavor, Southern Rhodesian authorities made extensive efforts to gather information showing that, in spite of the ban, many people from north of latitude 22° south crossed the border and took up employment in different parts of South Africa. They then presented such information to the South African authorities and urged them to act. In one of several letters he wrote to South African officials, Southern Rhodesia's chief native commissioner expressed his government's appreciation of their counterparts' efforts to prohibit "illegal" recruiting in the border zone. However, he also pointed out that government officials were concerned by reports indicating that a large number of "Rhodesian natives" were still being engaged at the mines of the Rand and Natal. Reminding his counterparts of the ban, the chief native commissioner wrote, "as these natives come from areas North of latitude 22° south, they are, as stated . . . prohibited immigrants in the Union."[64] He went further to argue that it should not have been difficult for South African officials to tell that these migrants came from restricted areas because their registration certificates contained their names and those of their chiefs. Although it is possible that the chief native commissioner did not know that recruiters often misled South African officials about the identities of the migrants, he cited some correspondence relating to the estates of migrants who died in the mines as evidence that it was possible to trace their true origins.

The chief native commissioner further revealed that Southern Rhodesian officials were disappointed by the lack of cooperation from their South African counterparts:

> It does not, however, appear that up to the present at any rate, any serious attempt has been made to exclude them from the Union. . . . Indeed, if any

serious attempt had been made to observe the law making Rhodesian natives prohibited immigrants and to prevent their employment in the Union, it is difficult to suppose that the NRC, which represents the Transvaal Chamber of Mines and which has been in constant touch with your department, could have acquiesced in, or been permitted to acquiesce in, practices such as those to which your letter refers; still less that an official in the position of the Director of Native Labour could even 'under momentary misapprehension' have suggested, in effect, the exploitation of Southern Rhodesian labour in opposition to the known policy of this Administration, *vide* his letter to yourself of the 28 March, 1918.[65]

He ended his letter by pointing out that the Southern Rhodesian leadership strongly supported the ban on "tropical" migrants and were prepared to do everything possible to fight illegal recruiting in the border zone. He also emphasized that efforts to regulate the recruitment and importation of northern migrants into South Africa would not succeed unless and until the two territories started working together. However, he and his South African counterparts knew very well that implementing such an agreement would not benefit South African employers who badly needed foreign workers.

After further correspondence in which senior officials from the Southern Rhodesian and South African departments of native affairs accused each other's government of not doing enough to stop *clandestine* mobility in the region, a bilateral conference was held in Pietersburg in September 1918. As the notes of the conference reveal, there were major differences between the two countries' approaches to managing migration in the region. Whereas Southern Rhodesia's chief native commissioner spoke strongly about the need to cooperate in fighting border jumping, the South African authorities argued that it was not their responsibility to stop Africans from leaving their homes for better paying jobs anywhere in the region. In this respect, the native commissioner for Louis Trichardt pointed out that absolute prohibition of migration from north of the border was "outside the region of practical politics."[66] With that in mind, the South African director of native labor proposed a resolution affirming that it was not possible to stop border jumping between the two countries. Part of the resolution read, "While we recognise that the Union and Southern Rhodesian Governments have accepted the policy of prohibiting the entry into the Union of Natives from north of latitude 22° S, we are of the opinion that it is not practicable to give effect to this policy in respect of natives from Southern Rhodesia who voluntarily enter the Transvaal through its northern borders; nor do we consider it practicable to effectively deal with the repatriation of such natives who enter the Union."[67] After another round of heated exchanges during which Southern Rhodesia's representatives repeatedly called for cooperation in dealing with unlicensed recruiters in the border zone, the resolution was adopted.

Although Southern Rhodesian authorities revived the proposal for joint police operations in the border zone, South African officials argued that there was nothing their government could do about illegal recruiting that took place north of the boundary. As the native commissioner for Louis Trichardt put it, again, South African officials understood that it was "a matter of wide concern to Rhodesia to conserve its native labour for its own benefit," but they expected their northern neighbor to realize "how impossible it is to prevent this voluntary infiltration of natives from Southern Rhodesia."[68] The South African director of native labor further pointed out that when Union authorities recognized that migrants filtered through the border, they allowed them to obtain employment under conditions that the government regarded as sustainable and not prejudicial to their health.[69] Despite being custodians and authors of the ban on migrants from north of latitude 22° south, South African authorities were reluctant to put real barriers on workers from Southern Rhodesia and other areas north of the Limpopo River. Instead, they gave a green light for the employment of "tropical" migrants who entered their country without permission from authorities in colonial Zimbabwe. In the words of one Southern Rhodesian official, the attitude of South African authorities was "keep your Natives on your side: we do not want them, but do not expect us to put a ring of police posts along the border."[70]

The South African officials' refusal to adopt a more aggressive approach to controlling labor recruiters' activities in the border districts also infuriated mine owners, farmers, and other employers in Southern Rhodesia. As the numbers of Africans leaving the colony for South Africa increased in the early 1920s, the Rhodesia Chamber of Mines piled pressure on government officials to find ways of stopping loss of labor. In one of several letters that mine owners wrote to government officials, F. D. Roscoe of Antelope Gold Mine in Matopos (in south western Zimbabwe) claimed that he had information indicating that many "boys" were taking passes for Francistown (Botswana) from which they proceeded to the Transvaal. He therefore urged the government to "consider the advisability of curtailing the number of passes issued to natives in this way, and so retain the labour within the territory."[71] Similarly, the secretary for the Rhodesia Chamber of Mines wrote the chief native commissioner asking why the South African government did not strictly enforce the ban on "tropical natives" and what plans Southern Rhodesian authorities had to assist the mining industry with retaining labor.[72] Southern Rhodesian mine owners also urged their government to establish permanent police posts in the border districts. However, this did not happen because the country was short of manpower, finances, and other resources needed to establish new posts. As in previous years, Southern Rhodesia's police department could dispatch only occasional patrols to intercept border jumpers and labor recruiters. What complicated matters was that the border could be easily crossed at any point during most of the year when the Limpopo River was not in flood.

Southern Rhodesian officials and employers blamed their South African counterparts for encouraging border jumping between the two countries by not strictly enforcing the ban on "tropical" migrants, but they also did very little to address the factors that led Africans to look for work in South Africa. In 1921 the chief native commissioner pointed out that a good proportion of "Rhodesian natives" who proceeded to the Union did so for the purpose of visiting friends and relatives.[73] Given that the Venda, Shangani, Sotho, and other communities astride the border strove to keep social ties with their relatives by regularly moving back and forth across the Limpopo River, the chief native commissioner's observation could not be said to be off the mark. As discussed in chapter 1, cross-Limpopo mobility was the way of life for the majority of residents of the border districts. It was common for people to marry, worship, and attend social events across the border. Those forms of mobility, which involved closely connected groups, were not easy for Southern Rhodesian authorities to regulate.

Nevertheless, government officials and employers could surely do something about the conditions of work in both the mining and agricultural sectors in colonial Zimbabwe. It was no secret that Southern Rhodesian mine owners paid workers far less than their counterparts in South Africa did. Despite employers' insistence that Africans left the colony because of the administration's failure to enforce pass laws and police the border area, many officials in the Native Affairs Department knew that low wages contributed significantly in driving workers out of Southern Rhodesia. In 1915, for example, the chief native commissioner pointed out that the paltry 5 to 10 shillings per month which most Africans earned from local employers did not help them to fulfill their obligations, including paying government-stipulated taxes.[74] Reiterating the same point in 1916, the chairman of the Rhodesia Native Labor Bureau wrote, "The native cannot fulfill his obligations satisfactorily, and if there is a better market for his labour further south or further north, he will go there in increasing numbers."[75] Ten years later, the superintendent of natives in Fort Victoria said, "The lure of high wages in South Africa was so strong that our natives continue to go there in the face of difficulties," adding, "I was told of cases in which natives had persisted in going on, notwithstanding being imprisoned two or three times."[76] As the Southern Rhodesian officials explored ways of responding to the Rhodesia Chamber of Mines' criticisms, the chief native commissioner pointed out that "the only remedy of a permanent nature is to make conditions of employment more attractive."[77] His views resonated with those of the minister of native affairs, who said, "There is no provision of law under which we can prevent Natives proceeding to the Transvaal if they wish to do so, nor could we enforce such a law if it existed." He added, "It would appear to be an economic question, fine and simple. The attraction of higher wages."[78] Statements such as these go a long way to show that government officials in Southern Rhodesia knew that what the local employers paid their African employees was not enough to live on. However, they did nothing to try to correct that situation and ensure that few Africans left the territory in search of employment. They were simply powerless when it came to holding employers, especially the Rhodesia Chamber of Mines and the Rhodesia Farmers Association, accountable for their business choices. These two organizations controlled a very large section of the white community in early colonial Zimbabwe, making them very powerful political constituents.

Southern Rhodesian authorities also did very little to address African workers' complaints about ill treatment by their white employers. As noted in chapter 1, it was common for employers and, at times, native commissioners to whip Africans in an attempt to force them to work. But the abuse of African workers took different forms. Sometimes employers would deny their workers even the right to quit when they felt like doing so. The experience of one Amon Makufa Mlambo sheds more light on how some employers treated African workers. Recounting his experience as a domestic servant in Southern Rhodesia's second largest city of Bulawayo, Mlambo said:

> For a time I was there working for my employer then I informed him that I wanted to resign. He said I should give him the notice to resign. I gave him one month's notice. At the end of that month I told him I wanted to go, and he said you are not going. . . . I told him there is little money here so I gave him another month's notice. . . . In the second month I told him, I want to go. . . . He said you cannot go, whereupon he called the police. Meanwhile I had already packed my clothing. He told them, my servant has packed up his clothing he wants to desert.[79]

The police arrested Mlambo but only for a brief period because they realized he had given his employer enough notice in line with the laws governing African employment contracts. However, Mlambo's employer would not sign his pass. After this experience, Mlambo left for South Africa. Rather than focusing too much on South Africa's controversial ban on "Rhodesian natives" and other "tropical" migrants, it would have helped Southern Rhodesian officials to encourage local employers to improve work conditions for Africans.

It is also important to note that in times of drought, the colonial government extended grain loans to Africans and expected them to pay back the loans when the situation improved. Instead of waiting for good harvests to demand reimbursements, sometimes government officials sent out messengers to round up indebted people so they could work to settle their debts. Large numbers of people in the Victoria Circle (now Masvingo Province), for example, left for South Africa in 1917 when the government started collections for grain debts. As the chief native commissioner noted, the districts that were most affected were Ndanga (Zaka) and Chibi (Chivi), where people had to earn money to pay back debts to the government for grain advanced them when they faced famine. What is interesting about this case is that in addition to those who went to work in South Africa so they could pay their debts, others crossed the Limpopo to avoid paying back debts. In addition, some people refused government support and sought work in South Africa to support their families in times of famine.[80]

What complicated matters was that few opportunities for employment existed in the southern districts of Southern Rhodesia. The mines and farms in northern Transvaal were the nearest employment centers where the residents of the border region could find employment. Commenting on this situation, the native commissioner for Zaka wrote, "The distance to the North Transvaal from the natives' homes compares favourably with the distance to the larger labour centres in Southern Rhodesia such as Gwelo, Gatooma, Bulawayo, Salisbury, etc.," and added, "I may mention that were any attempt made by the local Government to prevent natives from these parts from proceeding to the Transvaal to work as hitherto, it would be strongly resented by them and would adversely affect Native Tax collection."[81] Consequently, the chief native commissioner was not surprised to find that the Messina Copper Mine employed large numbers of African workers from Southern Rhodesia. Instead of demanding the repatriation of such migrants, he argued that his government would appreciate it if the Messina Copper Mine helped with the collection of taxes from the "Rhodesian natives" they employed.[82]

Although multiple factors compelled Zimbabweans to leave their country for South Africa, state officials' attempts to stop cross-border migration made it more difficult for migrants to use official channels. As was the case when the BSAC administration started controlling mobility across the Limpopo River in the 1890s, the attempt to prevent people from leaving the colony through official channels fueled "clandestine" emigration. Given that South African officials allowed employers to engage migrants from north of latitude 22° south who "filtered" through the Southern Rhodesia–South Africa border, thousands of Zimbabweans found various ways to cross the border. In this respect, Southern Rhodesia's endorsement of South Africa's ban on "tropical natives" could not help but promote border jumping between these two countries.

Migrant Workers' Evasion of the Ban

When Creswell asked the South African native affairs minister to clarify the government's strategy for ensuring effective enforcement of the ban on "tropical natives," he predicted that migrants from the restricted areas would deploy clandestine means to continue entering the country. His prediction was spot on. The implementation of the ban, along with Southern Rhodesian authorities' modification of the pass system in an effort to further restrict Africans' migration to South Africa, resulted in an upsurge of border jumping between these two countries. Although the early twentieth-century records of population movements between Zimbabwe and South Africa are imprecise, official estimates indicate that the number of Zimbabweans working in South Africa increased from 2,526 per year in 1911 to more than 5,000 by 1925.[83] These statistics include migrants who crossed the border through the legal channels, but it is possible that they do not include everyone. Most people walked across the Limpopo at various crossing points and obtained employment of one kind or another without being formally registered or attested. It is therefore very likely that the number of Zimbabweans who worked in different parts of South Africa by the mid-1920s was much larger than projected in these statistics.

In 1925 the minister for mines and public works in Southern Rhodesia pointed out that there was "a fairly steady stream of natives from north of the Limpopo River proceeding to the Transvaal."[84] It is tempting to dismiss this comment as simply speculation by officials from a country that wanted to prevent loss of labor; however, the reports coming from South Africa around the same time pointed toward the same scenario. The sub–native commissioner for Louis Trichardt noted that 95 percent of migrants from Southern Rhodesia and "British Central Africa" in general entered the Transvaal without passes.[85] This was inevitable. As Michel Foucault argues, the existence of a legal prohibition on any human activity almost always creates a field of illegal practices.[86] In this case, South Africa's ban on so-called tropical migrants did not exactly create illegality, but it encouraged a phenomenon that already existed. With the Union of South Africa's participation in the control of migration in the region (despite its refusal to cooperate with Southern Rhodesia), crossing the Limpopo River took on a different meaning. Previously, travelers only had to worry about Southern Rhodesia's strategies for restricting mobility between the two territories; now they had to think about ways to evade South Africa's ban as well.

When state authorities in Southern Rhodesia stopped issuing passes for South Africa, citing the ban and supposed health risks on the Transvaal mines, potential migrants changed their strategies. Instead of applying for a permit that would enable them to buy a train ticket for South Africa (via Botswana), people sought passes for border districts such as Gwanda, Bulilima-Mangwe, Matobo, and Plumtree. In those areas, job seekers targeted mines such as West Nicholson and Jessie in Gwanda and Legion and Antelope in Matobo, where they worked for varying periods of time before sneaking across the border. When Southern Rhodesian authorities stopped issuing passes to the border districts, the routes and strategies of border jumping shifted accordingly. As Southern Rhodesia's chief native commissioner observed, the refusal of passes for South Africa had "the result that Natives intending to go to the Transvaal were diverted to use illegal means of crossing the Limpopo River."[87]

Because most migrants walked the entire journey from different departure points to the border, it was not difficult to evade Southern Rhodesia's migration control measures. In this respect, migrants often followed what police officers characterized as "devious paths" that avoided the Native Affairs Department stations and European settlements where the police were usually stationed. Migrants' routes often passed through networks of villages where travelers would rest and/or replenish supplies. Experienced travelers who knew the routes and the location of resting places usually led the way. As Mlambo narrated, "The routes were well known by the pioneer migrants who had been there before. . . . We went with someone who had been there before. He is the one who told you, 'the place is like that and that.'"[88] Once they got into the border zone, they connected with labor recruiters who handed them over to potential employers in South Africa. Sometimes migrants were assisted by villagers from communities astride the border who gave them directions and, at times, helped them cross the Limpopo River. In so doing, migrants not only simply succeeded in dodging the official systems of migration control but also developed important social networks on which future generations of border jumpers depended.

When they realized that they could not get passes for Southern Rhodesia's border districts, which would make it easier to sneak into South Africa, migrants shifted attention to Botswana. Because Botswana had not been a popular destination for migrants from Southern Rhodesia for a long time, officials did not restrict migration to that region. As such, people obtained passes for Francistown, from which they then proceeded to South Africa. In some cases, Zimbabwean and other "northern" migrants worked in Francistown for as long as it took to get onto the Botswana tax registers. They would then present their tax receipts and buy train tickets for South Africa, as if they were originally from Botswana. Other migrants bribed community leaders in the Tati Concession who falsely testified that the concerned migrants were indeed from Tati. Doing that allowed such migrants to register and pay local taxes so they could obtain receipts to use as proof of identity when traveling to South Africa.[89]

Migrants originating from Southern Rhodesia's southeastern districts such as Chipinga (now Chipinge) and Melsetter (Chimanimani) deployed a similar strategy by first crossing into southern Mozambique, where they obtained identity documents as if they were "Portuguese natives," before proceeding to South Africa. The real identities of such migrants were often revealed after they died and officials tried to resolve the deceased's estates. One of several cases that officials in South Africa and Southern Rhodesia had to handle concerned a man called Lunch Mapenya. Although he was originally from Chipinge, Mapenya lived and worked in South Africa as a "Portuguese native" until he died sometime in 1924.

Following his death, someone simply identified as Mbika, who held a Southern Rhodesian passport—despite also being registered as a Portuguese native—came forward and testified that the deceased was from Southern Rhodesia.[90] Because Chipinge, Chimanimani, and other areas in southeastern Zimbabwe were part of the precolonial Gaza state, which extended into southwestern Mozambique, it was easy for people like Mapenya to pose as Mozambicans. By adopting Mozambican or Botswanan citizenship, which allowed people to "legally" enter and work in South Africa, migrants did not simply subvert South Africa's ban on "tropical" migrants and Southern Rhodesia's pass laws but also made creative use of historical, linguistic, and cultural identities that transcended colonial borders in the region.

As was the case before 1913, migrants often worked with labor recruiters, touts, and runners who were camped at Crooks' Corner and other parts of the border zone. Because most of these recruiters did not have the permission to register "tropical natives" with South African officials, labor recruiters "sold" migrants to various employers who would then register such workers with the Native Affairs Department officials in the Transvaal. For example, within a few years of the introduction of the ban, a recruiter named Cecil Barnard (whom the Shangani called *Bvekenya* (because he swaggered as he walked) and another known simply as "Roux" became well known for the violent means they used in obtaining workers from areas around Crooks' Corner. As Southern Rhodesia's chief native commissioner observed, Barnard and Roux "terrorized natives in the surrounding districts by flogging them and threatening to shoot them, [so much that] the natives [were] afraid to stay in their kraals on account of these men."[91] Interestingly, the NRC once engaged Barnard as one of its recruiters. This triggered a seemingly angry reaction from a South African official who argued that Barnard collected "gangs of boys, more often than not, with a rifle leveled at their heads," adding that the methods he used were "similar to those adopted by the Australian bushrangers except that instead of specie, Bernard's object is the acquisition of gangs of natives."[92]

As violence intensified, representatives of the NRC and other recruiting agents operating in the Pafuri Triangle held several meetings hoping to self-regulate their activities, but none of them respected the agreements they negotiated. One of the recruiters' meetings, which the sub–native commissioner for Sibasa attended in 1915, produced a seemingly progressive list of agreements. For example, recruiters agreed that they needed to eliminate violence and competition by paying salaries instead of commissions to their agents stationed at Crook's Corner. They also agreed that there should not be recruiting within Southern Rhodesia's borders—apparently in line with the 1913 prohibition on such kinds of activities in areas north of latitude 22° south.[93] However, these agreements were not implemented because none of the parties were willing to give up what they perceived as their comparative advantages over the others.

In addition to adopting more aggressive and violent means to obtain migrant workers, labor recruiters developed creative ways of evading South Africa's ban on "tropical natives." Taking advantage of the migrants' ability to assume fake identities, labor agents often engaged border people, especially the Shangani speakers from areas around the Pafuri Triangle, who coached migrants on what to say when they went for attestation. At times, recruiters engaged "native" employees at the Makuleke store to take "tropical" migrants through crash courses on the local identities and cultures they were supposed to adopt. When recruiters took migrants for attestation, they often mixed "tropical natives" with migrants from nonrestricted areas and then selected spokesmen from among those originating south of latitude 22° south to speak on behalf of the group when questioned by state authorities. To misrepresent information, recruiters would urge "tropical" migrants to destroy their registration certificates and obtain fake ones or simply lie to state officials that they lost their original identity documents.[94] Such practices were not just by-products of the policy inconsistences that surrounded the implementation of South Africa's ban on "tropical natives"—they simultaneously benefited from and worked against the ban.

Opening the Floodgates: Lifting the Ban

Debates and contestations about the recruitment and employment of "tropical" migrants in South Africa took a major twist following the modification of the 1896 Labor Agreement between South Africa and Mozambique. Through what came to be known as the Mozambique Convention of September 11, 1928, the government of South Africa conceded to the Portuguese colonial officials' request to reduce the number of Mozambican migrants who could be legally employed in South Africa in any given year. Although the 1928 convention's effect on agriculture and other sectors of the South African economy remained unclear, the number of Mozambicans that mining companies could employ in any given year was reduced from 100,000 to fewer than 80,000.[95] Given that Mozambique was a major source of cheap labor for South African businesses, the Transvaal mining companies argued that a 20-percent reduction in labor supplies from that country placed their operations in danger because they were forbidden from employing migrant workers from north of latitude 22° south. This development bolstered calls for relaxation of labor recruitment policies in general and especially the removal of the ban on northern workers.

Mining company representatives wrote several petitions in the wake of the 1928 Mozambique Convention. In one of those petitions, the president of the Transvaal Chamber of Mines argued that despite the economic depression, which affected many parts of the world, the Witwatersrand mining industry was expanding and thus in urgent need of between 10,000 and 15,000 workers. He also complained that the Portuguese curator in Johannesburg was turning down applications for the renewal of passports for Mozambicans whose work contracts had expired. For these reasons, the Transvaal Chamber of Mines asked the government to lift the ban and allow the WNLA to provide facilities for the importation of workers from north of latitude 22° south. He further argued that the pneumonia vaccine that the SAIMR produced had been so effective that employment at the mines posed no further health risks to "tropical natives."[96] The Transvaal Chamber of Mines' request was supported by the South African government's mining engineer, who argued that the time had arrived for policy makers to revisit the ban. For his part, the engineer pointed out that it did not make sense to deny the chamber's request on health grounds because many "tropical" migrants were already employed at several mines. He also argued that removing the ban would serve not just the interests of the gold mining industry but also the South African economy as a whole.[97]

After some further lobbying and debates in and out of the House of Assembly, the South African government yielded to the mining companies' request. However, instead of removing the ban completely, the prime minister went back to the proposal that the Transvaal Chamber of Mines made in 1917. Therefore, on October 21, 1933, the South African government gave the Transvaal Chamber of Mines permission to employ 2,000 workers from north of latitude 22° south. Emphasizing that the lifting of the ban was just an experimental measure intended to assess whether health conditions were now suitable for the employment of "tropical natives," the prime minister instructed the Department of Public Health to make sure the experiment was carried out under conditions that were not dangerous to migrants' health. He also stressed that "the importation of Native labourers outside the Union is permitted on condition that all available Native labourers in the Union who desire employment on the mines and are suitable, are employed."[98] Nevertheless, despite the government position about the ban being partial and temporary, the prime minister effectively opened the way for the Transvaal mining companies, farmers, and other South African employers to hire job seekers from Southern Rhodesia and other areas north of latitude 22° south who entered the country without following official channels.

The timing of the removal of the ban was also strategic in that South Africa's economy experienced steady growth in the 1930s after recovering from the Great Depression, which affected the world between 1929 and 1932. The South African economy managed to recover more quickly than most in the region because the country's industries did not suffer as much as those in other countries in

Sub-Saharan Africa. The removal of major restrictions on the importation of unskilled workers was therefore timely, coming as it did—as the recession wound down. In addition, the state assisted investors in the mining sector to secure modern technological equipment and invested in agricultural extension programs and other projects that helped the economy to grow.[99] In this respect, lifting the ban went a long way toward addressing the labor supply situation in South Africa. However, it took the region back to the scenario that prevailed between 1890 and 1913, when state authorities in Southern Rhodesia and the Transvaal did not share the same sentiments regarding the meaning of the border and movements across it. For almost three decades—from 1933 to about 1960—Southern Rhodesian authorities struggled to control migration to South Africa while their counterparts on the other side of the border covertly encouraged and promoted "illegal" immigration from north of the Limpopo River.

Notes

1. British Library (BL) C.S.D.252, Union of South Africa House of Assembly Debates, November 8, 1910.

2. Ibid.

3. BL, C.S.D.252, Union of South Africa House of Assembly Debates, February 10, 1911.

4. BL, C.S.D.252, Union of South Africa House of Assembly Debates, February 10, 1911.

5. BL, C.S.D.252, Union of South Africa House of Assembly Debates, May 14, 1912.

6. BL, C.S.D.252, Union of South Africa House of Assembly Debates, May 8, 1913.

7. Randall M. Packard, "The Invention of the 'Tropical Worker': Medical Research and the Quest for Central African Labor on the South African Gold Mines, 1903–36," *Journal of African History* 34 (1993): 271–92. For further discussions on medical sciences and disease control in colonial Africa, see Tamara Giles-Vernick and James L. A. Webb, eds., *Global Health in Africa: Historical Perspectives on Disease Control* (Athens: Ohio University Press, 2013); Ruth J. Prince and Rebecca Marsland, eds., *The Making and Unmaking of Public Health in Africa* (Athens: Ohio University Press, 2014).

8. BL, C.S.D.252, Union of South Africa House of Assembly Debates, May 14, 1913.

9. BL, C.S.D.252, Union of South Africa House of Assembly Debates, May 14, 1913.

10. Union of South Africa, Immigrants Regulation Act (No. 22) 1913, sec. 4.1.

11. NASA, GNLB, vol. 123, file 950/13/240, Extract from Speech of Minister of Native Affairs on May 23, 1913.

12. For more details on these correspondences, see NASA, GNLB, vol. 30, file 3260/11/240, Secretary for Natives, Pretoria, to Director of Native Labor, Johannesburg, June 9, 1913.

13. NASA, GNLB, vol. 30, file 3260/11/240, Director of Native Labor, Johannesburg, to Pass Officer, Randfontein November 5, 1913.

14. BL, C.S.D. 252, Union of South Africa House of Assembly Debates, March 13, 1911. See also, Peberdy, *Selecting Immigrants*; Klotz, *Migration and National Identity*.

15. NAZ, S482/468/39/2, Emigration and Immigration, 1937 to 1939.

16. Kalsheker, "1908 Asiatics Ordinance"; Patel, *Indians in Uganda and Rhodesia*; Dotson and Dotson, *Indian Minority.*

17. Union of South Africa, Immigration Regulation Act (No. 22) 1913, sec. 4.1.

18. NASA, GNLB, vol. 30, file 3260/11/240, Secretary for Native Affairs to Director of Native Labor, Johannesburg, August 22, 1913.

19. NASA, GNLB, vol. 123, file 1950/13/240, Secretary for Justice, to Secretary for Native Affairs, April 3, 1914.

20. NASA, GNLB, vol. 30, file 3260/11/240, Director of Native Labor, to the Portuguese Curator, Johannesburg, November 7, 1913.

21. NASA, GNLB, vol. 30, file 3260/11/240 (Part 2), Secretary for Native Affairs, Pretoria, to Hendrick Mentz, Pietersburg November 14, 1913.

22. NASA, GNLB, vol. 123, file 1950/13/240, Director of Native Labor, Johannesburg to Secretary for Native Affairs, Cape Town, May 30, 1914.

23. NAZ, N3/22/4 vol 2, Director of Native Labor, Johannesburg, was quoted in a report by the Superintendent of Natives, Fort Victoria, after his visit to the Transvaal, September 17, 1917.

24. NASA, GNLB, vol. 123, file 1950/13/240, Notes of a Conference held at Pietersburg on Tuesday September 10, 1918 for the Purpose of Discussing the Best Means of Giving Effect to the Instructions of the Union Government that the Introduction of Tropical Natives should as far as Possible Cease, and of Over-coming, if Possible, the Difficulties Experienced with Casual and Clandestine Immigrants from Rhodesia.

25. NASA, GNLB, vol. 122, file 1950/13/D240, Sub-Native Commissioner, Louis Trichardt, to Native Commissioner Zoutpansberg, December 1, 1920.

26. NASA, GNLB, vol. 30, file 3260/11/240 (Part 2), Director of Native Labor, Johannesburg, to Secretary for Native Affairs, February 10, 1914.

27. NASA, GNLB, vol. 123, file 1950/13/240, Sub-Native Commissioner, Louis Trichardt to E.K. Whitehead, Louis Trichardt, August 10, 1915.

28. NASA, GNLB, vol. 123, file 1950/13/240, Director of Native Labor, Johannesburg, to Secretary for Native Affairs, Pretoria, November 25, 1915. See also, Murray, "'Blackbirding' at 'Crooks' Corner"; Jeeves, "Over-Reach."

29. NASA, GNLB, vol. 123, file 1950/13/240, Notes of a Conference held at Pietersburg on Tuesday September 10, 1918. See also NAZ, N3/22/4 vol.1, Employment of Southern Rhodesia Natives in the Union of South Africa (1914–1923).

30. NASA, GNLB, vol. 120, file 1950/13/240, Acting Director of Native Labor, Johannesburg, to NCs and Sub-NCs for Louis Trichardt, Pietersburg, Sibasa, etc., January 6, 1919. Emphasis mine.

31. NASA, GNLB, vol. 120, file 1950/13/240, An Affidavit Statement Made by Native Sukwayo of Chipinge (Melsetter District), June 27, 1918.

32. NASA, NTS, vol. 2062, file 112/280 (Part 2), J.A. Starke to Senator Dr. Roberts, Cape Town, May 18, 1921.

33. NASA, GNLB, vol. 123, file 1950/13/240, Director of Native Labor, Johannesburg to E. Lazarus, Middleburg, August 18, 1921; Director of Native Labor, Johannesburg, to Medalie Brothers, Trichardt, June 1, 1921. See also, NASA, GNLB, vol. 122, file 1950/13/240, Director of Native Labor, Johannesburg, to Messrs Spain and Stein, Bethal, April 3, 1922.

34. NASA, GNLB, vol. 30, file 3260/11/240 (Part 2), Chief Pass Officer, Johannesburg, to Director of Native Labor, Johannesburg, December 12, 1922.

35. NASA, NTS, vol. 2061, file 107/280, Rex Versus W.P. de Villiers, December 19, 1923.

36. NASA, NTS, vol. 2061, file 107/280, Rex Versus W.P. de Villiers, December 19, 1923.

37. NASA, NTS, vol. 2061, file 107/280, District Commander, Pietersburg, to Deputy Commissioner, Transvaal Division, South African Police, January 19, 1924.

38. NASA, NTS, vol. 2061, file 107/280, Attorney General, Pretoria, to Secretary for Native Affairs, Pretoria, February 2, 1924.

39. NASA, GNLB, vol. 122, file 1950/13/240, Sub-Native Commissioner, Louis Trichardt, to Director of Native Labor, Johannesburg, September 4, 1924.

40. NASA, GNLB, vol. 122, file 1950/13/240, Director of Native Labor, Johannesburg to Secretary for Native Affairs, Pretoria, March 4, 1926.

41. Jeeves and Crush, "Introduction"; Martin J. Murray, "'Burning the Wheat Stacks': Land Clearances and Agrarian Unrest Along the Northern Middelburg Frontier, c. 1918–1926," *Journal of Southern African Studies* 15, 1 (1988): 102–22.

42. J. F. Murray, "History of the South African Institute of Medical Research." *South African Medical Journal* (April 1963): 389–95.

43. NASA, GNLB, vol.30, file 3260/11/240 (Part 2), Secretary, WNLA, to Director of Native Labor, Johannesburg, May 20, 1913. See also, Packard, "Invention of the 'Tropical Worker.'"

44. NASA, GNLB, vol. 30, file 3260/11/240, Secretary WNLA, to Director of Native Labor, June 2, 1913.

45. NASA GNLB 30/3260/11/240 (Part 2), Memorandum: Mortality From Disease Amongst Tropical Natives Employed on Mines (Members of the Witwatersrand Native Labor Association only) in the Proclaimed Labor Districts of the Transvaal. See also, GNLB, vol. 30, file 3260/11/240, Secretary WNLA, to Director of Native Labor, September 5, 1913.

46. NASA, GNLB, vol. 30, file 3260/11/240 (Part 2), Medical Officer, WNLA to the President, Chamber of Mines, Johannesburg, July 12, 1917.

47. NASA, NTS, vol. 2062, file 112/280 (Part 1), President, Transvaal Chamber of Mines, Johannesburg, to the Prime Minister's Office, Cape Town, June 7, 1917.

48. NASA, NTS, vol. 2062, file 112/280 (Part 1), Director of Native Labor, Johannesburg, to Secretary for Native Affairs, Pretoria, July 18, 1917; NASA, NTS, vol. 2062, file 112/280 (Part 2), Prime Minister's Office, Cape Town, to President of the Chamber of Mines, Johannesburg, April 10, 1918.

49. NASA, GNLB, vol. 122, file 1950/13/240, Sub-Native Commissioner, Louis Trichardt, to Secretary for Native Affairs, Pretoria, February 11, 1926. See also, Mavhunga, "Navigating Boundaries."

50. NASA, GNLB, vol. 122, file 1950/13/240, Director of Native Labor, Johannesburg, to the Magistrate, Bethal, April 3, 1922.

51. NASA, GNLB, vol. 122, file 1950/13/240, Medalie Brothers, Louis Trichardt, to Director of Native Labor, Johannesburg, December 30, 1921.

52. NASA, GNLB, vol. 123, file 1950/13/240, L. E. Krause, Pietersburg, to Secretary for Native Affairs, Pretoria, July 15, 1921. See also, Martin J. Murray, "Factories in the Fields: Capitalist Farming in the Bethal District, c.1910–1950," in Jeeves and Crush, *White Farmers, Black Labor,* 75–93.

53. NASA, GNLB, vol. 123, file 1950/13/240, Petition for Removal of Restrictions in Conditions Governing Labour Agents' and Employers' Recruiting Licenses.

54. NASA, GNLB, vol. 122, file 1950/13/240, Secretary Low Veld Farmers Association, Nelspruit, to Secretary for Native Affairs, Pretoria, October 1, 1924.

55. NASA, GNLB, vol. 122, file 1950/13/240, A Copy of the Resolution Passed at a Meeting of the Low Veld Farmers' Association Held on October 4, 1924.

56. NASA, NTS, vol. 2062, file 112/280 (Part 1), Director of Native Labor, Johannesburg, to Secretary for Native Affairs, Pretoria, July 16, 1925.

57. NASA, GNLB, vol. 122, file 1950/13/240, Director of Native Labor, Johannesburg, to Sub-Native Commissioner, Louis Trichardt, July 24, 1924. See also, Murray, "Factories in the Fields."

58. NAZ, A3/21/57, Southern Rhodesia, Natives Pass Consolidation Ordinance no.15, 1913. See also, NAZ, SRG 2, Southern Rhodesia: Legislative Council Debates, December 14, 1911 and May 14, 1912.

59. NAZ, A3/21/57, Southern Rhodesia, Natives Pass Consolidation Ordinance no.15, 1913.

60. NAZ, N3/22/4 vol.1, Chief Native Commissioner, Salisbury, to Superintendents of Natives, September 16, 1918.

61. NAZ, 1226, Chief Native Commissioner, Salisbury, to Superintendents of Natives, December 2, 1922.

62. NAZ, S480/83, Statement by HON. H. U. Moffat (Minister of Mines and Public Works) Regarding Emigration of Rhodesian Natives into the Union, November 16, 1925.

63. NAZ, N3/22/4 vol. 2, A Draft Dispatch by Chief Native Commissioner for Submission to the South African High Commissioner, February 7, 1916.

64. NAZ, N3/22/4 vol. 1, Chief Native Commissioner, Salisbury to Secretary for Native Affairs, Pretoria, May 17, 1918.

65. NAZ, N3/22/4 vol. 1, Chief Native Commissioner, Salisbury to Secretary for Native Affairs, Pretoria, May 17, 1918.

66. NASA, GNLB, vol. 123, file 1950/13/240, Notes of a Conference held at Pietersburg on September 10, 1918.

67. NASA, GNLB, vol. 123, file 1950/13/240, Notes, September 10, 1918.

68. NASA, GNLB, vol. 123, file 1950/13/240, Notes, September 10, 1918.

69. NASA, GNLB, vol. 123, file 1950/13/240, Notes, September 10, 1918.

70. NAZ, S138/203, Assistant Chief Native Commissioner, to the Secretary to the Premier, Salisbury, September 7, 1925.

71. NAZ, S138/203, F.D. Roscoe, Matopos, to Secretary for Mines and Works, July 14, 1925.

72. NAZ, S138/203, Secretary, Rhodesia Chamber of Mines, to Chief Native Commissioner, Salisbury, September 2, 1925.

73. NAZ, S480/83, Chief Native Commissioner, Salisbury, to the Secretary for Native Affairs, Pretoria, November 4, 1921.

74. NAZ, N3/22/4, CNC to the Secretary, Department of the Administrator, April 29, 1915.

75. NAZ, N3/22/4, The Rhodesia Native Labour Bureau to the Chief Native Commissioner, Salisbury, January 26, 1916.

76. NAZ, S480/83, Superintendent of Natives, Fort Victoria, to Acting Chief Native Commissioner, Salisbury, August 30, 1926.

77. NAZ, S138/203, Assistant Chief Native Commissioner to Secretary to the Premier, September 7, 1925. The Minister of Native Affairs made a similar observation when he wrote: "It would appear to be an economic question, fine and simple. The attraction of higher wages." See also Minister of Native Affairs to Secretary to Premier, September 8, 1925, in the same file.

78. NAZ, S138/203, Minister of Native Affairs, to Chief Native Commissioner, Salisbury, September 8, 1925.

79. NAZ, AOH/46, Amon Makufa Mlambo, interview with Dawson Munjeri, Rhodesdale Estate, December 13, 1978.

80. NAZ, S246/716, Chief Native Commissioner to the Secretary, Department of the Administrator, October 11, 1917; NAZ N3/22/4 vol. 3, Superintendent of Natives, Fort Victoria, to Chief Native Commissioner Salisbury, June 6, 1917.

81. NAZ, S480/83, Native Commissioner Zaka to the Superintendent of Natives, Fort Victoria, April 19, 1926.

82. NAZ, N3/22/4, Chief Native Commissioner to Secretary Department of Administrator, Salisbury, January 10, 1917.

83. For a summary of the South African Census data for 1911–1985, see Crush, "Migrations Past." For estimates of Zimbabweans in South Africa between 1917 and 1925 see NAZ, N3/22/4, Chief Native Commissioner, Salisbury to Secretary, Department of the Administrator, Salisbury, October 11, 1917; S138/203, Chief Native Commissioner, Salisbury to Secretary Rhodesia Chamber of Mines [not dated: c. 1925].

84. NAZ, S480/83, Statement by Hon. H.U. Moffat (Minister of Mines and Public Works) Regarding Emigration of Rhodesian Natives into the Union, November 16, 1925.

85. NASA, GNLB 120/1950/13/240, Sub-Native Commissioner, Louis Trichardt, to Director of Native Labor, Johannesburg, May 26, 1926.

86. Foucault, *Discipline and Punish.*

87. NAZ S138/203 Chief Native Commissioner, Salisbury, to the Secretary to the Premier, November 2, 1925.

88. NAZ, AOH/46, Mlambo, interview. See also NAZ, S1226 British South Africa Police, Mtetengwe, to Superintendent CID, Bulawayo, January 4, 1926.

89. NAZ, S138/203, Resident Commissioner, Mafeking, to Chief Native Commissioner, Salisbury, February 17, 1927.

90. NASA, GNLB 122/1950/13/240, Native Sub-Commissioner, Krugersdorp, to Director of Native Labor, Johannesburg, December 30, 1924.

91. NAZ, N3/22/4 "Illicit Recruiting of Native Labour-Rhodesia, Transvaal, Portuguese Territory: A Draft Dispatch by the Chief Native Commissioner for Submission to the South African High Commissioner, February 7, 1916. See also, Bulpin, *Ivory Trail;* Mavhunga, "Navigating Boundaries."

92. NAZ, N3/22/4, Acting Sub-Native Commissioner, Sibasa, to Native Commissioner, Zoutpansberg, February 7, 1918. See, also Murray, "'Blackbirding' at Crooks' Corner."

93. NAZ, N3/22/4, Native Commissioner Zoutpansberg, to Director of Native Labor, Johannesburg, October 26, 1915.

94. NASA, GNLB, vol.123, file 1950/13/240, Sub-Native Commissioner, Sibasa, to Director of Native Labor, Johannesburg, June 14, 1915. See also Sub-Native Commissioner, Louis Trichardt to K.K. Whitehead, August 10, 1915.

95. NASA, NTS, vol. 2117, file 225 280, Mozambique Convention.

96. NASA, NTS, vol. 2117, file 225 280, President, Transvaal Chamber of Mines, Johannesburg, to the Prime Minister's Office, Cape Town, August 27, 1929.

97. NASA, NTS, vol. 2117, file 225 280, Government Mining Engineer, to the Minister of Mines and Industries, Pretoria, October 2, 1929.

98. NASA, NTS, vol. 2138, file 249/280, Secretary for the Prime Minister, Cape Town, to the President of the Chamber of Mines, Johannesburg, October 21, 1933.

99. Nicoli Nattrass and Jeremy Seekings, "The Economy and Poverty in the Twentieth Century," in *The Cambridge History of South Africa*. Vol 2, *1885–1994*, ed. Robert Ross, Anne Kelk Mager, and Bill Nasson (Cambridge: Cambridge University Press, 2011).

3 Border Jumping and the Politics of Labor

Barely a year after obtaining the South African government's permission to employ "tropical" workers on an experimental basis, the Transvaal Chamber of Mines successfully negotiated an arrangement that allowed the WNLA to import up to two thousand workers from Nyasaland in any given year. In a separate agreement, the WNLA also got permission to recruit a maximum of ten thousand workers annually from Northern Rhodesia. As part of these agreements, the WNLA established recruiting depots in both countries and pledged not to engage migrant workers who independently traveled from Nyasaland and Northern Rhodesia to South Africa. Along with these developments, the South African Parliament voted in favor of removing the statutory bar on the recruitment and employment of so-called "tropical natives," which had been in place since 1913. In addition, following the publication of Government Notice No. 1170 dated August 6, 1936, South African officials resumed issuing permits to employers' agents and licensed recruiters to operate in the country's northern border areas. Through the same notice, the South African government lifted the embargo on recruiting within twenty miles of the border with Southern Rhodesia, which had also been in place since the announcement of the ban.[1] Although the notice stated that only the licensed agents and registered touts and runners were permitted to recruit tropical workers, it effectively opened up the border zone to licit but not authorized recruiting.

By the late 1930s, hundreds of licensed and unlicensed labor recruiters had established camps and depots in South Africa's northern border districts. Among the licensed agents who became well known in the border zone were retired army officers and former employees of the South African Native Affairs Department with extensive knowledge of the country's labor recruitment regulations. For example, Retired Colonel Stubbs, a former native commissioner for Louis Trichardt, teamed up with Retired Major Leifeldt, who had served as a magistrate in the same district, and organized a recruiting syndicate that operated in areas around Crooks' Corner. They often engaged tropical migrants who were rejected by the WNLA staff on medical grounds and "sold" them to farmers in the Transvaal Province.[2] Another retired colonel, identified as D. Swarts, secured a contract to supply approximately five thousand African workers per annum to the

Zebedelia and Leteba Estates in the Transvaal, whereas Sacks, Labuschagne, and Durr supplied workers to farmers, citrus estates, and several mines in the Transvaal Province.[3] With the involvement of individuals with knowledge and connections in the South African law enforcement system, labor recruitment activities in the border zone became highly competitive.

As was the case in earlier years of the twentieth century, South African employers also deployed touts who intercepted migrants in Southern Rhodesia's southern districts before they reached the border. In this respect, employers particularly preferred to work with former "police boys" and so-called "detective natives" who understood the border landscape and Southern Rhodesia's migration control systems quite well. In so doing, South African employers relied on people with insider knowledge to beat the system of migration control in Southern Rhodesia. At times the touts went further into the country, targeting places such as the mining towns of Gwanda and West Nicholson, which were serviced by trains from Bulawayo. Because migrants often used the Bulawayo–Mafeking routes and disembarked before the trains got to the border with Botswana, touts working for different agents or employers also intercepted them in the Plumtree area and directed them to various places in South Africa. In one of more than a dozen cases that the police in Southern Rhodesia reported, a man called Cookson, who owned a farm near the confluence of the Pai and Limpopo Rivers (on the South African side), engaged three touts who advised and directed migrants on specific routes to follow from Gwanda to his farm.[4]

In addition to the independent recruiters and those working for individual employers, the Native Recruiting Corporation also deployed its agents in the northern Transvaal area, with the view to recruiting migrants who entered the country independently. Around the same time, there were widespread rumors that the Transvaal Chamber of Mines had a contract with a man named Impey, who established a recruiting station on a farm known as "C to C Dairy," about three miles south of the border. As did other labor agents, Impey subcontracted touts, who regularly crossed the Limpopo River to recruit workers from Southern Rhodesia.[5] Although they did not have permission to recruit from Southern Rhodesia, the Transvaal Chamber of Mines also used media campaigns to encourage "Rhodesian natives" to consider working in South Africa. This approach became public knowledge in 1938 when a weekly newspaper—the *Bantu Mirror*—published a series of articles in English, Sindebele, and Chishona advertising some alleged benefits enjoyed by the African migrants working at the Witwatersrand mines. In the same spirit, other employers such as the Messina Copper Mines, which relied heavily on tropical workers, believing them to be better skilled and more prepared to work in harsh environments than locals, engaged thousands of Zimbabweans regardless of whether they had official permits to be in South Africa.[6] Given that Southern Rhodesian mine owners, farmers, and other employers competed for the same pool of regional workers, the 1930s witnessed the intensification of contestations over the control of cross-Limpopo mobility. Along with that was the continuation of border jumping in the region.

Southern Rhodesia's Increased Surveillance of the Border Zone

Southern Rhodesian authorities' initial response to South Africa's suspension of the ban on migrants from north of latitude 22° south was to increase police surveillance of the border zone. In doing so, they took advantage of the Alfred Beit Bridge, which was built across the Limpopo River in 1929.[7] Although South African authorities extended the railway line from Messina (via the bridge) to what became the Beitbridge location on the Southern Rhodesian side of the border, they did very little to control the movement of pedestrians and vehicular traffic that welcomed the bridge as a safe route to move between the two countries. In contrast, Southern Rhodesian authorities installed gates at both ends of the bridge, marking the birth of the Beitbridge border post. Speaking at the official opening of the bridge, Southern Rhodesia Prime Minister H. U. Moffat said that installing the gates would "provide a suitable barrier to facilitate the examination of persons entering Southern Rhodesia."[8] The same authorities deployed customs officers who acted on behalf of the South African government during the day because the latter kept only night security staff at the bridge. Furthermore, Southern Rhodesian authorities insisted that all Africans traveling to South Africa should first present their registration certificates and travel permits for inspection at the police station established not far from the bridge.[9] Whereas European travelers simply had to deal with the customs officials and border guards when they passed through the Beitbridge border post, Africans had to go through the police before they presented themselves at the border gates.

In line with renewed efforts to curb "illegal" emigration to South Africa, Southern Rhodesian authorities also utilized the police station in Beitbridge to coordinate most operations in the border zone. In that respect, the British South Africa Police (BSAP) deployed regular police patrols along the Limpopo River, particularly in places that had become popular crossing points for border jumpers. During the first two decades of the twentieth century, Southern Rhodesia's border patrols focused on the Pafuri triangle and the surrounding areas, in the mid-1930s, police patrols were occasionally deployed along the Bechuanaland border as well. Most migrants using trains plying the Bulawayo–Mafeking route tended to disembark before the train got to the border with Bechuanaland and then used bush paths to cross into South Africa. In this respect, the BSAP also deployed regular patrols in areas around Gwanda and West Nicholson, two small mining centers where Africans heading to South Africa would normally get off the trains. The police often randomly stopped and searched residents of the border districts and anyone they met in areas adjacent the Limpopo River, frequently arresting those found without passes.[10]

In addition to regular border patrols, the BSAP created what it called *special border patrol units*. These were specialized forces composed mainly of African detectives and informers who did not wear uniforms, making it difficult for other people to identify them. Members of the special border patrols were deployed in strategic places such as Beitbridge town's "native compound," which quickly became a hiding spot for border jumpers, unlicensed recruiters, and transport operators who helped travelers dodge the police in the border zone.[11] At times, these undercover African detectives were deployed in mining centers and farms near the border that border jumpers often used as fueling stations before slipping into South Africa. The major task of these specially trained detectives was to study the routes, strategies, and networks that migrants used to evade Southern Rhodesia's efforts to restrict migration to South Africa. To gather information, the African police details often posed as desperate migrants in need of assistance on how to cross the boundary without official documents. It was also common for African detectives to pose as passengers on trains that plied the Bulawayo–Mafeking and Bulawayo–West Nicholson routes. In the process, they studied and reported on "clandestine" activities involving migrants, recruiters, train crews, and other actors in South Africa and Southern Rhodesia.[12] From the information obtained in this way, Southern Rhodesian police managed to arrest some potential border jumpers and other people involved in activities that promoted border jumping, but this approach was not enough to eradicate the practice.

A Tripartite Coalition against Border Jumping

Along with the deployment of police patrols in the border zone, Southern Rhodesian authorities sought a diplomatic solution to unlicensed recruiting and clandestine emigration to South Africa. If Southern Rhodesian authorities learned anything from the 1918 Pietersburg Conference and other earlier attempts to persuade their South African counterparts to restrict immigration from north of the Limpopo, it was that they needed to approach this issue regionally. In particular, Southern Rhodesian authorities wanted the leaders of Nyasaland and Northern Rhodesia to join the fight against border jumping in the region. Although the three countries enjoyed different statuses as labor units in an integrated regional economy, they shared "an interest in controlling, restricting, and profiteering from labour export to South Africa."[13] The combined demand for labor in Northern Rhodesia and Nyasaland was probably less than that of Southern Rhodesia alone. However, the governments of both of these countries preferred to have an arrangement that allowed them to collect taxes from thousands of their people who worked in Southern Rhodesia and South Africa. Consequently, the two countries signed the Tripartite Labor Agreement with Southern Rhodesia in August 1937. Among the key elements of the agreement, which became a precursor to the Central African Federation of 1953–63, was that Nyasaland and Northern Rhodesia would direct their surplus labor to Southern Rhodesia and not to South Africa. In turn, Southern Rhodesian officials pledged to ensure that employers in their country engaged only those migrant workers who possessed passports or other official identity documents from their home countries.

In proposing the tripartite agreement, Southern Rhodesian authorities hoped that they would have more influence in the other two British colonies' "native" labor policies. Not only did Southern Rhodesia want to have an official guarantee of its position as the first port of call for all surplus labor from the other two territories, but also it hoped to undermine South Africa's comparative advantage. The idea of forming the alliance followed South Africa's removal of the ban on northern migrants. Southern Rhodesia, therefore hoped to use the alliance to undercut the WNLA's hegemonic control of the region's labor supplies. However, the Tripartite Labor Agreement did not help with the issue of border jumping from Southern Rhodesia to South Africa. A review meeting of the three governments' representatives in December 1937—four months after the agreement was signed—revealed that, "clandestine" emigration of African workers to South Africa had not just increased but "reached alarming proportions."[14] At the same meeting, the three countries came to an unsurprising conclusion that without South African authorities' cooperation, it would be very difficult to control migration across the Limpopo. More important, they agreed that they needed South Africa's help to stop unlicensed labor recruiters from operating in Southern Rhodesia's border districts.

Although South Africa's removal of the ban on northern migrants was probably the main cause of the rise of border jumping across the Limpopo River, other factors militated against successful implementation of the Tripartite Labor Agreement between Southern Rhodesia and its partners. As was the case when the importation of African workers from Northern Rhodesia and Nyasaland commenced at the beginning of the twentieth century, migrants still did not make Southern Rhodesia their final destination. Instead, they continued to view the territory between the Zambezi and Limpopo Rivers as a mere stopover en route to higher paying jobs in South Africa. In the same way that local Africans strove to escape low wages and poor working conditions at Southern Rhodesian mines and farms, migrants from Northern Rhodesia and Nyasaland were not satisfied with the living and working conditions in Southern Rhodesia. Rumors about higher wages and better working conditions in South Africa, which drove thousands of Zimbabweans to leave their country, had the same effects in Nyasaland and North Rhodesia. While returning migrants did a lot to spread the information about wages and working conditions in South Africa, the Transvaal Chamber of Mines (through the WNLA) did its part to lure people from Nyasaland and North Rhodesia to seek employment on the Rand. Similar to what they did in Southern Rhodesia, the Transvaal Chamber of Mines placed advertisements in major newspapers in the two central African territories. Using vernacular languages such as ChiChewa and Nyanja, the advertisements highlighted higher wages, free food, and leisure time as some of the benefits that migrant workers would enjoy if they went to South Africa. Apart from WNLA ads, migrants returning from the Transvaal spread the news about the money, food, free cinema, and nice clothes that they allegedly enjoyed in South Africa.[15] In this context, most migrant workers from Northern Rhodesia and Nyasaland went to Southern Rhodesia prepared to proceed across the Limpopo River at the slightest available opportunity.

In a development showing that diplomatic calculations had less influence than market forces, some migrant workers from Nyasaland and Northern Rhodesia spent less than one week in Southern Rhodesia. They simply checked in with the local Native Affairs Department officials in order to obtain work permits and, at times, travel permits, which allowed them to travel to different parts of the country in search of employment. Once in possession of such permits, most went straight to Gwanda, Beitbridge, or any of the southern districts, where they enlisted with several recruiters who helped them cross the border into the Transvaal. Some migrants destroyed the work permits they obtained in Southern Rhodesia as soon as they got to Beitbridge, where they presented their Northern Rhodesian or Nyasaland passports as if they had never obtained any documents in Southern Rhodesia. On October 8, 1938, for example, forty-three migrants arrived at the Beitbridge border post with the intention of crossing the border into South Africa. Although all of them possessed Nyasaland passports endorsed "proceeding to Southern Rhodesia," they stated that they had boarded the train at Dondo in Mozambique and then traveled via Umtali, Salisbury, and Bulawayo before they disembarked at West Nicholson and then walked to the border.[16] Although it is not clear how such a big group of migrants would travel for such a long journey throughout the country without being caught, it is highly likely that they were brought into Southern Rhodesia under the Tripartite Labor Agreement but then decided to proceed to South Africa.

That the governments of Northern Rhodesia and Nyasaland kept separate agreements with the Transvaal Chamber of Mines, which permitted the WNLA to recruit in those two countries, also weakened the Tripartite Labor Agreement. By 1938 the South African mines had obtained permission to increase the number of migrants they could recruit in Nyasaland from two thousand to eight thousand five hundred per annum. In line with that development, the WNLA established "a string of [recruiting] stations in Malawi from the top to the bottom of the country."[17] These stations were in addition to the outposts that the WNLA set up in Northern Rhodesia, Bechuanaland, South West Africa (Namibia), and as far north as Tanganyika (Tanzania). Although the Transvaal Chamber of Mines had not obtained permission to establish recruiting stations in Southern Rhodesia at that time, putting WNLA camps in the border zone on the South African and Bechuanaland sides was enough to lure people from Southern Rhodesia to enlist with the mining industry's agents. People who wanted to work on the South African mines had only to cross the colonial borders and present themselves at various WNLA camps. To improve its recruiting machinery, the Transvaal Chamber of Mines also developed a regional transport network linking WNLA's various outposts. Northern Bechuanaland became a strategic base of this regional network specifically meant to tap into the previously out-of-reach areas.[18]

Faced with all these challenges, Southern Rhodesia and its northern partners could not effectively enforce the Tripartite Labor Agreement. As such, many a migrant from Nyasaland and Northern Rhodesia who obtained a passport and assistance with transport into Southern Rhodesia eventually found a way into South Africa. As a result, both Nyasaland and Northern Rhodesia, which hoped to benefit through labor export fees and taxes, and Southern Rhodesia, which subsidized the importation of migrants from the north, lost out to South Africa, which was not officially included in the agreement. By 1938, Southern Rhodesian officials estimated that approximately thirty-four thousand Africans were leaving the country for South Africa annually without following official channels.[19] As this situation shows, the three countries' efforts to control border jumping under the auspices of the Tripartite Labor Agreement failed. Despite the efforts, the practice continued with the assistance of both the Transvaal Chamber of Mines and the South African administration.

South Africa's Implicit Promotion of Border Jumping

Having realized the limits of the Tripartite Labor Agreement, Southern Rhodesian authorities became more convinced that without South Africa's cooperation, efforts to control cross-Limpopo mobility would not yield desired results. With that in mind, they initiated another round of talks hoping to build a broader coalition with South Africa and the other two countries. In so doing, Southern Rhodesian authorities hoped that the four states would develop a joint mechanism of controlling labor migration in the region and possibly reduce the rate of border jumping. After a series of negotiations in which South African authorities and representatives of the Transvaal Chamber of Mines used threats to extract concessions from Southern Rhodesian authorities, the four states reached an agreement in 1939. In a bid to get South Africa to cooperate in the control of cross-Limpopo mobility, Southern Rhodesian officials (naively) accepted the Transvaal Chamber of Mines' request to establish the WNLA's regional headquarters in Salisbury. As part of the same agreement, Southern Rhodesian authorities gave the WNLA a green light to establish depots, camps, outposts, and roads in Northern Rhodesia and Nyasaland. In turn, South African authorities reassured their counterparts that the WNLA would engage only people with "permits to seek work in the Union" that would be issued by officials in the other three countries.[20] However, the South African mining companies did not keep their promise.

When it emerged that migrant workers continued to travel from the three British territories into South Africa through unofficial channels, representatives of Southern Rhodesia, Northern Rhodesia, and Nyasaland met again, separately, in March 1940 to review the terms of the 1939 agreement with South Africa. Operating under the banner of the Interterritorial Council of Central Africa, the three states resolved to hold further meetings with the South African administration to encourage it to take steps to control the influx of border jumpers from north of the Limpopo River. However, showing that it was not willing to cooperate with representatives of the other states, South Africa turned down the request for a proposed meeting.[21] It maintained that Southern Rhodesia was responsible for discouraging what it considered to be illegal crossings of the Limpopo boundary. The Pretoria administration's snub of the proposed conference in 1940 must have come as a huge setback for Southern Rhodesia, whose demand for labor was on the increase. In addition to the agricultural sector, which was expanding steadily, the British government invested large amounts of capital in Southern Rhodesia at the height of the World War II, particularly in the manufacturing sector. Under pressure from these developments, which increased the demand for labor, Southern Rhodesian authorities sought other ways of stopping migration to South Africa.

In a further attempt to find common ground with their neighbors, Southern Rhodesian authorities convinced the South African government to send representatives to what came to be known as the African Manpower Conference, which took place in 1943. The manpower conference came up with four major resolutions that were meant to reduce border jumping in the region. The first was that the northern states would tighten their railway transport systems to ensure that itinerant Africans respected pass laws, especially in Southern Rhodesia. Second, the four governments agreed that if Southern Rhodesian authorities stopped issuing passes for South Africa, that would make it difficult for northern migrants to travel across the Limpopo boundary. They also agreed that the prosecution of unlicensed labor recruiters who operated in the Southern Rhodesia–South Africa border zone would help reduce unauthorized migration in the region. Finally, the conference resolved that Southern Rhodesia should charge duty on all taxable goods brought into the colony by Africans returning from South Africa, both locals and those en route to Northern Rhodesia or Nyasaland.[22] Although and perhaps because none of these resolutions was particularly new, South Africa remained uncommitted to cooperating with Southern Rhodesia on the implementation of the conference resolutions. Consequently, the 1943 agreement, like previous ones, did not achieve the intended objectives.

With Southern Rhodesian authorities piling pressure on government representatives of the other three countries, another round of talks took place in 1947. At that time, labor demands in Southern Rhodesia had reached an all-time high because of the economic boom triggered by the World War II investments into both the agriculture and manufacturing sectors. In addition, authorities in Northern Rhodesia and Nyasaland were increasingly concerned about the criminal activities associated with unlicensed recruiting in the Southern Rhodesia–South Africa border zone. However, given South Africa's unwillingness to commit to an arrangement that would have made it difficult for border jumpers to cross the Limpopo River, two other conferences held in 1947 failed to produce any meaningful agreement among the four countries. When another conference was called for in December 1947, the South African representatives pointed out that the Pretoria administration would agree to detaining border jumpers from north of the Limpopo River only on condition that the 1937 Tripartite Labor Agreement's provision for Southern Rhodesia's preferential access to migrant workers from Northern Rhodesia and Nyasaland was revoked.[23] This did not go down well with the other three countries, especially Southern Rhodesia, which preferred a situation in which each government undertook to ensure that no migrant would find work without possessing the official identity documents and travel permits from his country of origin. Once again, the four countries failed to come up with a workable plan for the control of cross-Limpopo mobility.

After a few months, the Interterritorial Council of Central Africa met again and came up with five major proposals it thought would reduce border jumping in the region. The first was that if South African employers engaged migrants without the necessary documents, such employment should be for limited periods of time. Second, they proposed that South African authorities should conduct regular inspections of places of employment and prosecute both employers and employees who breached the provisions relating to possession of identity documents and travel permits. The third proposal was that South African employers should take necessary steps to improve the conditions of service of legal migrants, especially regarding housing, food, hours, and conditions of work. Fourth, the council submitted that no deductions should be made from the pay of legal migrants for the cost of their transportation to the place of employment. Finally, they requested South African authorities to repatriate all legal migrants who completed three consecutive contracts of 180 days each within twenty-seven months to the Southern Rhodesian border.[24] Had South African authorities agreed to these measures, the incentives for border jumping in the region probably would have been reduced. However, Southern Rhodesia would have come out as the major beneficiary of the labor deal.

Because the South African economy benefited immensely from the flow of border jumpers from north of the Limpopo, the Pretoria administration did not agree with the Interterritorial Council of Central Africa's proposals. This compelled Southern Rhodesia and its northern neighbors to accept a watered down memorandum of understanding among the governments of the four countries, hoping that a more favorable arrangement would be worked out in the future. As the minutes of the December 2–3, 1947, meeting show, the representatives of the northern states "realised the difficulties of the Union Government in the matter, and fully appreciated that Government's willingness to arrive at a satisfactory solution to the common problem."[25] Once again, South African officials managed to convince their counterparts from the other three countries that it was practically and politically impossible to come up with a permanent solution to the problem of "illegal migration" in the region. Ultimately, the four governments agreed that instead of seeking to completely stop the flow of unauthorized migration to South Africa, they could put measures in place to regulate labor movements in the subregion. To that effect, Southern Rhodesian officials agreed to the idea of increasing migration control through nonobstructive legalization of cross-border flows, which South African authorities had proposed.[26] In accepting a deal that gave them far less than they had anticipated, Southern Rhodesian authorities thought that the agreement would at least help to reduce "illegal" emigration to South Africa. They might have naively thought that they were getting half of the loaf, which was better than nothing at all. However, the agreement did nothing to stop the movement of border jumpers to South Africa, where they continued to access work permits in obvious disregard of the 1947 memorandum of understanding.

Although Southern Rhodesia, Northern Rhodesia, and Nyasaland came up with another set of proposals in April 1948, the election and change of government in South Africa hampered prospects for meaningful consideration of a regional migration management strategy. For two years after winning the election in South Africa, Daniel F. Malan and his National Party government declined Southern Rhodesia's calls for meetings to discuss the issue of border jumping in the region. To the apartheid administration, the control of cross-Limpopo mobility was not a priority. That left the other three territories with no option other than to proceed without South Africa. In further efforts to find the solution to the issue of border jumping, the representatives of the three governments met again on October 7, 1950, and drafted another proposal for a regional labor deal. Realizing that it was not practical to obtain total control of labor emigration to South Africa, the three states toned down their demands. Among other things, they proposed a deal under which each government would issue identity certificates valid for two years to adult male Africans applying to work in South Africa. They also wanted to establish an organization in South Africa to inspect the working conditions of their people and to represent their governments' interests. In a similar fashion with the Portuguese curator, which the Portuguese colonial officials deployed in Johannesburg, this arrangement would have allowed Southern Rhodesia, Northern Rhodesia, and Nyasaland to have an ambassador in South Africa who would represent their interests so far as labor issues were concerned.

In devising these proposals, representatives of the three countries expected South African officials to stop issuing permits to border jumpers and to take steps that would prevent the employment of northern migrants without permits and "to arrange for safe travel of northern natives in possession of identity certificates both into and out of the Union through central transit depots sited on or near the Union border."[27] Furthermore, they expected South Africa to organize what they termed a "satisfactory" system to register migrants from north of the Limpopo at the time of their entry into the Union and to repatriate them after two years of working in South Africa. Determined to make the agreement work, representatives of the three countries agreed to establish an intergovernment advisory council to oversee the operation of the agreement. The proposed council, which was to be headed by an independent chairman, would consist of equal members representing the three countries and the Union of South Africa.[28] Had it been adopted, such an agreement would have allowed each country to control the number of permits it issued and to benefit from labor export through a proposed deferred pay system. At this point, it was clear that Southern Rhodesia had shifted its focus from trying to prevent loss of labor to trying to draw financial gains from Zimbabwean migrants who worked in South Africa.

Like several previous attempts to reach an agreement, this arrangement did not materialize owing to the South African authorities' unwillingness to give away their advantage in the region. When representatives of the four countries met again in 1952, the South African delegation, comprising the country's high commissioner, director of native labor, secretary of native affairs, commissioner of immigration, and representatives of the Chamber of Mines and the South African Agricultural Union, maintained that it was not willing to accept any agreement that would impede the "free" movement of labor in the region. It rejected the other three delegations' proposal that South Africa should not welcome workers coming from north of the Limpopo unless they possessed exit permits. The South Africans argued that accepting such a proposal would give power to Southern Rhodesia "to limit as it liked the number of natives permitted to enter the Union."[29] Furthermore, they argued that the proposal would make it difficult for South African employers to access not only migrants from Southern Rhodesia but also those from Nyasaland and Northern Rhodesian who, in most cases, had to pass through Southern Rhodesia to enter the Union. At the very least, the South African delegation preferred a scenario in which economic laws of supply and demand prevailed. They wanted the African workers from the whole region to choose where to work, so they expected representatives of the other three countries to uphold that position. By projecting their government as a champion of free labor, South African authorities barely disguised the real reason for their reluctance to restrict cross-Limpopo migration: they did not want to let go of the advantage they enjoyed in the regional labor market.

Migrants' Evasion of Southern Rhodesia's Control of Cross-Limpopo Mobility

If anything was achieved by Southern Rhodesia–South Africa competition for regional labor and contestations over the control of cross-Limpopo migration during the 1930s and 1940s, it was the escalation of border jumping in the region. What complicated matters for Southern Rhodesian authorities was that the Transvaal gold mines continued to enjoy the reputation of being the highest paying employers in the region, thus the labor market remained tilted in South Africa's favor. In this context, returning migrants commanded a lot of respect in their communities. As Amon Mlambo, a Chipinge former migrant worker, put it, "People derided those who worked in here. They encouraged such people to go afar and see places. No-one even noticed you if you worked in the country."[30] Migrants returning from South Africa also brought back new clothes, bicycles, blankets, watches, and other items that most peasants could not afford in Southern Rhodesia. On this point, Mlambo said:

> The kind of clothes you brought from the south were very different from the ones the local workers brought. Even the blankets that you had, the shirts, the coats, the suits, all these were of super value. The clothes in the south came from Palace [Paris?] and these were the latest fashions. . . . It was from Palace that trends were formulated. Not from London, but from Palace. Some material was so good that even if you took out matches and tried to light that material, it would not burn out but would simply crumble. Then if you pulled it straight, it was again all right. The locally available materials would burn.[31]

Given that African workers on the mines and farms in Southern Rhodesia continued to receive low wages, many considered migration to South Africa as the most viable way of improving their lifestyle and social standing.

Poor working conditions and ill treatment of African workers by employers in Southern Rhodesia also continued throughout the 1930s and 1940s, thereby presenting challenges to the administration's efforts to prevent migration to South Africa. At one point the BSAP was forced to raise these issues with the

Native Affairs Department officials after they uncovered cases of violence and ill treatment of workers by one Eilardus Conrad Bruins. This discovery came out of the police investigations of alleged desertions of workers from the Clifton Gold Mining Company and other mines in the Midlands and southwestern regions of the country. In a report that castigated Bruins as a supporter of the Nazi and Fascist movements in Europe, the head of the BSAP's Criminal Investigations Department (CID) indicated that

> natives on the Clifton and Great Belingwe . . . are subjected to cruelty, sjam-bokings [whipping] being administered out of hand for the slightest breach of Bruins's instructions. Fines, I understand are also imposed upon native employees for sundry minor misdemeanours. It is a well-known fact in the district that local natives are now endeavouring to get leave in order that they may visit their kraals for the purpose of tending their lands. On the last two Mines, this privilege has been refused them. Bruins will not allow natives to brew beer in the compound. This man is feared throughout the district by the Native population. . . . The Natives have named Bruins "Majerman" [a cruel man] which speaks for itself and Kumuchiza which means "He who holds the sjambok."[32]

Contrary to what they experienced in Southern Rhodesia, Zimbabwean peasants received information about "attractive" working environments in South Africa from friends and relatives who had lived and worked on the other side of the Limpopo. As Louis Samuel Glover, a former recruiting agent for the De Beers Company, pointed out, South African companies offered "good hospitals and good treatment," and "supervisors who struck natives were dismissed instantly."[33] Although working conditions in some parts of South Africa may not have been as good as Glover put it or even better than those in Southern Rhodesia, returning migrants' accounts played an important role in encouraging others to look beyond Southern Rhodesia for better wages and working conditions.

Furthermore, occasional droughts, especially those in the country's southern districts, continued to push people to seek employment in South Africa. The situation was particularly bad during the 1934–35 and 1935–36 planting seasons when districts such as Bikita, Melsetter (present-day Chimanimani), and Chipinge received far-below-average rainfall. Faced with food shortages caused by poor rains, large numbers of people from these areas, which have long histories of supplying migrant workers to South Africa, moved south of the Limpopo. In Melsetter, where there was an almost total failure of crops, "it was estimated that 60% of the male tax payers went to the Union."[34] Although there was probably very little that the colonial government could do to avert droughts, developments such as these put pressure on state-centered restrictions on migration to South Africa.

As people from various parts of the country tried different ways and means to evade Southern Rhodesian authorities' efforts to prevent migration to South Africa, the 1930s and 1940s witnessed the adaptation of informal networks, routes, and channels that had been in existence for generations to suit the prevailing situation. For example, use of fraudulently obtained travel documents increased. As the BSAP's CID records show, there were several cases in which Africans returning from South Africa were found to unlawfully possess packs of signed and stamped employment contracts without the holders' names filled in.[35] Whoever came up with this strategy, which appears to have emerged during the period when South African authorities tried to enforce the ban on "tropical" workers, knew that returning migrants could be effective recruiters among their friends and relatives. In using this strategy, South Africa-based employers continued to sponsor networks that sustained border jumping in the region.

Whereas some people used employment contracts they received from returning migrants, others mailed their RCs to relatives and acquaintances who were already in South Africa so that they could obtain work permits on their behalf. Those in South Africa then mailed back the work permits and stamped RCs to prospective migrants or simply handed them over when they returned home on holidays or at the end of their work contracts. A prospective migrant would then present these documents to the pass officers and obtain travel permits for South Africa. Alternatively, one would bypass the pass officers, present the South African work contract to the railway officials and obtain a train ticket, which would facilitate a hassle-free journey to the Botswana border or to West Nicholson. Southern Rhodesia's policy pronouncements stating that authorities would give passes only to people with special permits from South Africa might have encouraged this behavior.[36]

In June 1942 the BSAP intercepted some letters that African workers at the Premier Portland Cement (in Bulawayo) wrote to relatives and friends in South Africa. The letters provide more details about how these networks of illegality worked. In a letter to Chimota Manda of P. P. Rust Mine in Rustenburg, for example, one writer pleaded, "Send me money as soon as possible please father, when you send money . . . send me also a leave pass; you can take all particulars of mine from my old tax receipt of £1.0.0 tax. When receiving my letter please send the above mentioned pass very urgent."[37] Another letter read, "I need no money from you but I only want your leave pass thus all. Send it to me as soon as possible please. . . . When you get it please go to the Compound Manager's Office and stamp it and put inside envelope. I have failed to take train because of having no pass."[38] Emphasizing the urgency with which these "deals" had to be executed, a third letter writer stated:

I am writing the second letter but story is still just the same. Please try to help me very quick; send your leave pass that which you had given to Loisi Nkwazi; then when you send a pass send also a passport and the pass of this month which you are walking with there, so I can go with it at the office. I am enclosing herewith my train ticket for Mafeking, who did bought it for me is another man from Nyasaland who had his pass from Nyasaland and leave pass. He is there in U.S.A. [Union of South Africa] that's why I am sending my train ticket so that you see yourself . . . look here brother, when you send me pass send also my train ticket. I have send this to make you quick posting the passes, please make haste when the time still, it may be finished please.[39]

Through these letters, we can see how the network theory of migration worked to undermine Southern Rhodesia's efforts to prevent loss of labor.[40] Although the police managed to intercept these specific letters, it is quite likely that they depict a widespread practice that migrants used to circumvent Southern Rhodesia's migration control mechanisms.

Responding to the demand for travel documents, some enterprising Africans sold the documents they either forged or fraudulently obtained. In a case that speaks to this strategy, on February 4, 1942, the Bulawayo Magistrates Court convicted a man called Mutawale after he pleaded guilty to selling passes to three Malawian migrants who intended to leave Southern Rhodesia. In its ruling, the court found that Mutawale, who was messenger in the Native Affairs Department, "committed the crime of fraud by wrongfully and unlawfully, falsely and fraudulently giving out or pretending to Josamu Mwale, a Nyasaland native who wished to proceed from Bulawayo . . . to the Union of South Africa, that he could supply the said Josamu Mwale with a pass which would enable him to leave the colony."[41] During the trial proceedings, the court heard that Mutawale received a total of 30 shillings from Josamu Mwale, Mohela Banda, and Nambalawani Mbewa and, in return, gave them passes that he knew were forged and would not enable them to enter South Africa. In a similar case, the same court found Noel Janitarie guilty of selling fake passes to three individuals who wanted to migrate to South Africa.[42] Apparently, the selling of passes was not confined to Bulawayo, which was the major departure point for the railways destined for South Africa. The same practice took place in South Africa, where the Johannesburg police arrested a migrant from Southern Rhodesia based on allegations that "he was supplying passes to Rhodesian natives at £8 per pass."[43]

In addition to those who used other people's RCs to obtain travel documents to cross the Limpopo border, some male travelers resorted to buying train tickets that were reserved for women. The idea of distinguishing between tickets for men and for women arose when Southern Rhodesian authorities recognized the fraudulent activities surrounding the acquisition of passes to leave the colony.

In this respect, the chief native commissioner instructed the railway ticketing officials to closely scrutinize the passes that male travelers presented when they purchased train tickets. Because female buyers were not subject to the same level of scrutiny, some male travelers connived with their female acquaintances who bought tickets for them. To avoid arrest for using tickets with specific markings that showed they were reserved for women, such migrants would disembark when the trains stopped at the Plumtree station where the police examined all passengers' tickets. From Plumtree, they either walked to various crossing points along the Limpopo River or got into Bechuanaland and then proceeded to South Africa when the situation allowed them to do that.[44]

This period also witnessed the rise of the *layitsha* concept, which has since played a major role in fueling border jumping across the Zimbabwe–South Africa border. The word refers to the transportation of border jumpers and various kinds of goods across the Zimbabwe–South Africa by individuals without official licenses to do that (see chap. 5 for more discussion of this activity). In most cases, the transporters (*malayitsha*) use private vehicles that also are not licensed to carry out these functions. Although this word only became part of the Zimbabwe–South Africa border lingo over the past two decades, when border jumping reached unprecedented levels, the practice itself grew in the 1930s and 1940s. It followed the erection of the Alfred Beit Bridge across the Limpopo River, which coincided with the suspension of South Africa's ban on "tropical" workers and the intensification of Southern Rhodesia's and South Africa's competition for labor. Whereas Southern Rhodesian authorities used the bridge as a focal point in their effort to control cross-Limpopo mobility, some owners of motorized vehicles saw the bridge as an opportunity to make money by transporting migrants between the two countries. Transport operators joined the networks of recruiters and South African employers who helped migrants to clandestinely move from Southern Rhodesia to South Africa.

In November 1935, the *Bulawayo Chronicle* ran a story indicating that some private vehicles regularly transported migrants from Bulawayo to Beitbridge. Providing more details on how the *malayitsha* of the 1930s dodged Southern Rhodesian authorities, the paper argued that the drivers of these vehicles picked their passengers from areas around Bulawayo and dropped them off within a mile of the rudimentary border post that had emerged at the bridge and let them walk across the border at undesignated points. They would then drive their vehicles through the bridge, pick up their passengers on the other side of the border and hand them over to labor recruiters.[45] In December of the same year, the chief superintendent of police in Bulawayo made a similar observation when he pointed out that prospective migrants regularly boarded "motor lorries" from Bulawayo to Legion Mine in Gwanda and then proceeded "through the veldt in a South Easterly direction, crossing the Shashi and Limpopo Rivers, and make for

Bandolier Kop, south of Louis Trichardt," adding that "large numbers of natives have used this route."[46] In another report, a BSAP trooper deployed in the border zone pointed out that an African woman called Nonia (or Mary Gamble) used her car to carry migrants from the West Nicholson railway station to the Beitbridge border post. On crossing the border through the bush, concerned migrants would link up with Nonia's daughter, who transported them to various places in the Messina area.[47]

Unlicensed transporters also took migrants out of Southern Rhodesia through the Bechuanaland route, which gained prominence in the 1920s. Although the Bulawayo–Mafeking trains continued to be a viable option for the migrants who chose this route, some received assistance from individuals such as Mahomed Ismael Lehar, an Indian businessman who transported border jumpers between Bulawayo and the Bechuanaland border. On April 6, 1939, the BSAP arrested Lehar after discovering a truck carrying twenty-three African passengers at his house in Bulawayo. On the day of Lehar's trial in court, all twenty-three passengers revealed that they possessed no permits to leave the country. Furthermore, they confirmed that the accused had planned to take them to Francistown, where they hoped to work briefly before proceeding to Johannesburg.[48] Apart from Lehar, other motorists dropped migrants near the Limpopo–Shashe confluence, from which they walked to Bobonong, an African village in Bechuanaland where there was a store for them to replenish their food supplies. From there, they proceeded to Johannesburg. Commenting on this practice, the Bechuanaland Police Department wrote that there was "a regular route via the Bobonong area leading to the Transvaal Border which natives from Southern Rhodesia [were] in the habit of taking."[49]

Furthermore, drivers of the Railway Motor Services (RMS) vehicles, which carried various kinds of goods between West Nicholson and Beitbridge, also transported border jumpers to the border area. To avoid apprehension by the police in Beitbridge, the RMS drivers emulated private transporters who dropped passengers a mile or so north of the border post to allow them to proceed through the bush and evade the authorities at the bridge.[50] Besides drivers, other employees of the RMS also helped border jumpers evade the system of migration control in Southern Rhodesia. As several police reports revealed, some passengers on the trains destined for West Nicholson disembarked in Gwanda (one stop before West Nicholson) with chits issued by the station master in Bulawayo. After disembarking, these migrants proceeded to the Jessie Mine Store, where a white storekeeper called Jacob Sacks gave them free food on presentation of the chits. Another white man named Turner would then use his car to transport migrants from there to the border town where they crossed through various bush paths.[51] Given that RMS was a state entity, its employees had a responsibility to ensure that the government's migration laws were respected. Its employees' involvement in these activities not only shows the extent of the networks that facilitated border jumping in this period but also indicates that corruption has been part of this phenomenon for a long time. The assistance that these employees rendered to migrants who moved within and out of the colony without official permission was also a subversion of the state's authority.

Some drivers of the South African Railways (SAR) plying the Bulawayo–Mafeking route also helped undermine Southern Rhodesia's migration control efforts by facilitating illicit crossings of the border. In 1941, for example, the Southern Rhodesian chief immigration officer observed that it was common for the SAR drivers to hide migrants in "a goods truck, the caboose or the guards van, or even the engine, according to the necessities of the situation."[52] Another strategy that train drivers used was to disguise their passengers as servants of the train crew. In that respect, a traveler would board at Bulawayo and pose as a personal employee of one of the crew members throughout the entire journey, only to part ways with his "employer" as soon as the train reached Mafeking. In some cases, which the police reported, train drivers gave aprons to border jumpers and disguised them as caboose workers in order to smuggle them across the border. The more valiant drivers often instructed relief guards to sit on the caboose platforms when the train stopped at search points and chase away the African constables who usually performed the searches, telling them that they could not search the caboose without warrants. In other cases, the train guards asked travelers to purchase tickets for Plumtree, where the migrant passenger would disembark and rejoin the train immediately after the police finished their routine inspections.[53]

It was also common for border jumpers to travel on South Africa–bound trains without the knowledge or permission of the drivers. This was particularly so with goods trains, which often contained some open wagons. Sometimes migrants jumped onto the wagons as the trains took off from any of the stations or check points along the railway line. Once on the train, border jumpers would cover themselves with whatever might be carried on the wagons and then jump off when the trains got near the border area. This undoubtedly risky practice cost some lives. For example, on July 15, 1944, a group of migrants jumped off a South Africa–bound train at Coldridge Siding (one stop before Plumtree), leading to the death of one man identified as Paul Makoni. The police investigations of circumstances surrounding Makoni's death revealed that migrants commonly used this strategy to evade the system of migration control in Southern Rhodesia. To avoid detection by the police who checked all trains at the Plumtree Siding, migrants who used this strategy jumped off the train at Coldridge and proceeded to the border on foot. However, on the day in question, the train did not stop at Coldridge, prompting Makoni and his group to jump off while it was in motion.[54]

Despite the presence of the police guards at the Alfred Beit Bridge and border gates, it was also possible for migrants to slip through without the required documents or permissions. The South African guards at the border post were focused on protecting the bridge "against sabotage," so they did not "normally interfere with traffic or pedestrians."[55] This approach made it less difficult for "undocumented" migrants to pass through. However, such people still had to devise strategies of dodging the Southern Rhodesian guards at the bridge. An incident that took place January 13, 1939, reveals one of the strategies that migrants used to slip into South Africa via the bridge. Having arrived in Beitbridge that afternoon, a group of three migrants connected with Axon, an African employee of the Beitbridge Hotel, and another African man called Togo and headed to the bridge. Before they crossed onto the Transvaal side, the police guards on the Southern Rhodesian side intercepted them and asked where they were going. All four said they were tourists who had come to have a look at the bridge, and Axon, whom the police guards knew very well, said he was accompanying them on a walk across the bridge to the South African customs post. After asking all four to produce their RCs, the police guard detained Togo on suspicion that he was the individual that the police had wanted to question regarding the theft of a suitcase. Although the police guard ordered Axon and the other three men to go back to the Beitbridge Native Compound, he later reported that he "found no trace of the four natives who had been in company with Togo," but he did not clearly say that they crossed the bridge at night.[56]

However, Axon's report on this case provides more details of the networks that border jumpers utilized to dodge Southern Rhodesian guards at the bridge. He said:

> On Friday 13/1/39 in the Native Compound at Beitbridge I met a brother native of the same tribe as myself from Nyasaland. I do not know his name or anything about him, he was with three other natives, two alien natives and one indigenous, I could tell by their talk. . . . All these four natives arrived at Beitbridge that day on native Kamba's Road Services Lorry and they were staying at Kamba's hut in the Compound. I met them at about 4pm and the four of us went for a stroll across the Beitbridge to the Union Customs about 5pm. They told me they were going to cross into the Transvaal that night. When we were crossing into the Transvaal we met N/L/Cpl. Sinyelo of the BSA Police, he stopped us and asked to see the RCs and passes of the natives I was with. He did not ask to see my RC or Pass as he knows that I live in Beitbridge.[57]

This account gives the impression that Axon was part of a network that helped migrants to cross the Southern Rhodesia–South Africa border through the border post without the necessary documents. The way he used the term *brother* to refer to someone whose name or background he did not actually know underscores the importance of fictitious familial relationships that people forge to build networks of trust. It was particularly important in such situations where they needed to evade the official systems of migration control. It is also possible that the concerned police guard did not only know what was going on but indeed was part of the same network. As it turned out during further investigations, the police department suspected that Togo was a tout working with Kamba on behalf of labor recruiters in South Africa.[58] It is possible that Kamba, the transporter, used his "house" in Beitbridge as a place for border jumpers to rest or hide while waiting to cross the border when it was most convenient to do so.

In another case that took place on March 19, 1943, a group of border jumpers attacked a police guard at the bridge and forced their way across the border. The incident began with the migrants refusing to stop when the guard at the Southern Rhodesian end of the bridge ordered them to. Instead, they ran across the bridge, prompting the same guard to fire some shots in the air. When another guard, who was at the southern end of the bridge, tried to stop the migrants, they assaulted him with knobkerries. In the scuffle that ensued, the majority succeeded in getting through into the Transvaal, leaving one whom the two guards overpowered and apprehended.[59] My research in the Zimbabwean and South African archives and fieldwork in the border zone did not reveal many other similar cases where border jumpers used violence to cross the border. This incident says more about the season of the year it happened than the significance of violence as a tool that migrants used to achieve their objectives. The Limpopo River is usually in flood and difficult to cross at points other than the bridge from December to March, which is the rainy season in southern Africa. Rather than trying to swim across a flooded Limpopo, these migrants chose to assault the guards who were the symbol of the state that sought to prevent them from exercising their freedom of movement.

As Southern Rhodesian authorities intensified efforts to stop migration to South Africa during the 1930s and 1940s, border jumpers became more determined to evade the system. In addition to using the Botswana and Mozambican routes, which we discussed in chapter 2, a new route emerged that took migrants from the eastern districts of Southern Rhodesia via the junction of Save and Runde Rivers where a man named Mahambayedwa had built a store. A report compiled by an African detective deployed in the Chipinge area at the time shows that by 1944, Mahambayedwa's store had become a major refueling station for migrants. From there they proceeded to Crooks' Corner, which continued to be a popular meeting place for border jumpers and recruiters of different kinds. As was the case in the Beitbridge district and along Southern Rhodesia's border with Botswana, such migrants were assisted by private motorists who transported them to Crooks' Corner and beyond.[60]

Free-for-All: Unregulated Recruiting and Violence in Northern South Africa

As the 1940s went by, it became harder for Southern Rhodesian authorities to control the movement of people to South Africa. Having lifted the ban on tropical workers in 1933, South African authorities did very little to control the activities of labor recruiters who camped in the country's northern border region. In a bid to maximize their ability to compete for migrant workers, several farmers' groups engaged storekeepers in the Zoutpansberg region to act as their recruiting agents. This alliance was strategic because stores in the sparsely inhabited border districts were among the few places where migrants would go in search of food, water, and other supplies as they made the long journey across the Southern Rhodesia–South Africa border. Interestingly, stores in the border area also functioned as important markers on migrants' routes. Experienced border jumpers used them as mapping tools, rest camps, and strategic points to meet with recruiters and potential employers. In this respect, storekeepers who doubled as part-time recruiters were well positioned to persuade migrants to sign work contracts with employers willing to pay for their recruiting services. As such, the epicenter of unregulated recruiting gradually shifted from Crooks' Corner to the area around Messina Town to the south of the Beitbridge border post and the Waterberg area along the South Africa–Bechuanaland border.[61]

Given that storekeepers were paid for every worker they recruited, some subcontracted touts and runners who intercepted border jumpers on the banks of the Limpopo River. As South Africa's chief native commissioner pointed out in December 1948, most touts and runners who operated in areas such as Messina, Sibasa, Louis Trichardt, and the Waterburg "bushveld" were former migrant workers from Southern Rhodesia and Nyasaland who had intimate knowledge of the routes and camping sites used by migrants in northern Transvaal. Because they could speak the same languages with most of the migrants, such people were better able than white storekeepers and licensed labor agents to persuade job-seeking migrants to accept contracts with the employers they represented. Often touts pretended to be un-uniformed officers of the South African Police Services (SAPS) on patrol in the border zone. In this disguise, touts were able to stop, search, and "arrest" migrants they found with or without passes and then force them to accept work contracts with specific employers.[62]

This scenario not only gave rise to an environment in which labor recruitment in the border zone had different meanings and legal connotations depending on which side of the border it took place but also fueled violence and lawlessness. As the demand for unskilled workers increased in response to South Africa's growing economy, competition among labor recruiters in the northern Transvaal intensified. In a repeat of what transpired at Crooks' Corner during the early twentieth century, labor recruiters often combined deception, threats, and outright force to get migrants to sign work contracts with employers willing to pay the recruiters' fees. One case that sheds some light on how recruiters interacted with migrants concerns a man called Swelisile Ncube who was kidnapped in 1947. In his testimony, Ncube said a "native" posing as a police officer intercepted him immediately after he crossed the Limpopo River and asked to see his traveling pass. When Ncube said he did not have a pass, his kidnappers searched his pockets and took away his pass and some money. As if that was not enough, they told Ncube that he was under arrest and placed him in a hut where he found seven other "arrested" border jumpers. After spending three nights in that place, a white man came and loaded Ncube and the other migrants in a truck with several other people. They were taken to a farm that Ncube said was owned by P. P. Rust. There they were asked to choose between accepting work contracts or paying for all the food they had been fed since the day they were kidnapped and reimbursing the costs of being (forcibly) transported from the Limpopo River to Rust's farm. As Ncube explained, the migrants did not have any choice because the people who kidnapped them also threatened to beat up anyone who refused to sign a work contract.[63]

It was also common for recruiters to use firearms to scare migrants and forcibly load them into vehicles that took them to specific employers in the Transvaal region. Inevitably, the use of guns resulted in serious injuries and even deaths of work-seeking migrants. In one of the recorded cases of violence against migrants, which the Nylstroom Court dealt with between 1947 and 1950, the magistrate sentenced an unlicensed labor recruiter called Zacharias Koekemoer to a fine of £50 or three months in prison for assault with intent to do grievous bodily harm. This sentence came after Koekemoer and his runners went on a night raid of migrants who had camped on the banks of the Limpopo River. As the migrants tried to run away, Koekemoer fired some shots and hit a man called Jim Nyindu on both of his legs. Although Nyindu was lucky to survive, some border jumpers were killed for refusing to follow recruiters' instructions or trying to fight back or escape from detention.[64] Sometimes migrants were placed in bush carts, which functioned like mobile detention camps, instead of fixed huts. The touts would then keep moving the carts as they gathered more migrants before forwarding them to the recruiting agents, who moved around the border zone in trucks.

The SAPS also reported cases of recruiters who raided farm compounds, mostly at night, with the intention of taking away migrants already working for other employers. This tactic was particularly common in the Louis Trichardt area, where the police received several complaints from farmers who had their migrant employees taken away in this manner.[65] As such, the Limpopo Valley witnessed the continuation of activities that closely resembled various aspects of the transatlantic slave trade. In addition to being forcibly recruited and trafficked, work-seeking migrants were often sold two or three times before they got to the place where they were forced to accept work contracts with terms they barely understood. As the *Sunday Times* of South Africa reported in March 1949, recruiters went out to get "as many heads as farmers and industrialists [were] prepared to pay for."[66] In a repeat of what had happened in 1918 (see chap. 2), the

South African government amended the Native Labor Regulation Act (1911) in 1949, requiring employers' agents who operated outside their districts to obtain special permits. The idea was to reduce competition among recruiters and eradicate violence in northern Transvaal. However, violence continued in this region. In February 1950, for example, the CID in Rustenburg received a report that some recruiters had beaten a work-seeking migrant to death and buried his body in a hole on a farm in Nylstroom District. On further investigation into this case, the police unearthed more kidnappings and violent killings of migrants. In one of the reports, the police revealed that a white man identified simply as "Coetzee" who lived on Stokpoort Farm had the habit of robbing migrants who passed by the farm as they traveled to other places in South Africa or back to their home countries.[67]

As disagreements over the control of cross-Limpopo mobility raged on between Southern Rhodesian policy makers and their counterparts in South Africa throughout the 1950s, border jumping thrived in this region. However, as this discussion suggests, the situation likely benefited South African business owners the most because they could employ cheap migrant workers from north of the Limpopo River without major restrictions. As for border jumpers, they continued to exhibit a high level of determination to conquer the odds, but the stakes were also getting higher and higher. The near free-for-all environment that prevailed in South Africa's northern border regions exposed them to various forms of abuse and violence. This scenario not only shows the extent to which violence had become an inseparable partner of border jumping in this region by the 1950s but also reveals what often happens when business interests override other considerations in border management processes.

Notes

1. NAZ, S1226, Chief Superintendent, BSAP, Bulawayo, to Staff Officer, BSAP, October 11, 1937.

2. NAZ, S1226, Chief Superintendent, BSAP, Bulawayo, to Staff Officer, BSAP, October 11, 1937.

3. NAZ, S1226, Detective Sergeant Barfoot, Beitbridge, to Chief Immigration Officer, Bulawayo, April 12, 1937.

4. NAZ, S1226, P. Hurdles, Circular to the Gwanda Small Workers Association, February 1935; Native Commissioner Gwanda to Chief Native Commissioner, June 24, 1937.

5. NAZ, S1226, CID Bulawayo, to Chief Superintendent CID, November 29, 1935; See also Detective Sergeant Stephenson, to Chief Superintendent CID Bulawayo, September 9, 1936.

6. NAZ, S1226, Chief Superintendent CID Bulawayo, to the Staff Officer, BSAP, January 4, 1938. See, also *Rand Daily*, "Banned Natives Enter Union: Immigration Laws Not Enforced: Thousands Cross Northern Border," April 5, 1934.

7. The bridge was named after Alfred Beit who was the benefactor of the Beit Railways Trust, which sponsored its construction. In 1935, the Southern Rhodesian government proclaimed the area along the Limpopo River, from the Shashe-Limpopo confluence down to Chikwarakwara, as the administrative district of Beitbridge.

8. NAZ, S482/203/39/1, Copy of the Premier's Speech on the Occasion of the Opening of the Beit Bridge on August 31, 1929. See also, The Premier, Salisbury, to the Minister of External Affairs, Pretoria, January 26, 1931 (same file).

9. NAZ, S1226, H.W. Clemow, Chief Superintendent CID, to the Staff Officer BSAP, November 24, 1937.

10. NAZ, S1226, Detective Sgt Elliot, CID Bulawayo, to Chief Superintendent, CID Bulawayo, November 30, 1939.

11. NAZ, S1226, Tpr L.L.A. Seward, BSAP, West Nicholson to Chief Superintendent CID, Bulawayo, December 2, 1935.

12. See report by one such "secret police": NAZ, S1226, Statement by Austin Makawa Regarding Illegal Emigration of Natives, March 21, 1939. See also (in the same file), Chief Superintendent CID's letter to Assistant Superintendent CID, in which he sanctioned the deployment of a plain cloth Native Constable in trains to investigate alleged illegal movements of Africans from Southern Rhodesia to South Africa, May 26, 1939.

13. Crush et al., *South Africa's Labor Empire*, 48.

14. NAZ, S1561/4, Minutes of Proceedings of a Meeting of the Standing Committee held in Salisbury, December 3–4, 1937.

15. NAZ, S1561/5, Migrant Labour: Recruitment of Natives in Nyasaland and Northern Rhodesia, 1938–1939.

16. NAZ, S1226, B. E. Bulstrode, Cpl. B.S.A.P, Beitbridge, to Chief Superintendent B.S.AP, October 11, 1938.

17. Victor L. Allen, *The History of Black Mineworkers in South Africa*. Vol. 1, *The Techniques of Resistance, 1871–1948* (West Yorkshire: Moore Press, 1992): 232.

18. Paton, *Labour Export Policy*.

19. Paton, *Labour Export Policy*.

20. Crush et al., *South Africa's Labor Empire*.

21. Crush et al., *South Africa's Labor Empire*.

22. Paton, *Labour Export Policy*.

23. Paton, *Labour Export Policy*.

24. NAZ, S1226, Central African Council: Minutes of a Meeting between Representatives of the Governments of the Union of South Africa and the Governments of Southern Rhodesia, Northern Rhodesia and Nyasaland, held in Salisbury on December 2 and 3, 1947.

25. NAZ, S1226, Central African Council: Minutes, December 2 and 3, 1947.

26. Paton, *Labour Export Policy*.

27. NAZ, F146/12, Central African Proposals for a Migrant Labour Agreement with South Africa, October 7, 1950.

28. NAZ, F146/12, Central African Proposals for a Migrant Labour Agreement with South Africa, October 7, 1950.

29. NASA, NTS, vol. 2246, file 603/280, Northern Governments' Delegation to Pretoria on Clandestine Emigration of Natives to the Union.

30. NAZ AOH/46, Mlambo, interview. For further discussions on how the migrant labor system related to issues of masculinity and honor in colonial Africa, see John Iliffe, *Honour in African History* (Cambridge: Cambridge University Press, 2005); David B. Coplan, *In the Time of Cannibals: The Word Music of South Africa's Basotho Migrants* (Chicago: University of Chicago Press, 1994); Dunbar Moodie, *Going for Gold: Men, Mines and Migration,* with Vivienne Ndatshe (Berkeley: University of California Press, 1994).

31. NAZ AOH/46, Mlambo, interview.

32. NAZ, S1226, Statement by the CID, Gwelo, November 18, 1941.

33. NAZ, ORAL GL/1 Louis Samuel Glover, interview with D. Hartridge, Salisbury, February 4, 1969.

34. NAZ, S1542/E2/2 Vol 2, Assistant Native Commissioner, Melsetter, to Native Commissioner, Chipinga, June 26, 1935.

35. NAZ, S1226, Lieutenant Staff Officer, BSAP, to the Commissioner of Police, Salisbury, February 22, 1939. See, also (in the same file) H. W. Clemow, Chief Superintendent, CID, to the Staff Officer, BSAP, November 24, 1937; Detective Sergeant C. Stephenson, Beitbridge, to Chief Immigration Officer, Bulawayo, November 29, 1935.

36. NAZ, S1226, H. W. Clemow, Chief Superintendent, CID to the Staff Officer, BSAP, November 24, 1937.

37. NAZ, S1226, These letters were included in several correspondences between the Civil Security Officer Southern Rhodesia and the Provincial Native Commissioner, Bulawayo, June 12, 1942.

38. NAZ, S1226, Wazelu Mbove, to Senter Mbove, 1942.

39. NAZ, S1226, Isaac Mkolongo Mhuka, to Bible Nkwazi, 1942.

40. For further discussions of the networks theory of migration, see Douglas S. Massey, et al., "Theories of International Migration: A Review and Appraisal," *Population and Development Review* 19, no. 3 (1993): 431–66; Frank D. Bean and Susan K. Brown, "Demographic Analyses of Immigration," in *Migration Theory: Talking Across Disciplines,* ed. Caroline B. Brettell and James F. Hollifield (New York: Routledge, 2015).

41. NAZ, S1226, Rex vs Mutawale *alias* Alick, Native Affairs Department Messenger: Trial in the Court of Magistrate for the District of Bulawayo, March 17, 1942.

42. *Bulawayo Chronicle,* "Fined for Selling Passes," January 14, 1944.

43. NAZ, S1226, Chief Inspector District Commandant, Johannesburg, to the Officer Commanding CID, BSAP, Southern Rhodesia, February 26, 1951.

44. NAZ, S1226, Detective Sergeant CID Bulawayo, to Detective Inspector in Charge CID Bulawayo, March 18, 1944. See also (in the same file) South African Railway Guards, Mafeking, to System Manager, Kimberley, November 10, 1944.

45. *Bulawayo Chronicle,* "Labour Smuggled Over the Border," November 29, 1935.

46. NAZ, S1226, Chief Superintendent CID, Bulawayo, to the Staff Officer BSAP, December 10, 1935.

47. NAZ S1226 Trooper L.L.A. Seward, BSAP, West Nicholson, to Chief Superintendent CID Bulawayo, December 2, 1935. See, also (in the same file) letter from the Native Commissioner Gwanda, to Southern Rhodesia's Chief Native Commissioner (dated June 24, 1937) in which he reported that there were about ten vehicles, which moved people daily between Beitbridge and Messina, adding that these vehicles were usually full at night.

48. NAZ, S1226, A Summary of a Court Trial: Rex vs Mahomed Ismael Lehar- Bulawayo Town C.R.276.4.39.

49. NAZ, S1226, Officer Commanding Palapye, Bechuanaland Protectorate Police, to Chief Superintendent CID, BSAP, Bulawayo, November 7, 1939. See also, NAZ S1226 Chief Superintendent CID, to the Commissioner BSAP, October 24, 1939.

50. NAZ, S1226, H. G. Seward, Chief Superintendent, Divisional Criminal Investigation Officer, Salisbury, to the Inspector General, BSAP Bulawayo December 2, 1944.

51. NAZ, S1226, Trooper L.L.A. Seward, BSAP, West Nicholson, to Chief Superintendent CID Bulawayo, December 2, 1935; See also (in the same file) Detective Sergeant Elliot CID Bulawayo, to Chief Superintendent CID Bulawayo, November 30, 1939; Statement by Austin Makawa Regarding Illegal Emigration of Natives, March 21, 1939.

52. NAZ, S1226, Major H. W. Clemow, Chief Immigration Officer, Bulawayo, to the Commissioner for Immigration and Asiatic Affairs, Pretoria, November 12, 1941.

53. NAZ, S1226, Detective Sergeant K. D. Leaver, CID, Bulawayo, to Assistant Commissioner CID Bulawayo, March 29, 1944.

54. NAZ, S1226, Captain Harrison, Divisional Criminal Investigation Officer, CID Bulawayo, to Sub-Inspector in Charge, BSAP Plumtree, July 31, 1944.

55. NAZ, S1226, Chief Superintendent of Police, Bulawayo, to the Staff Officer to the Inspector General BSAP, April 25, 1941.

56. NAZ, S1226, BSAP Investigation Diary on Alleged Illegal Recruiting of Natives, January 13, 1939.

57. NAZ, S1226, BSAP Investigation Diary, January 13, 1939.

58. NAZ, S1226, BSAP Investigation Diary, January 13, 1939.

59. NAZ, S1226, BSAP Monthly Intelligence Summary: Bulawayo District, March 1943.

60. NAZ, S1226, "Clandestine Migration of Natives to the Union: Spraggon Route- Report by Native Biyasi, December 4, 1944.

61. NASA, NTS, vol. 2246, file 564/280 Secretary for Native Affairs, to Attorney General, Pretoria, August 11, 1947. See also, NAZ, AOH/46, Mlambo, interview.

62. NASA, NTS, vol. 2246, file 564/280, South African Police, Office of the Public Prosecutor, Nylstroom, to the Attorney General, Pretoria, July 15, 1947. See, also (in the same file) Chief Native Commissioner, Pietersburg, to Secretary for Native Affairs, Pretoria, September 15, 1947; Secretary for Native Affairs, Pretoria, to Director of Native Labor, Johannesburg, October 28, 1947.

63. NASA, NTS, vol. 2246, file 564/280, Statement taken from Swelisile Ncube, *alias*, Dick, Unit No.C874, Dist. Matobo, S.R. April 17, 1947.

64. NASA, NTS, vol. 2246, file 564/280, Recruiting of Natives Criticized: Comment by a Magistrate in Assault Case, January 30, 1950.

65. NASA, NTS, vol. 2246, file 564/280, Chief native Commissioner, Louis Trichardt, to Chief Native Commissioner, Pietersburg, March 2, 1949.

66. *Sunday Times* (Johannesburg), "Police Drive Against Border 'Blackbirders': 'Recruiters's Use of Violence in Trade in Human Bodies," March 20, 1949.

67. NASA, NTS, vol. 2246, file 564/280, Office of the CID, Rustenburg, to District Commandant, South African Police, Rustenburg, February 6, 1950.

4   Apartheid, African Liberation Struggles, and the Securitization of Cross-Limpopo Mobility

After decades of ambivalence about and sometimes subtle encouragement of "clandestine" migration from Zimbabwe, the South African government changed course in the 1960s when it adopted several measures to reduce the country's reliance on foreign workers. In a dramatic shift of priorities, South African authorities took the leading role in fighting border jumping in the region while their counterparts in Southern Rhodesia played only a supportive role. This scenario was largely a result of the policies that the Afrikaner-dominated National Party, which won the 1948 general elections in South Africa, began to implement in the 1950s. Although previous administrations had used racial segregation and exploitation of nonwhite groups to stay in power, the National Party government went steps further by adopting apartheid as the official ideology of governance. In simple terms, apartheid was no different from the policy of segregation that prevailed in parts of the United States around the same period. The idea was to enforce geospatial separation of the country's population along racial lines with a view to entrenching the dominance of white people at the expense of black, Indian, and other groups.

In pursuit of its segregationist agenda, the South African government devised and deployed numerous legal instruments (e.g., the Group Areas Act of 1950 and the 1951 Elimination of Squatting Act) to forcibly relocate black people from cities and other areas set aside for the white population to the so-called tribal homelands or *bantustans*. As a result, millions of black people lost their prime lands, which had provided stable sources of livelihood, while those who had survived on informal trading and other income-generating activities in the urban areas found themselves in overcrowded bantustans with few resources and minimal support from the government. In this respect, forced removals led to the rise of unemployment among the black population of South Africa, the livelihoods of which were grossly destabilized. This led in turn to increasing calls for South African businesses (mostly mine owners and farmers) to replace migrant workers with locals. In addition to members of the Labor Party and leaders of some native associations that had advocated for the banning of foreign workers since the first decade of the Union government (see chap. 2), the 1950s witnessed the rise of workers unions among the black population in South Africa. They, too, joined the chorus for the creation of employment opportunities for millions of black people who bore the brunt of forced removals and apartheid policies in general.[1]

What made it difficult for the South African government authorities to ignore the calls for a shift in labor recruitment priorities was the growing radicalization of African political activities in the country. African political activism in the past had focused on reforming oppressive systems of governance, whereas the 1950s witnessed increasing calls for the end to white rule in South Africa. Unsurprisingly, apartheid policies fueled the flames of black liberation movements. In response to growing political activism among the black people, the South Africa government invoked the Suppression of Communism Act, which was introduced in 1950—to ban the South African Communist Party (SACP), which was formed in 1921; the African National Congress (ANC), which emerged in 1912; and the Pan African Congress (PAC), which was formed in 1959. By banning these organizations, the government did not miss the point that unemployed black youths constituted the majority of their supporters.

In addition to concerns about African migrant workers taking up jobs that the squeezed local population could benefit from, critics of the South African government also worried about the increasing numbers of what it viewed as unwanted migrants. These migrants were foreign African women who entered the country either in the company of male migrant workers or on their own.[2] Because mining companies and farms, which were the biggest employers of African migrant workers at the time, did not provide family housing in their compounds, women migrants and children lived in informal settlements dotted around Johannesburg, Pretoria, Durban, Cape Town, and other major cities. With the number of such migrants standing at about 186,000 in 1960, serious concerns were raised about them being an unnecessary expense for the nation. Despite the fact that they did not enjoy similar rights and protections as white people, African women migrants and their dependents practically enjoyed the same kinds of (limited) rights to education, health, and other social services as the local black population.[3] In addition, there were concerns that the increasing numbers of foreign African women indicated migrant workers' intention to settle permanently in South Africa. Furthermore, the country's predominantly white electorate was convinced that African migrant workers prejudiced the South African economy by exporting large amounts of money to their home countries instead of reinvesting it to help with the creation of more jobs for the local people.[4]

Another factor that contributed to the change in perception toward African migrant workers in South Africa was the unmistakable shift in the region's political landscape. The impending independence of Botswana, Lesotho, and

Swaziland was publicly discussed in the late 1950s. Together with Mozambique, Malawi, and Zambia, the former High Commission territories had also been major suppliers of labor for the South African mines and farms. Although South African authorities envisioned a situation in which mine owners and farmers would continue to employ migrant workers from these countries, they were concerned about the influence that migrants from independent states would have on local Africans. More important, the 1950s and 1960s also witnessed the militarization of anticolonial movements in Southern Rhodesia. The last thing that South African authorities wanted to see happening was the cross-Limpopo movement of people actively involved in the fight against white supremacy in the region. In this respect, migrants from north of the Limpopo ceased to be a mere reservoir of cheap labor in South Africa. Instead, they became a security threat to the apartheid government, which devised several ways of blocking their entry into the country.

Influx Control and the Displacement of Foreign Workers in South Africa

In an effort to reduce the country's reliance on foreign workers, the minister of Bantu administration and development appointed an interdepartmental committee "to consider the problem of foreign natives in the Republic" on May 20, 1961.[5] After more than a year of gathering data from various sectors of the South African population, the committee—commonly referred to as the Froneman Committee—recommended a policy of preventing permanent settlement by African migrants. A key pillar of this policy, as the committee explained, was the compulsory repatriation of all foreign "Bantu" women and children back to their countries of origin. In the minds of the committee members, such a policy stance was necessary to compel male migrant workers to leave South Africa at the end of their contracts. Along with this proposal, the Froneman Committee suggested that, "the admission of Bantu children and juveniles from outside the Republic to educational institutions in the Republic and under the control of Bantu Education must be stopped."[6] Furthermore, the committee encouraged the government to take away citizenship rights of children born to African migrants while in South Africa by classifying them as foreigners and modifying their birth certificates to reflect that status. To enforce this policy, the committee recommended that "Bantu" children should produce their birth certificates in order to be enrolled in school and that their parents should not only accompany them at the time of admission but also produce their own identity documents and marriage certificates.[7]

Realizing that the number of African migrant workers employed in South Africa (approximately 836,000 at the time) exceeded the number of local Africans who were considered to be unemployed (about 505,000), the Froneman Committee proposed a policy of replacing all African migrant workers with a local workforce. The committee proposed, for example, that people of Indian heritage, who constituted the majority of nonwhite citizens of Durban, would replace African migrant workers in that part of the country, and people of mixed race (locally referred to as *coloreds*) do the same in the Western Cape. Furthermore, the committee recommended that South African employers (companies and individuals alike) should not engage or continue to employ African migrants except with the permission of the director of Bantu labor, who was previously referred to as the director of native labor. In line with this proposal, employers who engaged African migrants without official permission would be charged for the costs of deporting such prohibited immigrants. The committee also recommended cash payments for traditional African leaders (the so-called Bantu authorities) who induced their followers to take up jobs at the mines, on farms, and in the manufacturing sector.[8] In so doing, the Froneman Committee envisioned a situation in which foreigners came into the country only as supplements to the local African workforce.

Another key recommendation of the Froneman Committee was for the compulsory registration of all African migrants regardless of employment status. This proposal was not particularly new because the 1939 Aliens Registration Act and the Population Registration Act of 1950 had made similar provisions. For example, the Aliens Registration Act required employers to ensure that all suspected alien workers were registered with the SAPS. The objective was to give South African authorities the power to monitor the movements and activities of all foreigners as World War II began. In doing so, the employers were required to submit a concerned employee's full name, presumed nationality, workplace, residential address, nature of work, remuneration, and dates when employment was supposed to begin and end.[9] In the same fashion, the Population Registration Act required that all persons aged eighteen years and older who lived in South Africa permanently or temporarily be registered and issued with identity document. Although Europeans, coloreds, Indians, and local Africans were required to have only numbers and photographs on their identity cards, African migrants were also supposed to have their fingerprints taken. Furthermore, the Population Registration Act stipulated that African migrant workers should be allowed to stay for up to only two years per visit.[10] The fact that the Froneman Committee brought up this issue suggests that South African authorities had not seriously enforced it.

In what became the first major attempt to restrict the influx of African workers from areas south of latitude 22° south, the committee recommended the setting up of immigration control posts manned by armed police officers at Mbabane and Ficksburg along South Africa's borders with Swaziland and Lesotho, respectively. Previously, South African authorities had tried to regulate only the entry of migrant workers from areas north of latitude 22° south through the highly contested ban on "tropical natives," discussed in chapter 2. As such, South Africa maintained only three border posts prior to the 1960s. One was located at Mafeking, along the boundary with Botswana; another was at Beitbridge, along the border with Southern Rhodesia; and the third one at Komatipoort on the South African border with Mozambique. However, the country kept very minimal staff at these border posts. That the committee recommended the establishment of border posts and the deployment of armed police guards along the country's borders with Lesotho and Swaziland was truly a game changer. Taking this enforcement a little further, the Froneman Committee also recommended that migrant workers from the former High Commission territories be required to possess official passports from their home governments by July 1963 to enter South Africa.[11]

As far as migration from Zimbabwe, Mozambique, Malawi, and other (tropical) areas was concerned, the Froneman Committee recommended that work contracts for people from such countries be limited to two years. In the past, the government allowed such workers to stay beyond the expiry of their contracts; now they had to be repatriated. Under the proposed dispensation, all foreign workers were also required to produce identity documents and travel permits from their home governments before they could be allowed to enter South Africa. Interestingly, this proposal was not the first of its kind. Back in the 1930s and 1940s, Southern Rhodesian authorities begged their South African counterparts to require travel permits from all northern migrants, without success. Regardless, the committee also recommended that all foreign workers be recruited in their countries of origin within the frameworks set out in intergovernmental agreements that South Africa would negotiate with specific countries. To reduce the rate of border jumping, the committee recommended summary arrests, detention, and deportation of African migrants who entered the country without following prescribed procedures. In addition, the committee recommended the establishment of detention centers in the border areas to facilitate speedy apprehension and deportation of border jumpers.[12]

In a development that resembled the bumpy implementation of the 1913 ban on "tropical" migrants, the apartheid government did not formally adopt or publish the Froneman Committee report, fearing that doing so would offend mining companies and other employers who benefited from engaging unskilled migrant workers.[13] Instead, the South African authorities quietly implemented several of the committee's recommendations over the course of the 1960s and 1970s. For instance, more than fifty checkpoints were established on South Africa's borders with Botswana, Lesotho, and Swaziland. In this respect and in line with the committee's recommendation, migrants from these territories were reclassified as "foreign Bantu natives" and were required to possess passports issued by their home governments in order to enter South Africa.[14] Migrants from territories to the south of latitude 22° south previously traveled to and from various points in South Africa without major hindrance; now they were required to cross the country's borders only at designated checkpoints to avoid arrest, detention, and possibly deportation.

In line with the shift in perception toward "foreign Bantu natives" from the former High Commission territories, the South African government signed bilateral agreements with the governments of Botswana (in 1973), Lesotho (in 1973), and Swaziland (in 1975).[15] Although the primary objective of these agreements, which contained the same wording, was to facilitate the opening of these three countries' government labor offices in South Africa, they also included various other arrangements meant to restrict the flow of migrants across South Africa's borders. The agreements stipulated, for example, that in addition to passports issued by their home governments, citizens of these countries were required to obtain visas and certificates of small pox vaccinations before they could be allowed to enter South Africa only through designated checkpoints. The agreements also stated that migrant workers from Botswana, Lesotho, and Swaziland were supposed to obtain work contracts (for not more than two years) attested in their countries of origin and completed sets of fingerprints taken under the supervision of government officials in their countries. If found in South Africa without passports and other required documents, citizens of these countries would be arrested, detained, and deported. This was a major departure from previous practice, where recruiting companies such as WNLA, the Native Recruiting Corporation, and others signed interterritorial labor agreements and recruited from these countries without the direct involvement of the South African government.

In the same vein, South Africa also signed labor deals with countries that supplied the bulk of "tropical" workers in the country. For example, the South African government signed a new agreement with the Portuguese colonial administration in Mozambique in 1964. Building on the Mozambique Convention of 1928—the only intergovernmental labor deal that South Africa signed before the 1960s—the 1964 agreement prohibited South African employers from recruiting workers in Mozambique except for affiliated businesses located in that country. More important, the new arrangement stipulated that only Mozambican recruiters were allowed to recruit workers in that country and forward them to employers in South Africa.[16] In the past, South African recruiters affiliated with the WNLA had the permission to recruit in areas of Mozambique that were south of latitude 22° south. By making such changes, the new agreement was intended to make it more complicated and expensive for South African employers to import workers from Mozambique.

In 1967 the South African government signed another labor agreement with the government of independent Malawi (formerly Nyasaland). This agreement built on several labor deals that previous colonial administrations in that country had signed with the WNLA. Among other things, the 1967 South Africa–Malawi agreement prohibited South African companies from actively recruiting in Malawi. Although Malawian migrant workers could still enlist "voluntarily" with the WNLA agents and other labor recruiters from South Africa, they were now required to be in possession of Malawian identity documents and passports to enter the country. In an effort to regularize the status of Malawian migrants who were in South Africa before the agreement was signed, the latter pledged to employ Malawian citizens in the offices of Bantu affairs commissioners in many parts of the country. The main duty of such employees was to assist migrants in completing required forms and other necessary steps to obtain a Malawian passport without having to leave South Africa. However, Malawian citizens who applied for and obtained passports while in South Africa were issued with work permits valid for only six months. At the expiry of their work permits, such migrants were supposed to travel back to Malawi before they could apply for new permits.[17]

The agreement also stipulated that every Malawian migrant worker had to be issued with an employment record book containing the holder's passport number, photograph, employment details, and records of tax payments. As was the case with the Mozambique agreement, this labor deal was intended to make it hard for Malawians to go to South Africa for work purposes. In a move meant to prevent permanent settlement of Malawian migrant workers, article 16 of the South Africa–Malawi agreement stated that "wives and children from Malawi of Malawi citizens employed in South Africa shall not be allowed to enter South Africa, save with the prior approval of the Government of South Africa for humanitarian reasons," adding that "any Malawi citizen wishing to visit the Republic of South Africa (including a Minister of Religion who wishes to take up employment) shall require a visa."[18] To help with the administration of this agreement, the two countries arranged for the government of Malawi to appoint a labor representative who functioned as the country's ambassador in South Africa. Among other tasks, the Malawi government labor representative was responsible for making sure that the migration, employment, and repatriation of Malawians in South Africa took place within the framework laid down in the labor agreement.

By signing labor agreements with other countries in the region, the South African authorities sought to control regional migration in a way they did not prior to the 1960s. In addition to channeling human traffic through designated checkpoints, the apartheid regime also made efforts to control and monitor the activities of private recruiters in the country. Unlike previous South African governments that did very little to restrict the entry of African migrants into the country (even during the time of the ban on so-called tropical migrants), the National Party government was determined to regulate the entry of foreign workers and to monitor those who were already in South Africa. As these measures made it more difficult for African migrants to enter South Africa through the formal channels, the number of foreign-born workers who were in the country legally declined significantly over the course of the 1960s and 1970s. Whereas official estimates put the number of African migrants between 484,000 and 550,000 in 1960, the figures decreased to between 210,000 and 290,000 by 1977.[19] Nevertheless, South African authorities became more concerned about migrants who continued to enter the country through unofficial channels.

Southern Rhodesia–South Africa Border as a War Zone

Along with efforts to restrict the influx of migrants from other territories in the region, South African authorities invested more toward cooperation than competition with their northern neighbor. This was particularly so after Ian Smith's white minority government made the Unilateral Declaration of Independence (UDI) from Britain and changed the country's name from Southern Rhodesia to simply Rhodesia in November 1965.[20] As part of the new strategy, South Africa stood with Rhodesia when Britain, other Western powers, and the United Nations responded to the UDI with trade embargos and other economic sanctions. More important, the South African Defense Forces (SADF) became actively involved in the control of people's movements within and across the Limpopo border zone. The decision to deploy the military along the Limpopo River came in the wake of the militarization of antiapartheid struggles in South Africa. Despite being proscribed in 1960, the ANC and the PAC had teamed up with the SACP in forming a military organization called Umkhonto we Sizwe (MK), which sent hundreds of youths to China, the Soviet Union, Algeria, Ethiopia, and other countries where they received military training.[21] Mindful of the fact that the MK planned to bring back its trained fighters to execute the struggle within the country, the South African government adopted a more vigilant and militaristic approach to border enforcement.

Around the same time that the MK began exporting South African youths to other countries for military training, the liberation storm was also brewing in Rhodesia, where the UDI had become a copycat of the apartheid administration. Following the banning of several African nationalist organizations between 1959 and 1964, the Zimbabwe African People's Union (ZAPU), formed in 1961, and the Zimbabwe African National Union (ZANU), which emerged in 1963, made the decisions to take up arms and fight for the country's independence. In this respect, despite also being proscribed, the two organizations established military units—the Zimbabwe People's Revolutionary Army (ZIPRA) for ZAPU and the Zimbabwe African National Liberation Army (ZANLA) for ZANU—which also sent some young men and women to the Soviet Union, China, Iran, and Algeria for military training.[22] To South African authorities, this development did not simply reflect the obvious point that white domination in the region was under assault; it increased their concerns about uncontrolled movements between the two countries. The concern was that a war-torn Rhodesia had a heightened danger of infiltration by MK fighters, proliferation of arms, and the spread of what the apartheid regime viewed as the communist scourge in the region.

Making the securitization of South Africa's border enforcement and migration control apparatuses more imperative was the decision of the first black president of Zambia, Kenneth Kaunda. After assuming power at the end of colonial rule in 1964, Kaunda quickly emulated other African leaders, such as Ahmed Ben Bella of Algeria, Julius Nyerere of Tanzania, or Haile Selassie of Ethiopia, who actively supported African liberation movements fighting against white minority rule in various parts of the continent. In addition to joining the Frontline States, a coalition of African countries publicly supporting antiapartheid struggles in South Africa, Zambia opened its borders to fighters affiliated with the MK, ZANLA, ZIPRA, and other liberation movements to coordinate their activities outside their countries. Given that such fighters had to reenter their respective countries to wage wars from within, Southern Africa witnessed the rise of a new group of cross-border travelers. For generations, the region had known migrants as traders, workers, or people visiting relatives separated by colonial borders. The movement of people from one part of the region to another for purposes of military training and fighting for regime change was a completely new phenomenon. Security concerns became a major component of state-centered controls of mobility across interstate borders in the region.

The earliest evidence of the danger posed by the new category of migrants in Southern Africa in the 1960s came in the form of MK and ZIPRA fighters who tried to infiltrate South Africa and Rhodesia from training bases in Zambia in 1967. Despite successfully training large numbers of fighters in exile since its formation in 1961, the MK found it difficult to smuggle them back into South Africa. Attempts to penetrate the country via Botswana after it attained independence in 1965 failed because its newly installed African leaders were reluctant to support forces fighting their more powerful neighbor.[23] Although the MK had also considered infiltrating South Africa via Mozambique, that task had also proved to be impossible owing to the distance involved and the cooperation between the apartheid administration and the Portuguese colonial officials in that country. Faced with limited options, the antiapartheid liberation forces struck a deal with ZIPRA forces, which were also trying to infiltrate Rhodesia from their base in Zambia.

In line with the plan that leaders of the two organizations drew, a joint unit of MK/ZIPRA fighters was going to cross the Zambezi River into Rhodesia and then travel southward along the border with Botswana until it reached the Rhodesia–South Africa border. At that point, the group would split, allowing the MK troops to cross the Limpopo River into South Africa while their ZIPRA counterparts moved further into Rhodesia.[24] However, things did not go as planned. Although the combined unit of about ninety MK/ZIPRA fighters successfully crossed the Zambezi River into Rhodesia, it clashed with the Rhodesian army before it reached the border with South Africa. During the fighting that ensued, the South African government dispatched a contingent of approximately one thousand two hundred police and paramilitary forces and approximately twenty military helicopters to assist the Rhodesian army. As John Vorster, who was South Africa's prime minister at the time, pointed out on September 4, 1967, the military involvement in Rhodesia was meant to block "terrorists who originally came from South Africa and were on their way back to commit terrorism in South Africa."[25] Although the SADF withdrew some of its military personnel from the border after helping scatter the MK/ZIPRA offensive, the South African government stepped up surveillance of the Limpopo border zone.

In another development that encouraged further militarization of the Rhodesia–South Africa border, fighters linked to the PAC attempted to enter the northern Transvaal through Mozambique in 1968. This led to what came to be known as the "Sibasa Operation," in which South Africa deployed a contingent of more than five thousand soldiers and airmen that swept through the entire stretch of the border zone from Botswana to Mozambique.[26] As part of the operation, the Pretoria administration also established five special "antiterrorist" camps and deployed about eight hundred white and three hundred nonwhite police officers to maintain regular patrols of the country's northern borders with Rhodesia and Mozambique. Furthermore, South Africa's Defense Minister P. W. Botha dispatched senior army officials to meet with African chiefs and village leaders in the border zone to enlighten them about the war situation and what the government expected of them.[27] Through such counterinsurgent measures, South Africa hoped to prevent not only the infiltration of trained fighters back into the country but also the smuggling of weapons. In addition, South African officials feared that people associated with African nationalist organizations fighting for independence in Rhodesia would influence the local population if allowed to move freely into the country. Such fears were fueled by media reports of migrant workers found in possession of ZAPU and ZANU pamphlets in South Africa.[28]

As the threat of infiltration by the MK and other forces increased, South African authorities persuaded their Rhodesian counterparts to accept an arrangement to jointly control the movement of migrant workers across the Limpopo

River. As part of this arrangement, which was not a formal agreement, the South African Department of Bantu Affairs and Development required migrant workers from Southern Rhodesia to regularize their status by applying for the Rhodesian workers travel document (WTD). Although the WTD was valid for five years and could be renewed for another five years, renewals could be approved only after the holder had traveled back to Southern Rhodesia for at least a month after the expiry of the first five-year period. Zimbabwean migrants who, for one reason or another, did not possess WTDs by March 1968 were permitted to work only in the mining and farming sectors, where their contracts were limited to eighteen months. At the end of their contracts, such workers had to be repatriated.[29] As part of this arrangement, the two countries also pledged not to allow African migrants to cross the border without carrying official identity and travel documents issued by state authorities on either side of the border. Furthermore, the South African government made a commitment to stamp out activities of unlicensed labor recruiters in northern Transvaal and to ensure that employers engaged only migrants with proper documentation. The arrangement also facilitated for the opening of Southern Rhodesia's diplomatic mission in Pretoria in 1970.[30] Although the Rhodesian diplomat dealt with many issues affecting the relationship between the two states, the management of labor flows was the main mission of the post.

Following the outbreak of a full-scale war in Rhodesia, government representatives from South Africa and Rhodesia signed a comprehensive labor agreement that formalized the arrangements they had made in 1968. Among other provisions of the labor deal signed in December 1974, the WNLA was given permission to recruit up to fifty thousand African workers from Rhodesia in any given year. By the end of 1975—the first year of the agreement—the WNLA had recruited more than seventeen thousand African workers who were entrained or flown to the Transvaal and Orange Free State.[31] In an effort to ensure proper monitoring of cross-border movements within the framework of this agreement, the two countries also agreed that only the WNLA and its agents would transport migrant workers from different parts of Rhodesia to South Africa. In this respect, the Ministry of Transport and Power in Rhodesia issued a permit to Africair Limited of Johannesburg for the purpose of operating "non-scheduled air service, on a strict charter basis for the carriage of contract labour and company freight to, from and within Rhodesia."[32] The WNLA was supposed to engage and transport only those Zimbabweans who passed stipulated medical examinations and obtained official travel permits. Furthermore, the two governments put in place a compulsory remittance system whereby a certain percentage of Zimbabwean workers' wages had to be deposited into their bank accounts in Salisbury. The deferred pay system was meant to ensure that workers returned to Rhodesia at the end of their contracts and that they met their tax obligations back home.

Another important aspect of this agreement was that any Zimbabwean who went to South Africa illegally after April 1, 1976, was liable to prosecution and repatriation. Moreover, South African employers who engaged undocumented Zimbabweans were to be fined.[33]

During a debate in the Rhodesian Parliament, Minister of Labor and Social Welfare Rowan Cronje gave a statement in which he praised his government for signing what he argued was a very good deal. In particular, Cronje pointed out that the agreement benefitted "Rhodesian Africans" who wished to take advantage of the "excellent" work opportunities on the South African mines. He also noted that enlisting with the WNLA was a purely voluntary venture on which Zimbabweans were free to decide and argued that doing so came with free training and very high standard accommodation, food, and medical facilities. In saying so, the minister stressed that potential recruits had employment conditions fully explained to them at the time of entering into work contracts with the WNLA so they could make up their minds before traveling to South Africa.[34] However, when asked to explain the government's motive for signing the labor agreement and encouraging Zimbabweans to enlist with the WNLA, Cronje dodged the question. He said that "migrant workers have been the future of Southern Africa and of Western Europe and the rest of the world throughout the existence of mankind. It is a practice, which is followed everywhere. . . . If there is an African who voluntarily wants to go and work in South Africa and they are prepared to accept him, why should we prohibit him from doing so? This is a free country."[35] What is interesting about his response is that he did not fully address the main issue at stake. Given that Southern Rhodesia had previously tried everything to prohibit labor migration to South Africa, why did it change its policy and formally accept its status as a supplier of labor for South Africa?

The answer to this question lies in the changing economic and political situation in Rhodesia itself but also in South Africa and surrounding countries. In addition to the economic recession that hit the continent of Africa and other parts of the world in the wake of the oil crisis of the early 1970s, the sanctions that the British government and the United Nations imposed on Rhodesia following its adoption of the UDI had taken a toll on the country's economy. Unemployment was on the rise, especially among black high school graduates where it hovered around 15 percent. In this respect, the labor agreement, or the *joina* system, as it was known among Zimbabweans, provided much-needed employment opportunities.[36] Given that anticolonial struggles had turned into full-scale war, which was spreading throughout the entire country like veld fire, Rhodesian authorities also saw a safety valve in this agreement. Convinced that the shortage of jobs contributed to Africans' support for the war of liberation, the Rhodesian government signed the labor agreement hoping that many disgruntled African youths would prefer to work in South Africa than risk their lives by joining the war.

From South Africa's perspective, a labor agreement with Rhodesia provided opportunities for more systematic controls of cross-Limpopo mobility. The agreement was even more relevant because of developments taking place in other African countries that had, for generations, supplied South Africa with workers. For example, Julius Nyerere's administration, which recalled about fourteen thousand Tanzanians from South Africa soon after assuming control of the state in 1961, had withdrawn the bulk of its migrant workers by the mid-1970s. Similarly, the Kaunda administration recalled about six thousand Zambians in 1965 before closing all WNLA recruiting offices in the country by 1968.[37] Furthermore, Malawi, which by 1973 had emerged as the largest single supplier of legal "alien" workers to South African mines (with almost 120,000 of its people constituting about 31% of total mine labor force), changed its position completely after a WNLA aircraft crashed in April 1974, killing 75 Malawian migrants on board. Soon after the accident, Malawian leaders suspended all WNLA operations in the country.[38]

While these developments unfolded, the security situation in the Rhodesia–South Africa border zone further deteriorated following the end of Portuguese colonial rule in Mozambique in 1975. As was the case with the Kaunda administration in Zambia, Samora Machel's government gave logistical support to African liberation movements in South Africa and Zimbabwe and welcomed them to establish training camps in Mozambique. With Mozambique's independence and Machel's pledge of support, the forces fighting for African liberation in South Africa and Rhodesia had more convenient space to coordinate their operations. Whereas the Zambezi River made the movement from Zambia to Rhodesia very difficult, large portions of the Rhodesia–Mozambique border could be crossed without much difficulty. Capitalizing on this opportunity, ZANLA moved its headquarters from Lusaka (Zambia) to Maputo (Mozambique) and smuggled thousands of young men and women from various parts of the country to the training camps that the organization established in Mozambique. The MK, which had struggled to infiltrate South Africa for several years, also opened training camps in Mozambique. Although Mozambique's support provided opportunities for African liberation forces to better coordinate their activities, it resulted in the hardening of Rhodesia's borders with both Mozambique and South Africa.

As ZANLA forces began infiltrating the country from the eastern and southern districts early in 1976, the Rhodesian government established military camps in border districts such as Chipinge, Chiredzi, and Beitbridge. In further efforts to stop the infiltration, which intensified as the country plunged into full-scale war by mid-1977, the Rhodesian security forces planted land mines along the country's border with Mozambique. The land mines were planted in between two parallel game fences built along sections of the border about twenty-five meters apart. The main purpose of this war strategy, which Rhodesian forces referred to as *cordon sanitaire*, or *corsan* for short, was to detect, delay, and neutralize insurgency forces as they tried to enter Rhodesia from Mozambique.[39] This strategy changed the nature of the Rhodesia–Mozambique border from a largely invisible and porous boundary to a life-threatening instrument for controlling mobility.

In addition to planting land mines, the Rhodesian government forcibly resettled thousands of communities in the country's border districts in an effort to prevent interaction between insurgency forces and the ordinary people who provided them with food, clothes, intelligence, recruits, and moral support. In line with this strategy, the Rhodesian security forces, with the support of the Ministry of Internal Affairs, established what came to be known as "protected villages," which, for all intents and purposes, were internment camps.[40] Although in some areas the Rhodesian security forces shut down schools and converted them into "protected villages," most camps were built by constructing barbed wire fences around open fields into which surrounding villagers were relocated. For security purposes, every camp had military personnel who maintained twenty-four-hour guard over it and government employees who functioned as camp administrators. Although camp residents were allowed to build huts for their own use, they were required to store all food items in a common granary, which was protected and controlled by the administrators. Each day the administrators would give out food rations to camp residents (taken from each family's food bank) in line with the registered number of people per family unit.[41] By controlling the amount of food that camp residents took from their food banks on a daily basis, the Rhodesian security forces intended to make it hard for people to feed insurgent forces.

As Jakkie Cilliers notes, for resettlement to be effective as a military strategy, living conditions inside the camps should be improved so that inmates will see the benefits of being inside rather than outside the fences.[42] This was not the case in Rhodesia, where "protected villages" functioned more like prisons than anything else. Moreover, people lost large amounts of property because of the manner in which authorities moved them into camps. More often than not, Rhodesian authorities moved people without prior notice, insisting that they carry all their belongings from old homes in a single day. Sometimes the military personnel who supervised the relocation burned down people's huts and everything left behind as soon as the occupants removed whatever they could take with them. In some cases, the security forces actually burned people's huts as a way of forcing them to move into camps. As Alfred Ncube pointed out, an entire community in the Chabili village of Beitbridge had its houses burned in 1977 because the residents responded slowly to the order to move into a camp that authorities set up in the area.[43]

By 1978, the Rhodesian security forces had established more than fifteen "protected villages" in Beitbridge. Although the security forces allowed people to move out of the camps and tend to their fields and livestock, such movements were supposed to take place between 6 a.m. and 6 p.m. In other words, people were not allowed to move outside the camps between sunset and sunrise. Another condition was that every time inmates moved in or out of the camp, they had to report to guards at the gates who examined whatever inmates carried with them. In what appears to have been a desperate attempt to minimize the movements of people outside the camps, the Rhodesian security forces destroyed most of the boreholes that the government had drilled in this semi-arid district in the 1950s.[44] Although camp residents managed to smuggle food out of the fences and continue feeding and interacting with freedom fighters, it became difficult to move around the border zone. Given that the Rhodesian forces and those fighting for Zimbabwe's liberation needed communities' support to win the war, there was always a deep sense of mistrust and insecurity in their interactions with ordinary people. As Mathodzi Moyo put it, the first thing that the Rhodesian government soldiers thought when they came across an individual walking alone outside the camps was that he or she was an agent for the insurgent forces, yet the "comrades" would also suspect the same person to be a sellout intending to report their whereabouts to the "soldiers."[45]

As the war intensified in Beitbridge and the rest of Rhodesia, the SADF officially took over control of the country's northern borders from the SAPS. Building on arrangements made in the 1960s, the SADF stationed a company of what were called "citizen force territorial troops" at bases created on the outskirts of Messina. This was done to enhance the army's capacity to better patrol the Limpopo boundary and to respond quickly to any incidents. Along with this company, which operated on a three-month rotational basis, the South African army opened a permanent military headquarters for the entire Soutpansberg (formerly Zoutpansberg) area in Messina in 1976. Furthermore, the SADF appointed Lieutenant Andre van Rooyen, who was the second in command at the Messina military headquarters, to be its liaison officer to the Rhodesian security forces.[46] In so doing, and in line with the South Africa–Rhodesia agreement of 1974, the two countries also strengthened efforts to jointly monitor and control cross-border movements through the sharing of information.

At the Beitbridge border post, South African immigration officials also became stricter in their enforcement of the requirements for identity documents and travel permits. As revealed by an interview with Saratiel Muleya—a resident of Beitbridge district whose family lived in South Africa while he attended school in Rhodesia—there was a sudden change of protocol at the Beitbridge border post in 1976: "Certain documents were suddenly required for a Zimbabwean to cross the border. I only found that out when I was going back to South Africa from my boarding school in Rhodesia. My father, who worked for the South African Immigration Department, had to intervene for me to be allowed to cross the border."[47] Under the new dispensation, border officials also required residents of Beitbridge town who regularly crossed the border on work-related or shopping trips to Messina and other areas south of the Limpopo to obtain gate passes that stipulated where they were going and when they were expected to be back in Rhodesia. To get the passes, travelers were required to be in possession of Rhodesian identity documents. Unlike the past when travelers literally ignored the bridge, preferring to use their "traditional" bush paths to cross the border, the presence of armed security guards in the border zone compelled many people to go through the border post. Commenting on this issue, Tshabeni Ndou said that "crossing anywhere and everywhere got reduced during the war of liberation."[48]

As the 1970s came to an end, it became clear that the Rhodesian security forces could not contain ZANLA and ZIPRA forces that had gained ground and control over much of the country's rural areas, where the largest population of blacks lived. An attempt to end the war through what came to be known as the "Internal Settlement" of 1978 failed after the leaders of ZANU and ZAPU refused to accept the deal and urged their troops to continue fighting. Amid increasing calls for Ian Smith's regime to relinquish power and pave the way for independence in Rhodesia, the South African government took further steps to create physical barriers along the country's northern border. In this respect, the SADF commissioned a project to grow sisal plants on sections of the country's borders with Mozambique and Rhodesia.[49] Whereas military camps and border patrols could be moved at any given moment, the planting of sisals signified the South African state's intention to have a long-term presence in the border zone. Before the launch of that project, the game fence along Kruger National Park, together with those that borderline farmers put in place to prevent the movement of animals in and out of their farms, acted as de facto border fences. Although the South African authorities knew that sisal plants could be tampered with, they endorsed the idea in hope that it would force migrants to cross the border via the controlled checkpoints at Beitbridge.

Insurgent Forces and Refugees Join Migrant Workers as Border Jumpers

With the shift in South Africa's policy toward African migrants and the militarization of the Zimbabwe–South Africa border, the region witnessed significant changes in the nature of border jumping between the two countries. In the first place, the 1960s witnessed a major reduction in the flows of migrants across South Africa's northern border. As the South African government deployed the police and the army to control movements from areas north of the Limpopo River, it also enforced the agreements it signed with the governments of Malawi,

Mozambique, and Zambia as well as the 1968 informal arrangements with Southern Rhodesia. It became more difficult than previously for people to cross the border without identity and travel documents issued in their countries of origin. In the past, migrants needed only to dodge Southern Rhodesia's system of migration control, and they did, mostly with the help of South African employers and labor recruiters; however, from the 1960s onward, border jumpers also had to evade the systems that South African authorities put in place. More important, South Africa's arrest, detain, and deport policy—a major departure from previous practice, when the Pretoria administration turned a blind eye to illegal migrants in the country—served as an additional deterrent to border jumpers.

To circumvent the new enforcement regimes, which hinged on the National Party's labor recruitment policies, border jumpers did what previous generations of "clandestine" migrants did: they modified old strategies while devising new ones that helped them achieve their objectives under the new circumstances. For example, when the apartheid administration began enforcing the 1968 arrangement with Southern Rhodesia, some Zimbabwean migrants who were already in the country took South African identity documents. As Samson Moyo pointed out, obtaining the South African identity card was not difficult for many people who originated from Beitbridge and other areas in the border zone. Such people utilized their long-standing relations with and knowledge about people across the border to claim belonging in South Africa. Moyo, a Venda resident of Beitbridge, lied about his name, his father's name, and the name of his chief in order to obtain a South African identity card. He told South African officials that he was called Samson, the son of James Munyayi. Although Munyayi is a common last name among the Venda people in northern South Africa, Moyo said he chose that name because he knew a man called James Munyayi but was not in any way related to him. For his chief, Moyo chose Gumbu, who was a recognized traditional leader in northern South Africa, instead of Matibe, who was his chief on the other side of the border. Along with changing his surname, Moyo said he had to master the dialect of the Venda language spoken on the South African side of the Limpopo River.[50] In a repetition of previous scenarios when South African employers helped migrants to evade Southern Rhodesia's efforts to prevent cross-Limpopo mobility, other people changed their names with the help of their employers in South Africa. Although the desire to make a profit by keeping low-paid migrant workers might have motivated employers to behave in this way, some did so to avoid the taxes and other penalties that the apartheid government introduced in an effort to prevent the employment of undocumented migrants from Southern Rhodesia and other countries.

For residents of Chipinge, Chimanimani, and Chiredzi in the southeastern part of Zimbabwe, the Mozambican route remained a viable option during much of the pre-1975 period. As in previous years, it was common for people to get into Mozambique, where they changed their names and obtained identity documents purporting to be originally from that country, before proceeding to South Africa. For example, Paul Govhana from Chief Musikavanhu's area in Chipinge crossed into Mozambique in 1969 and presented himself as Paulo Govhana from Chief Garahwa in Mozambique.[51] What is interesting is that he simply added an "o" to his first name to make it sound Portuguese enough for him to get the Mozambican passport. In addition, he did not have to struggle to prove that he originated in that country because Chiefs Garahwa's and Musikavanhu's areas were part of the precolonial Gaza kingdom, so they were essentially one territory that fell victim to the political surgery that came with European conquest of the region. In addition to speaking the same dialect of the Ndau language, the inhabitants of these areas regularly crossed the border in either direction for beer parties, funerals, and other gatherings. Consequently, it was not too difficult for Govhana and many others in the same situation to assume Mozambican identity to evade South Africa's migration control mechanism. With Mozambican identity documents and passports, such people signed up for work contracts at various WNLA recruiting depots in Mozambique and proceeded to South Africa as Mozambican workers.

When the Rhodesian security forces planted land mines and started patrolling the Zimbabwe–Mozambique border in the late 1970s—at the peak of the liberation war in Rhodesia—it became very difficult for Zimbabweans to use the Mozambique route to go to South Africa. The same was true with clandestine movements across the Rhodesia–South Africa border, which became very difficult to undertake during the war. As Josiah Musheekwa of Chipinge explained, Zimbabwe's war of liberation and the attainment of independence in Mozambique entailed prison-like conditions in Zimbabwe's eastern border districts. Forced resettlements and curfews made it risky for people to move across the border. Often the Rhodesian security personnel forced the people who breached curfew conditions to strip naked so they could check if such people had any body markings that indicated that they had undergone military training or regularly carried weapons. Emphasizing that a lot of people died after making very simple mistakes during the war, Musheekwa narrated a story about a boy who got close to the security forces camp in Chief Mapungwana's area when he was tending his father's goats. The young man panicked and tried to run away but was shot dead on suspicion that he was a runner (locally referred to as *mujibha*) for the liberation fighters.[52] Under such conditions, it became quite risky for Zimbabweans to travel to South Africa through unofficial channels. The *joina* system, which the Rhodesian government encouraged and promoted, was the safest route for work seekers to leave the country during the war of liberation.

However, two new categories of border jumpers emerged during the 1970s. The first was made up of the young men and women who skipped the country to join the liberation forces. As already discussed, ZANLA and ZIPRA recruited some and smuggled them out of the country to Algeria, Angola, China, Russia, Cuba, and other places. However, as my interlocutors in Chipinge and Beitbridge revealed, many people who joined the training camps in Mozambique and Zambia left Rhodesia without much assistance from the liberation forces. In general, such people relied on border residents who knew the secret paths across the border. As Wilson Marange pointed out, the inhabitants of Chief Mapungwana's area and other parts of Chipinge helped thousands of young men and women who crossed the Mozambican border through a bushy and mountainous place called Chibawawa. The border people considered it more worthwhile to take the risk of helping the young fighters jump the border to receive military training than to help those who were going to South Africa via Mozambique during the war.[53] Although most fighters returned to the country armed and under the guidance of their commanders, they did so just as secretly as they left. In other words, they left as border jumpers and returned as border jumpers. This group was slightly different from some of the people who left clandestinely in search of employment or other purposes but then returned via the official channels because no one seemed to worry about returning migrant workers being in possession of official documents prior to Zimbabwe's independence.

The second category of border jumpers that emerged in the 1970s comprised refugees. These people fled their homes in Rhodesia at the height of the war of liberation. Although the majority went to Botswana, Mozambique, and Zambia, where they were officially welcome, some forced migrants "illegally" crossed the country's border with South Africa in search of safety. As an interview with Mutonga Ngwaxani revealed, some people enlisted with the *joina* system to escape Zimbabwe's war-ravaged areas. Once they got to South Africa, such people took the earliest opportunity to ditch their WNLA-assigned employers for other means of survival in South Africa.[54] Although desertion was an age-old strategy that migrant workers deployed to assert their freedom of choice under difficult circumstances, this was different. The primary objective of such deserters was to seek refuge from the war, not to find better paying jobs. Rather than returning to Rhodesia at the end of the WNLA contracts issued to them, many stayed until independence in 1980, and others never went back to Zimbabwe.

In addition to those who took advantage of the *joina* system, some border jumpers played hide-and-seek with the Rhodesian security forces as they escaped the country in search of refuge. In light of the challenges associated with traveling within and out of the border areas during the war, this approach was a huge risk that people took after considering many options. A story narrated by Mbazima Chauke of Chikwarakwara village shows some of the strategies used by refugees of Zimbabwe's liberation war to jump the country's border. After witnessing and experiencing several hardships in a protected village that the Rhodesian security forces established in the Chikwarakwara area in 1977, Chauke's father and three other men took their families out of the fence and moved into a nearby mountainous area. To avoid any suspicion, the four families left the camp at different times of day, carrying a few clothes, some blankets, a number of pots, and a few pockets of mealie-meal, which they managed to smuggle out of the camp. As Chauke recalled, they spent about three days in the bush before receiving word that the Rhodesian security forces had burned down their houses and granaries and the authorities had vowed to hunt down the four men and their families. The group then set off on a risky escape to South Africa.

Although they needed to travel for only about five kilometers to get to the Zimbabwean border with South Africa, the group took almost two days to cross the Limpopo River. The families started their journey at night and arrived at the Limpopo River in the morning, just before sunrise. In a bid to avoid detection by both the Rhodesian and South African security forces, the group camped at the banks of the Limpopo for the whole day and resumed the journey only after sunset. This approach was a major shift from the "traditional" practices of travelers in the region. A decade or two before the outbreak of Zimbabwe's liberation war, migrants would avoid traveling at night fearing wild animals. By the late 1970s, armed human beings had become the greatest cause for concern in the border zone. Although the group crossed the boundary river before midnight and were on the highway before sunrise, the families had to camp for another day as they looked for any form of transport that could take them to where their relatives lived. On the third night after they began their journey, Chauke and his group were relieved to board a bus, which took them to a place called Mlamleli. Because the apartheid regime was not a signatory to the United Nations 1951 Refugee Convention or the 1967 Protocol, which outlines states' obligations toward refugees, the Chaukes did not receive official status as refugees in South Africa. Instead, they self-settled among their relatives, who allowed them access to the land where they lived before they returned to Zimbabwe in 1981.[55]

Zimbabwe's Independence and South Africa's Border Fence

Following the end of white minority rule in Zimbabwe and the election of ZANU's leader—Robert Mugabe—as prime minister in 1980, the apartheid administration remained as the only white-minority government in Southern Africa. However, rather than yielding to increasing pressure (locally and internationally) to allow the majority people to enjoy their freedoms and citizenship rights in the country, the South African government—led by Pieter Willem Botha—dug in. The early 1980s witnessed a surge in state-sponsored violence and brutality in South Africa. On the northern side of the border, Mugabe and his government made a commitment to work alongside other African leaders who openly supported antiapartheid struggles in South Africa. In February 1981, the Zimbabwean government announced the termination of the 1974 labor agreement, which had helped South African authorities and their Rhodesian counterparts join hands in controlling migration across the Limpopo River. The Zimbabwean authorities also banned the WNLA's successor, the Employment Bureau of Africa (TEBA) from recruiting in the country, prompting the South African government to expel almost twenty thousand Zimbabwean migrant workers.[56] Although high rates of unemployment among the black population in South Africa made the closure of TEBA offices in Zimbabwe almost meaningless, the cutting of diplomatic ties between two countries that had supported each other in defending white supremacy changed the dynamics of migration control and border enforcement politics in the region.

As the rift between the governments of South Africa and Zimbabwe grew wider over the course of the 1980s, the Mugabe administration continued to support the MK fighters, who increased their activities in northern South Africa, where they planted land mines and staged hit-and-run operations against white farmers in the border zone.[57] Around the same time, the region witnessed an escalation of fighting in Mozambique, where a civil war had begun along the border with South Africa soon after the end of Portuguese colonial rule in 1975. Although the Pretoria administration supported RENAMO (Resistência Nacional Moçambicana) rebels, who were fighting against Machel's Liberation Front of Mozambique government, the influx of Mozambican refugees into northern South Africa raised the country's fears of further infiltration by MK and other forces opposed to the apartheid system. Feeling increasingly isolated and exposed, the South African government bankrolled the construction of an electrified fence along its borders with Zimbabwe and Mozambique. As with the growing of sisal plants, which was executed as a military undertaking, the construction of the border fence took place under the direct supervision of the SADF. Realizing that some portions of the sisal fence had succumbed to elephants and other wild animals, which destroyed the plants, the SADF erected a fence made up of two tiers of mesh wires flanking "a pyramid of coiled razor-wires that shields a series of electrified wires."[58] In devising such a design, the SADF intended to make it difficult for people to jump the fence from either side. Although a person could easily climb over the outer tiers without electric wires, one would need to tamper with the coiled razor wires to pass through the entire fence.

At the experimental stage, the fence ran for approximately 16 kilometers (10 miles) eastward from the point where the South Africa–Zimbabwe border intersected with the South Africa–Botswana border and was charged with about 4,000 volts of electricity. Although that made the barrier highly costly and deadly, the SADF increased the voltage to 20,000 volts as the border-fencing project expanded.[59] When it was completed in 1986, the fence stretched for more than

200 kilometers (125 miles) from Zimbabwe's border with Botswana to Kruger National Park and then covered another 60 kilometers (37 miles) from Kruger National Park along the South Africa–Mozambique border to a place known as Jeppe's Reef near Swaziland's border with South Africa. Consequently, the fence covered almost the entire stretch of the South Africa–Zimbabwe border and parts of the South Africa–Mozambique boundary. To enhance the effectiveness of the fence as a security measure, the SADF constructed brick-and-mortar guardrooms every ten kilometers along the fence. The guardrooms, also known as *echo stations*, were equipped with computer technology to monitor and report details of precise locations of any contacts or attempts to tamper with the border fence. More important, the buildings were big enough to accommodate about ten border guards at any given time.[60]

Along with the fence, the South African authorities put other measures in place to strengthen the barrier between their country and those to the north of the Limpopo River. For example, the apartheid regime launched a project to encourage white farmers to occupy vacant lands along the boundary from the Botswana border to Kruger National Park. As part of the arrangement, South African authorities marked out a five-mile strip of territory along the border and declared it a "designated area" where old and new white farmers would get financial support to stay or settle. To persuade more white people to settle in the designated area, which had become quite dangerous given MK insurgency activities, South African authorities offered military protection to borderline farmers. In this respect, the SADF posted soldiers to help with guarding of farms on South Africa's border with Zimbabwe and launched a program to teach farmers' wives how to handle semiautomatic weapons. The South African government also provided farmers with land mine–proof vehicles, which they used to transport their children to school.[61] Through this arrangement, farmers at South Africa's northern border became integrated into local commando systems.

In another indication that the border had become a highly securitized zone, the apartheid administration offered financial subsidies and military training and weapons to white people who were willing to take up farms along the banks of the Limpopo River. To ensure the strategy worked, the government warned that farmers who accepted financial aid under this program but failed to comply with the requirements to stay in the designated area would be fined up to R5,000 (approximately £2,100) or five years' imprisonment.[62] For its part, the SADF required all farm owners in the border area to check their properties every morning for signs of any trespassing by people suspected to be MK fighters and to make reports to the military camps quickly if they noticed anything. In this way, the South African government did not just integrate borderline farmers into the country's defense system but also used them as the first line of defense against the MK forces, who deployed several strategies including the planting of land mines in the border area in a bid to infiltrate the country. Farmer Piet Esterhuyse, who had a government-issued bulletproof and land mine–resistant pickup truck, an Uzi machine gun, and an R1 automatic rifle, said, "My farm is really big and I've got a lot of roads. . . . You look for any disturbance in the surface of the road which might indicate the laying of a land mine and you look for any tracks that you can find from someone's feet. . . . We find tracks quite often. . . . We follow them up and get the army in right quickly and they track them down."[63]

Furthermore, as part of a broader strategy to tighten border security, the South African government recruited and deployed high school students (mainly white) on occasional patrols of the border zone during school holidays.[64] The deployment of students on military internships along the Zimbabwe–South Africa border significantly helped further the SADF's objective of creating a hard border. Unfortunately for ordinary people, that came with the loss of many lives. As John Maramani pointed out, the inexperienced border guards shot willy-nilly at border jumpers. Unlike the professional soldiers, who sought to apprehend unlawful travelers and take them into police custody, the high school students simply shot at anyone they saw attempting to cross the border through undesignated points.[65] By implementing such programs, the South African authorities did not just seek to make it difficult for migrants to cross the border through undesignated points but also sent the message that they treated every border jumper as an enemy of the state. As was the case in the 1950s and 1960s, labeling such people as *terrorists* or *enemies of the state* was enough justification for the use of military approaches to border control.

By the mid-1980s, the status of the South Africa–Zimbabwe border had changed significantly from what it was before the 1960s. However, the flow of migration across the Limpopo River remained tilted toward South Africa despite apartheid rule in that country for fourteen more years after the end of colonial rule in Zimbabwe. While some people left the country through unofficial channels, continuing with a tradition that began almost a hundred years before, cross-border mobility changed in meaning and significance in the region. Border jumpers' previous strategies focused mainly on carrying sufficient water and food supplies to consume on the way, dodging wild animals that roamed the Limpopo Valley, knowing how and where to cross the Limpopo River, and evading the barriers that Southern Rhodesian authorities put in place to prevent migration to South Africa. Now they also had to worry about armed soldiers patrolling the border zone. More important, border jumpers had to deal with a border fence containing live electric wires that could kill instantly if tampered with.

The first evidence of border jumpers' determination to conquer the odds came March 30, 1985: members of the SADF on patrol at the country's northern border found the dead body of a man they suspected to be Zimbabwean. Near the corpse was a pair of wire clippers, an indication that the man was electrocuted after attempting to cut the electric fence that South Africa had erected along its border with Zimbabwe.[66] This incident was a precursor to many violent deaths linked to South Africa's border fence. By 1989, just four years after its construction, the fence had allegedly killed more people than those who died while trying to cross the Berlin Wall in twenty-three years of its existence.[67] Whereas the apartheid administration argued that eighty-nine people died as a result of tampering with the border fence, the South African Council of Churches and other organizations that campaigned for the removal of the electric fence put the number of victims—mostly Mozambicans trying to escape the civil war in their country—at between 200 and 900. Some people dubbed the fence "South Africa's fence of death," others called it a "snake of fire" or "the devil's fence."[68] Although the fence's voltage was reduced to a nonlethal level in 1993—just a year before the end of apartheid rule in South Africa—the region witnessed several more years of intensified contestations over South Africa's border fence in particular and control of cross-Limpopo mobility more generally.

Notes

1. Bill Freund, "Forced Resettlement and the Political economy of South Africa," *Review of African Political Economy* 29, (1984): 49–63; Cosmos Desmond, *The Discarded People: An Account of African Resettlement in South Africa* (Harmondsworth: Penguin, 1970); Laurin Platzky and Cherryl Walker, *The Surplus People: Forced Removals in South Africa* (Johannesburg: Ravan, 1985).

2. By referring to women and children as an "unwanted" or economically inactive group, South African authorities missed the point that some women did in fact work on the farms and as domestic servants in white people's homes. For a detailed discussion of this point, see Teresa Barnes, "Virgin Territory? Travel and Migration by African Women in Twentieth Century Southern Africa," in *Women in Africa Colonial Histories*, ed. Jean Allman, et-al., (Indianapolis: Indiana University Press, 2002), 164–190; Belinda Dodson, "Women on the Move: Gender and Cross-Border Migration to South Africa from Lesotho, Mozambique and Zimbabwe," in *On Borders: Perspectives on International Migration in Southern Africa*, ed. David A. McDonald (Ontario: SAMP, 2000).

3. Ken Owen and Gabriël Francois van Lingen Froneman, *Foreign Africans: Summary of the Report of the Froneman Committee, 1963* (Johannesburg: South Africa Institute of Race Relations, 1964). See also, Witwatersrand Native Labour Association (WNLA), File 45B/4, Pad 1, Extract of Findings and Recommendations of the Inter-department Committee in Connection with Bantu Natives in the Republic of South Africa.

4. NASA, BTS, file 14/33, Froneman Commission First Draft Report (1961). On this issue, the Froneman Committee estimated that in 1961 alone, migrants from the High Commission Territories exported about R5 million while those from other areas who worked in the mining sector sent more than R11 million back to their home countries.

5. WNLA, File 45B/4, Pad 1, Extract of Findings and Recommendations.

6. WNLA, File 45B/4, Pad 1, Extract of Findings and Recommendations.

7. WNLA, File 45B/4, Pad 1, Extract of Findings and Recommendations.

8. WNLA, File 45B/4, Pad 1, Extract of Findings and Recommendations.

9. WNLA, File 45A/3, Pad 1, Circular by A. J. Limebeer, Secretary of the Transvaal Chamber of Mines' Gold Producers Committee, September 21, 1939.

10. WNLA, File 45A/3, Pad 1, Union Gazette Extraordinary, July 7, 1950.

11. WNLA, File 45B/4, Pad 1, Extract of Findings and Recommendations.

12. WNLA, File 45B/4, Pad 1, Extract of Findings and Recommendations.

13. Crush, "Migrations Past"; Bolt, *Zimbabwe's Migrants*.

14. NASA BTS, File 14/33 Froneman Commission First Draft Report (1961); WNLA, 45B/4 Pad 1, Extract of Findings and Recommendations. See also, Duncan G. Clarke, "State Policy on Foreign African Labour in South Africa: Statutory, Administrative and Contractual Forms" (Development Studies Research Group Working Paper 4, University of Natal, September 1977).

15. See, Agreement between the Government of the Republic of South Africa and the Government of the Republic of Botswana Relating to the Establishment of an Office for a Botswana Government Labour Representative in the Republic of South Africa, Botswana Citizens in the Republic of South Africa and the Movement of such Persons across the International Border (December 24, 1973, https://treaties.dirco.gov.za/dbtw-wpd/exec /dbtwpub.dll?AC=GET_RECORD&XC=/dbtw-wpd/exec/dbtwpub.dll&BU=https%3A%2F %2Ftreaties.dirco.gov.za%2Fdbtw-wpd%2Ftextbase%2Ftreatywebsearch.htm&GI=&TN= TreatyWeb&SN=AUTO9568&SE=1844&RN=4&MR=20&TR=0&TX=1000&ES=0&XP= &RF=Printingformat2018&EF=Basic+Record+Form&DF=Web+full+record&RL=1&EL=1 &DL=1&NP=1&ID=&MF=&DT=&ST=0&IR=488&NR=0&NB=0&SV=0&SS=0&BG=&FG= &QS=TReaties+New+Master; Agreement between the Government of the Republic of South Africa and the Government of the Kingdom of Lesotho Relating to the Establishment of an Office for a Lesotho government Labour Representative in the Republic of South Africa, Lesotho Citizens in the Republic of South Africa and the Movement of such Persons across the International border (August 24, 1973), https://treaties.dirco.gov.za/dbtw-wpd/exec /dbtwpub.dll?AC=GET_RECORD&XC=/dbtw-wpd/exec/dbtwpub.dll&BU=https%3A%2F %2Ftreaties.dirco.gov.za%2Fdbtw-wpd%2Ftextbase%2Ftreatywebsearch.htm&GI=&TN= TreatyWeb&SN=AUTO8657&SE=1843&RN=2&MR=20&TR=0&TX=1000&ES=0&XP=&RF =Printingformat2018&EF=Basic+Record+Form&DF=Web+full+record&RL=1&EL=1&DL=1 &NP=1&ID=&MF=&DT=&ST=0&IR=483&NR=0&NB=0&SV=0&SS=0&BG=&FG=&QS= TReaties+New+Master; Agreement between the Government of the Republic of South Africa and the Government of the Kingdom of Swaziland Relating to the Establishment of an Office for a Swaziland Government Labour Representative in the Republic of South Africa, certain Swaziland Citizens in the Republic of South Africa, the Movement of such Persons across the Common Border and the Movement of certain South African Citizens across the Common Border, and Addendum thereto (August 22, 1975), https://treaties.dirco.gov.za/dbtw-wpd/exec /dbtwpub.dll?AC=GET_RECORD&XC=/dbtw-wpd/exec/dbtwpub.dll&BU=https%3A%2F %2Ftreaties.dirco.gov.za%2Fdbtw-wpd%2Ftextbase%2Ftreatywebsearch.htm&GI=&TN= TreatyWeb&SN=AUTO10133&SE=1845&RN=5&MR=20&TR=0&TX=1000&ES=0&XP=&RF =Printingformat2018&EF=Basic+Record+Form&DF=Web+full+record&RL=1&EL=1&DL=1 &NP=1&ID=&MF=&DT=&ST=0&IR=498&NR=0&NB=0&SV=0&SS=0&BG=&FG=&QS= TReaties+New+Master.

16. Duncan G. Clarke, "State Policy on Foreign African Labour in South Africa: Statutory, Administrative and Contractual Forms" (Development Studies Research Group Working Paper 4, University of Natal, September 1977).

17. See, Agreement between the Governments of the Republic of South Africa and Malawi Relating to the Employment and Documentation of Malawi Nationals in South Africa (August 1, 1967), https://treaties.dirco.gov.za/dbtw-wpd/exec/dbtwpub.dll?AC =GET_RECORD&XC=/dbtw-wpd/exec/dbtwpub.dll&BU=https%3A%2F%2Ftreaties .dirco.gov.za%2Fdbtw-wpd%2Ftextbase%2Ftreatywebsearch.htm&GI=&TN=TreatyWeb &SN=AUTO10381&SE=1846&RN=2&MR=20&TR=0&TX=1000&ES=0&XP=&RF= Printingformat2018&EF=Basic+Record+Form&DF=Web+full+record&RL=1&EL=1&DL=1 &NP=1&ID=&MF=&DT=&ST=0&IR=429&NR=0&NB=0&SV=0&SS=0&BG=&FG=&QS= TReaties+New+Master.

18. Agreement between the Governments of the Republic of South Africa and Malawi Relating to the Employment and Documentation of Malawi Nationals in South Africa (August 1, 1967), https://treaties.dirco.gov.za/dbtw-wpd/exec/dbtwpub.dll?AC =GET_RECORD&XC=/dbtw-wpd/exec/dbtwpub.dll&BU=https%3A%2F%2Ftreaties .dirco.gov.za%2Fdbtw-wpd%2Ftextbase%2Ftreatywebsearch.htm&GI=&TN=TreatyWeb &SN=AUTO10381&SE=1846&RN=2&MR=20&TR=0&TX=1000&ES=0&XP=&RF= Printingformat2018&EF=Basic+Record+Form&DF=Web+full+record&RL=1&EL=1&DL=1 &NP=1&ID=&MF=&DT=&ST=0&IR=429&NR=0&NB=0&SV=0&SS=0&BG=&FG=&QS= TReaties+New+Master.

19. Clarke, "Foreign African Labour Supply." See also, WNLA, File 45B/4, Pad 1, Recruitment in High Commission Territories. Extracts from Froneman Committee Report.

20. Luise White, *Unpopular Sovereignty: Rhodesian Independence and African Decolonization* (Chicago: University of Chicago Press, 2015).

21. Stephen Ellis and Tsepho Sechaba, *Comrades against Apartheid: The ANC and the South African Communist Party in Exile* (Bloomington: Indiana University Press, 1992); Ian Taylor, "The Ambiguous Commitment: The People's Republic of China and the Anti-Apartheid Struggle in South Africa," *Journal of Contemporary African Studies* 18, no. 1 (2000): 91–106.

22. Joseph Mtisi, Munyaradzi Nyakudya and Teresa Barnes, "Social and Economic Developments during the UDI Period," in *Becoming Zimbabwe: A History from the Pre-colonial Period to 2008*, ed. Brian Raftopoulos, and Alois S. Mlambo (Harare: Weaver, 2009); Zvakanyorwa W. Sadomba, *War Veterans in Zimbabwe's Revolution: Challenging Neo-Colonialism and Settler and International Capital* (Harare: Weaver, 2011); Maurice Nyagumbo, *With the People: An Autobiography from the Zimbabwe Struggle* (London: Allison & Busby, 1980).

23. Rendani M. Ralinala, Jabulani Sithole, Gregory Houston, and Bernard Magubane, "The Wankie and Sipolilo Campaigns," in *The Road to Democracy in South Africa*. Vol. 1, *1960–1970*, ed. South African Democracy Education Trust (Cape Town: Zebra, 2007); Nicole Van Driel, "The ANC's First Armed Military Operation: The Luthuli Detachment and the Wankie Campaign, July–September 1967" (Masters thesis, University of the Western Cape, 2003).

24. Ralinala et al., "Wankie and Spolilo Campaigns."

25. Bernard Magubane, "Introduction to the 1970s: The Social and Political Context," in *The Road to Democracy in South Africa*. Vol. 2, *1970–1980*, ed. South African

Democracy Education Trust (Cape Town: Zebra, 2007), 9. See also, South African History Online, "Balthazar Johannes Vorster," http://www.sahistory.org.za/people /balthazar-johannes-vorster.

26. Magubane, "Introduction to the 1970s."

27. Magubane, "Introduction to the 1970s."

28. John K. McNamara, "Black Workers Conflicts on South African Gold Mines, 1973–1982" (PhD diss., University of the Witwatersrand, 1985).

29. Clarke, "State Policy."

30. Clarke, "State Policy."

31. McNamara, "Black Workers' Conflicts."

32. *Rhodesian Herald*, "Charter Plane is Flying Mine Labour to South Africa," January 10, 1975.

33. Clarke, "State Policy"; Paton, *Labour Export Policy*.

34. Rhodesia Government, House of Assembly Debates, April 11, 1975.

35. Rhodesia Government, House of Assembly Debates, April 11, 1975.

36. Paton, *Labour Export Policy*. The word *joina* is a vernacular version of *join*. It was used in this context to stress the importance of the contract that one had to enter into before departing for South Africa.

37. Crush et al., *South Africa's Labor Empire*.

38. Allen, *History of Black Mineworkers*.

39. Jakkie Cilliers, *Counter-Insurgency in Rhodesia* (London: Croom Helm, 1985).

40. The term was really a misnomer given that the compounds exposed Africans to diseases and other kinds of problems. Because of the prison-like conditions in some of the camps, Africans called them "makipi," which literally means *keeps*. In some works and (sometimes) in general discussions, these were also referred to as "internment" or "concentration" camps. See, e.g., Martin R. Rupiah, "The History of the Establishment of Internment Camps and Refugee Settlements in Southern Rhodesia, 1938–1952," *Zambezia*, 22, no. 2 (1995): 137–52; Munya Munochiveyi, *Prisoners of Rhodesia: Inmates and Detainees in the Struggle for Zimbabwean Liberation, 1960–1980* (New York: Palgrave Macmillan, 2014).

41. Josiah Musheekwa, interview with author, Musheekwa Village, Chipinge, June 9, 2013. See also, Irene Staunton, "Sosana Marange," in *Mothers of the Revolution: The War Experiences of Thirty Zimbabwean Women*, ed. Irene Staunton (London: James Currey, 1990).

42. Cilliers, *Counter-Insurgency in Rhodesia*.

43. Alfred Ncube, interview with author, Chabili Village, Beitbridge, June 1, 2010.

44. I gathered stories of the Rhodesian Front's use of coercive measures to compel people to move into so-called protected villages from a focus group discussion I had with 12 residents of Makombe Village, Beitbridge May 25, 2010.

45. Mathodzi Moyo, interview with author, Limpopo Village, Beitbridge, June 15, 2010. In Zimbabwe's liberation war discourse, the terms *comrades* and *soldiers* are ordinarily used to refer to African nationalist-backed troops and Rhodesian security forces, respectively.

46. Ed Bird, *Special Branch War: Slaughter in the Rhodesian Bush Southern Matabeleland, 1976–1980* (West Midlands: Helion, 2014).

47. Saratiel Muleya, interview with author, Beitbridge Town, May 20, 2010.

48. Tshabeni Ndou, interview.

49. Kloppers, "Border Crossings."

50. Samson Moyo, interview with author, Chitulipasi Village, Beitbridge, July 12, 2013.

51. Paul Govhana, interview with author, Mukwakwami Village, Chipinge, June 6, 2013.

52. Josaih Musheekwa, interview, June 9, 2013.

53. Wilson Marange, interview with author, Musheekwa Village, Chipinge, June 9, 2013.

54. Mutongi Ngwaxani, interview with author, Musheekwa Village, Chipinge, June 9, 2013.

55. Mbazima Chauke, interview with author, Chikwarakwara Business Center, Beitbridge, June 29, 2010. For a detailed discussion of apartheid South Africa's handling of refugees see, Tara Polzer, "Adapting to Changing Legal Frameworks: Mozambican Refugees in South Africa," *International Journal of Refugee Law* 19, no. 1 (2007): 22–50.

56. See Ray Kennedy, "Zimbabwe Blacks Ordered to Leave South Africa," *Times*, August 5, 1981; Stephen Taylor, "Mugabe Attitude Blamed for Blacks' Expulsion," *Times*, August 7, 1981; Caryle Murphy, "S. Africa sets Ban on Jobs for Zimbabweans," *Washington Post*, August 7, 1981.

57. Patrick Laurence, "SA to Build Electric Fence on Zimbabwe Frontier / South Africa Reacts to Cross-Border Attacks by ANC Rebels," *Guardian* (London), January 13, 1986.

58. Sean O'Toole and Paul Botes, "Porous Border Is Smugglers' Paradise," *Mail and Guardian Online*, April 4, 2011, http://mg.co.za/article/2011-04-04-porous-border-is-smugglers-paradise.

59. See "Electric Fence," *Africa Research Bulletin, Political Series*, 22, no. 1 (1985): 7600.

60. *IRIN News*, "South Africa: Troops Reinforcing a Porous and Dangerous Border," May 26, 2010, http://www.irinnews.org/Report.aspx?ReportID=89262.

61. Laurence, "SA to Build Electric Fence."

62. See, "Designated Area," *Africa Research Bulletin, Political Series*, 22, no. 1 (1985).

63. *Toronto Star*, "Farmers Stand on Guard for South Africa," June 12, 1988; Bolt, *Zimbabwe's Migrants*.

64. Hugh McCullum, "South Africa's Fence of Death," *Horizon* (Harare), August 19, 1992.

65. John Maramani, interview with author, Limpopo Village, Beitbridge, June 15, 2010.

66. See *Globe and Mail* (Canada), "Electrocution Ends Border Crossing," April 2, 1985; *New York Times*, "South Africa Border Death," April 2, 1985.

67. Tania Monteiro, "Hundreds Killed by South Africa's Border Fence," *New Scientist*, January 27, 1990; "Electric Fence," *Africa Research Bulletin*; Griffiths, "Permeable Boundaries."

68. McCullum, "South Africa's Fence of Death." See also, *Globe and Mail* (Canada), "Wall of Razor Wire a Cruel Barrier to Freedom: Fenced in Frightened Mozambican Refugees Risk Capture, Injury or Death as they Attempt to Cross into South African Homeland," January 14, 1992.

5 Crossing the Boundary Fence

The Zimbabwe Crisis and the Surge in Border Jumping

IF ZIMBABWEANS RISKED their lives by tampering with South Africa's border fence in the 1980s, when their country enjoyed moderate economic growth, how did they engage with the border during the 1990s and early 2000s when Zimbabwe faced an economic decline and the rise of political violence? And how did postapartheid South Africa's immigration policies affect the movement of people between these two countries? Focusing on these questions, this chapter shows how the dynamics of border jumping changed in the period that some scholars view as the beginning of "illegal migration" in Southern Africa. A three-part argument helps to unpack this complex phenomenon. First, although Zimbabwe celebrated the end of white-minority rule fourteen years before apartheid rule came to an end in South Africa, migration between the two countries remained heavily tilted toward South Africa. From an economic point of view, this trend can be explained by the fact that South Africa's economy continued on a positive growth path throughout this period while Zimbabwe's slid into a double-dip recession in the first decade of the twenty-first century.[1] On the political front, the 1990s and early 2000s witnessed a relatively peaceful transition from apartheid to democracy in South Africa while Mugabe's autocratic leadership turned Zimbabwe into a dictatorship.

The second part of the argument this chapter makes is that despite the end of apartheid rule in 1994, South Africa continued to restrict migration and other forms of mobility from Zimbabwe until about 2009. This forced thousands of people running away from the deteriorating economic and political environment in Zimbabwe to enter the country illegally, causing an upsurge of border jumping in this period. Third, the strategies that border jumpers used to cross South Africa's border fence in the 1990s and early 2000s reveal a lot about the forces that pushed people out of Zimbabwe and those that made it difficult for travelers to enter South Africa through official channels during this particular period. The following discussion emphasizes several continuities from the past.

Zimbabwe's Troubled Economy and the Challenges of Migration to South Africa

Although the devastating effects of colonial rule continued to haunt Zimbabwe several years into independence, the policy choices that the Zimbabwe African National Union–Patriotic Front (ZANU-PF) government made in the 1990s significantly contributed to the challenges that the country faced in the first decade of the twenty-first century. One of those policy decisions was the launch of the International Monetary Fund and World Bank–sponsored Economic Structural Adjustment Program (ESAP) in 1990. Several other African countries that accepted loans from the two institutions in the 1980s and 1990s also implemented neoliberal reforms with varying degrees of success. In line with this program, the Mugabe administration undertook to reduce government expenditure by "removing subsidies on basic foodstuffs, reducing budgetary allocations, even to essential services such as education and health care, and downsizing the public service."[2] However, in sharp contrast to ESAP's projected outcomes (e.g., economic growth and reduction in poverty levels), Zimbabwe, like many other African countries, reaped largely negative results. Within two years of the program, Zimbabwe's unemployment rate rose from approximately 10 percent to more than 20 percent while the value of real earnings fell from approximately US$1,600 in 1990 to a paltry US$100 in 1991.[3] Over the course of five years of ESAP, the country witnessed more job cuts as hundreds of companies closed or scaled down production.

Coupled with job losses, the near-collapse of the manufacturing sector led to shortages of basic commodities such as soaps, toothpaste, cooking oil, salt, and sugar, which drove prices and inflation up. The country also witnessed rapid growth of the informal-sector economy, as the majority of people who lost jobs turned their backyards and street pavements into home factories and market stalls for all kinds of goods that were in short supply in the formal market. As the situation deteriorated over the course of the 1990s, the informal economy became the de facto mainstream economy in Zimbabwe. Because most raw materials used in the sprawling home industries and goods sold on the black market came from South Africa, ESAP changed the dynamics of mobility between the two countries in several ways. For starters, cross-border traders and subsistence shoppers became the most visible category of regular travelers across the Zimbabwe–South Africa border. Overloaded pickup trucks, cross-border buses, and trailer-pulling vehicles of different types and sizes became a common sight in the border zone.[4]

In previous years, Zimbabwean women generally remained behind when their male counterparts traveled to South Africa; however, ESAP led to the "feminization" of migration flows across the Zimbabwe–South Africa border. In efforts to fend for their families struggling with the effects of a shrinking economy, Zimbabwean women turned to cross-border trading. They played an important role as suppliers of basic food stuffs and even household equipment such as refrigerators, television sets, and kitchenware, much of which was no longer available in the Zimbabwean formal market. To raise the money they needed to buy items for resale in Zimbabwe, women "exported" different types of handicraft, especially crotcheted goods, that were in demand in South Africa. Some made a living by selling South African money and other currencies to potential travelers who could not obtain foreign currency through the formal channels in Zimbabwe. As the local currency increasingly lost its value over the years, the informal trade in foreign currency grew to an extent that some ordinary people and scholars called it the "World Bank of Zimbabwe."[5]

The 1990s also witnessed a surge in the number of skilled workers and professionals who left Zimbabwe for South Africa. As Elaine Fultz and Bodhi Pieris point out, by 1997 approximately sixty thousand Zimbabwean professionals (including teachers, university professors, doctors, nurses, engineers, accountants, and lawyers) were working in South Africa.[6] This was a major departure from previous years when a typical Zimbabwean migrant in South Africa was an unskilled man seeking the most basic form of employment on the mines and farms. Although it might have been relatively easy for Zimbabwean professionals and some shoppers to move in and out of South Africa through official channels in the 1990s, many others encountered various challenges. The South African Parliament introduced the Aliens Control Act in 1991, which imposed visa requirements for foreigners who were not covered by any of the interstate treaties or other special exemptions. It also considered foreigners who were in the country without the required documents as criminals. Although their only "crime" was breaching immigration restrictions as stipulated in this legislation, "undocumented" migrants and non–South Africans in general came to be viewed negatively. It was in this context that the South African media began to popularize the notion that the country was "swamped" or "flooded" by foreigners, especially Africans from Zimbabwe, Mozambique, and other countries with struggling economies.[7] Contrary to the widely circulated images of an increasingly progressive country, South Africa maintained a hard stance toward migrants from the region.

Several organizations that had campaigned for the removal of the electrified border fence celebrated when the SADF scaled down the voltage in 1993, but the postapartheid government did not capitalize on this opportunity to develop a migrant-friendly approach to cross-Limpopo mobility. In addition, the ANC government did very little to address the issues raised by immigration policy experts and migrants rights groups who argued that several clauses of the 1991 Aliens Control Act were either unconstitutional or racist. Instead, the Mandela administration bowed to pressure from groups that called for tighter controls of immigration and "took a draconian approach to border and heartland policing that has involved abuse of the rights of migrants and immigrants."[8] As such, the government kept the army, which was rebranded as the South African National Defense Forces (SANDF), in charge of the country's northern borders and reduced the number of ports of entry from fifty-two land border posts in 1994 to nineteen by 1997. Along with these changes, the government expanded the SANDF's border patrol unit from five thousand soldiers in 1994 to about eight thousand two hundred by 1995. To complement the SANDF's efforts, the SAPS launched a Border Police Division that specialized in prevention and detection of cross-border crime and enforcement of the country's immigration policies.[9]

Furthermore, the government launched a computerized surveillance system called the Movement Control System, which tracked the entry and exit patterns of foreigners, in a bid to enhance the effectiveness of the migrant-monitoring apparatus. As part of this initiative, the South African government also computerized the consular services at its embassies in major migrant-sending countries such as Zimbabwe and Mozambique.[10] Nothing was wrong with the computerization of migration control mechanism, but the project inhibited more than facilitated the legal entry of migrants from the region and forced many to resort to unofficial channels of entry. In further pursuit of the nation's protectionist approach, the South African Parliament passed the 1995 Aliens Control Amendment Act, which imposed more stringent requirements for people wanting to enter the country. Through this legislation, the South African government raised visa charges and deposit fees as well as skill requirements for potential visitors and migrants from most African countries and other parts of the world.

In the same year, South Africa, Botswana, and Namibia—three countries with the strongest economies in the region—led the region in rejecting a draft proposal that the Southern African Development Community (SADC) secretariat had compiled in a bid to promote free movement of people across interstate borders in Southern Africa. As shown in the 1995 Draft Protocol on the Free Movement of Persons in the Southern African Development Community, the SADC secretariat hoped to create a framework for the removal of all controls on SADC citizens who wished to enter any of the member countries and establish residence.[11] For all intents and purposes, the 1995 SADC protocol was modeled after the European Union's Schengen Agreement of 1985, which led to the abolition of border controls between member states and the adoption of a common immigration policy toward non–European Union citizens. Although the Mandela administration supported the idea of having an instrument to manage the mobility of people in the region, it was concerned that an open border policy would see South Africa flooded with migrants from Zimbabwe and other countries whose economies were not doing well. Although this concern was understandable given that the immediate postapartheid period witnessed a rise in unemployment and poverty among the nation's black population, the rejection of the 1995 proposal meant the continuation of contestations over the control of cross-border mobility in the region. As was the case with the regional alliances that Southern Rhodesian authorities proposed during the 1930s through 1950s, the proposed SADC protocol failed because the control of cross-border movements did not have the same appeal to all member states.

As the volume of migration from north of the Limpopo kept increasing, the South African High Commissioner in Harare announced a new set of requirements for Zimbabwean travelers to the country in October 1996. Depending on the purpose of one's trip, temporary visitors were now required to produce letters of invitation from business associates, friends, or relatives who were legal residents (not necessarily permanent residents) in South Africa before they could obtain visas. The invitation letter had to include the identity and contact details of the South Africa–based business or person inviting a Zimbabwean, such as a national identity number and physical address. In attempts to reduce cases of people who overstayed their visas, the new requirements stipulated that the invitation letters should clearly indicate the lengths of the planned visits. Those intending to visit the country without invitations from anyone had to show proof of confirmed and paid hotel accommodation at the time of applying for the visa. Zimbabwean travelers were also required to show that they could sustain themselves while in South Africa by providing bank statements or traveler's checks with amounts of money determined by the consular officials. In addition to these requirements, the South African immigration department also required visa applicants to produce letters from their employers confirming that they would return to their jobs in Zimbabwe after their intended trips. Those without formal employment were required to present copies of marriage certificates or affidavits from their spouses showing that they had "established roots" in Zimbabwe.[12]

While the visa requirements that the South African government imposed on Zimbabweans and other Africans reflected those implemented by countries such as the United States, the Pretoria administration was asking too much from people facing a multitude of challenges in their own country. Many Zimbabwean travelers could obtain invitation letters from relatives and friends living and working in South Africa, but they struggled to produce acceptable bank statements. Given that many were struggling to feed their families, they also found other requirements such as visa application fees and the cost of producing visa photographs and copies of various forms and documents to be exorbitant. What worsened the situation, especially for the people of Beitbridge and other districts close to the border, was that prospective travelers could apply for South African visas from only two places in Zimbabwe: Harare, the nation's capital, or Bulawayo—with a return trip to Beitbridge of approximately 1,200 kilometers (746 miles) or 700 kilometers

(435 miles), respectively.[13] This situation discouraged many borderland residents who wanted to obtain visas before they went to South Africa from doing so. For those who crossed the border on a regular basis for shopping, work, and simply to maintain long-standing connections with kith and kin on the other side of the Limpopo River, the new requirements were highly inconvenient.

A temporary solution came in 1997 after commercial farmers in the former Transvaal colony (now Limpopo Province), whose main source of labor comprised unskilled Zimbabwean migrant workers, successfully lobbied the Pretoria administration to create a special permit zone covering the South African border area within fifty kilometers of the Limpopo River. Within that zone, which incorporated the town of Musina and most vegetable and citrus farms in northern South Africa, Zimbabweans were exempt from visa and passport requirements if the purpose of their trip was to shop, visit relatives, or take up employment with farmers registered under the Transvaal Agricultural Union. They had only to present their Zimbabwean identification documents to obtain the permit, which, although it lasted for only twenty-one days, could be renewed multiple times. To facilitate this arrangement, South African authorities opened two small gates along the border fence. One, which could allow only pedestrian traffic to pass through, was at a place called Dite, about twenty-five kilometers east of the Beitbridge border post. The other was set up at a place called Weipe, about 40 kilometers west of the border post, and became known as Gate 17. South African border officials opened these gates on selected days and times of the week, and Zimbabweans would obtain what came to be referred to as a "B1-17 permit" to enter the special permit zone. Holders of B1-17 permits who went beyond the designated area risked arrest, detention, and deportation.[14]

This arrangement had the support of the Zimbabwean government, which designated the border district of Beitbridge as the primary beneficiary of the B1-17 permits. The Zimbabwean authorities insisted that such permits should be awarded only to the Venda-, Shangan-, and Sotho-speaking inhabitants of Beitbridge and any other person whose birth certificate indicated birth in Beitbridge District. Consequently, the B1-17 permits came to be known as "zero-two" permits, a nomenclature derived from the first two digits on Beitbridge residents' national identity numbers.[15] As MaSibanda, an elderly woman from the Panda Mine area (near Dite) observed, the zero-two arrangement came as a major relief to people of her village. It provided them and other inhabitants of Zimbabwe's border district a safe avenue not only to work or do regular shopping in South Africa but also to maintain ties with relatives across the border. By encouraging such people to cross the border through officially designated points, the special permits protected them from abuse by corrupt state functionaries and self-styled crossing "agents" in the border zone.[16] However, as Blair Rutherford observed, the South African media and various civic groups questioned the legality of B1-17 permits because the country's immigration laws did not make provisions for the creation of such arrangements.[17] Apart from the debate that this arrangement generated before it was abolished in 2004, Zimbabweans who struggled to meet the requirements for obtaining South African visas deployed several strategies to benefit from this facility and evade official channels of travel between the two countries.

At the regional level, the SADC secretariat modeled its revised proposal for managing people's movements into, within, and through the region after South Africa's 1997 Green Paper on International Migration, which kept in place most of the visa conditions and other restrictions contained in the country's 1995 Aliens Control Amendment Act.[18] Reflecting the shift from the idea of promoting "free" movement and travelers' rights of entry and residence in member countries, SADC's new framework—compiled in 1998—was entitled "Draft Protocol on the Facilitation of Movement of Persons in the Southern African Development Community." Among its key elements was the proposal for the progressive elimination of obstacles to the movement of SADC citizens in the region (within twenty years of the implementation of the protocol), the adoption of machine-readable passports by all member countries, and the improvement of infrastructure to manage cross-border movements of people.[19] Not surprisingly, the South African administration led other SADC heads of state and governments in adopting the 1998 protocol in 2005. However, only six (South Africa, Botswana, Mozambique, Lesotho, Swaziland, and Zambia) out of the fourteen member states ratified it.[20] Because of the clause that stipulated nine member states had to ratify the protocol before it becomes operational, its implementation was delayed. Therefore, the Pretoria administration continued to treat migrants from different countries differently depending on the relations that South Africa had with each of the countries in the region.

Crossing the Boundary Fence: Strategies of Border Jumping in the 1990s

Given that border jumpers used various strategies to evade official systems of migration control, it has not been possible to quantify the full extent of border jumping across the Zimbabwe–South Africa border during this period or at any given time. Available records suggest that 28 percent of the 47,031 people arrested by South African border officials for trying to enter the country illegally between 1994 and 1995 were Zimbabweans. In addition, the number of Zimbabwean illegal migrants deported from South Africa rose from 12,931 in 1994 to 45,922 in 2000.[21] Given that the Zimbabwean government—which struggled to provide jobs and other livelihood opportunities for its people—did very little to stop emigration in this period, border jumpers only had to worry about the South African border fence and agents patrolling the southern side of the boundary. As such, after crossing the Limpopo River, some people dug holes under the fence and crawled into South Africa, whereas others wore gloves or threw blankets over the fence to avoid direct contact with electrified wires as they climbed over it. These strategies were risky and probably contributed to some of the deaths recorded before the voltage of the border fence was reduced to nonlethal levels in 1993. To avoid arrests, travelers usually dug the holes at night when members of the SANDF and SAPS patrol units were either sleeping or away from duty. Quite often, as Muromoni Mbedzi—who grew up in the Dite area—pointed out, travelers used dry grass and leaves to cover the holes, making it difficult for border patrol teams to discover alternative crossing points.[22]

In a development that closely resembled the prevalence of unlicensed labor recruiters at Crooks' Corner in the early twentieth century, the 1990s witnessed the rise of maguma-guma who smuggled travelers across the South Africa–Zimbabwe border. Although some people working on the border farms and in the towns of Beitbridge and Musina would engage in similar activities during weekends or after work, maguma-guma were predominantly unemployed Zimbabwean men who saw an opportunity to earn a living by smuggling travelers across the border. In other words, maguma-guma responded to a thriving market of Zimbabweans trapped between a harsh economic and political environment on one hand and a border fence regularly patrolled by armed security guards on the other. Their main strategy involved cutting off portions of the South African border fence and charging anything from a few hundred to more than R1,000 for "undocumented" travelers to pass through.[23] In some parts of the border, maguma-guma removed the fence completely, creating alternative gates that they manned.

Although they roamed the entire stretch of the Zimbabwe–South Africa border, maguma-guma often targeted "traditional" crossing places such as Chikwarakwara, Dite, and Panda Mine on the eastern side of the border post and Makhakhabule, Tuli, Nottingham Estate, and Shashe on the western side of Beitbridge Town. To use the services offered by maguma-guma, travelers did not need to make prior arrangements. They usually just met at one or the other crossing point, negotiated the terms of the contracts, and paid the agreed fees while still on the Zimbabwean side of the border. This approach inevitably presented several challenges to desperate travelers because the maguma-guma often demanded more money, changed the terms of their unwritten contracts, or simply disappeared after receiving the payments. As discussed later in this chapter, it was quite common for these self-proclaimed border agents to abuse travelers, who were technically their clients.

Depending on the season of the year, the maguma-guma also charged fees for helping people to cross the Limpopo River. Given that they did not have boats or canoes, they often instructed their clients to join hands and slowly drag their feet until they crossed the river. Keeping the feet down and joining hands when crossing the river was a strategy to avoid being swept away. However, many people drowned as they tried to cross the Limpopo this way.[24] When the water level was too high, the maguma-guma often organized temporary accommodation for their clients among the border communities while they waited for it to subside. Sometimes they made such arrangements when they knew that South Africa's border patrol teams were in the areas they intended to use to smuggle travelers. To minimize the chances of arrest, the maguma-guma carefully studied the routine of South African border patrol units and avoided using a single entry point for more than two days in a row.

Along with the maguma-guma, the 1990s also witnessed the rise of unlicensed cross-border transport operators referred to locally as *malayitsha*.[25] These people helped Zimbabwean shoppers to bypass the official limits on imports and evade customs and taxation fees at the border post. Using various strategies, including hiding goods in their vehicles and giving bribes to customs and immigration officials on both sides of the border post, the malayitsha smuggled different kinds of goods that were in short supply in Zimbabwe. On their trips back to South Africa, the malayitsha often transported "undocumented" travelers whom they either smuggled through the border post or simply dropped at undesignated crossing points along the border. First-time travelers often engaged the malayitsha who visited several communal areas as they delivered goods from South Africa, whereas others met with them in the border zone. Despite being unlicensed transport operators, the malayitsha freely off-loaded smuggled goods and loaded border jumpers at a public bus terminus in Dulibadzimu Township and other open spaces in Beitbridge Town. In those unregulated spaces, where laws of the jungle ruled, negotiations for various kinds of deals and "contracts" between desperate travelers and unlicensed transporters took place. Some deals led to successful trips through the border post or alternative crossing points, and others took travelers into untold suffering.

As was the case with people who built bush stores in the border zone in the early twentieth century, some entrepreneurial individuals cashed in on Zimbabwean travelers' desperation in the 1990s and early 2000s. The story of Chabane, a Beitbridge businessman, is a case in point. After spending about three years running a cross-border bus route, Chabane settled in Beitbridge Town in 1995. As the Zimbabwean economy plunged into a recession, he regularly sent touts to places around the border town looking for people trying to cross the border without passports or visas. Chabane would then use his pickup truck to transport such travelers to specific unofficial crossing points where he paid bribes to border guards who let the people enter South Africa. Over time, Chabane bought a house in Beitbridge and another one in Musina, both of which he used to accommodate travelers who sought his assistance. After smuggling travelers across the border, Chabane's employees took those without prearranged accommodation to his house in Musina where they stayed (paying rent) until they found somewhere else to stay. Because he worked with several people in the South African border patrol units, Chabane prevented the arrest of most of his clients, making him a service provider of choice for many travelers.[26]

The special permit facility, which we discussed earlier, also provided an opportunity for Zimbabweans to enter South Africa through the back door. In itself, the B1-17 permit was technically a side door, given the controversies surrounding its legal status. Nevertheless, some people from outside the zero-two area gave bribes to staff at the registry office in Beitbridge and received identity documents purporting that they were born in the district. Others did not bother to obtain the Beitbridge identity documents, preferring to give bribes to the South African officials at the two small gates (Weipe and Dite) to obtain the B1-17 special permits. In this way, Zimbabweans who were ineligible to apply for the special permits benefited from the facility. As one elderly resident of Beitbridge Town put it, "MaHarare used cash to buy zero-two IDs in order to enter South Africa without passports and visas."[27] Then there were those who obtained the B1-17 permits and completely disregarded the restrictions attached to them. For instance, some people got the permits and proceeded to Johannesburg or other areas outside the designated 50-kilometer strip along the border, whereas others never bothered to renew expired permits, preferring to file for protection as refugees or explore other means of changing their status from within South Africa.[28]

In this respect, the late 1990s witnessed the invention of new strategies of border jumping and the modification of old ones. There was also the revival of most "traditional" crossing points (away from the border post), which border jumpers had found difficult to use at the height of Zimbabwe's 1970s liberation war and after the construction of South Africa's electric border fence. As Zimbabwe's economic and political situation further deteriorated, reaching a crisis point in the early 2000s, such crossing points and strategies became very popular with border jumpers from various parts of the country.

The Zimbabwe Crisis and the Surge in Border Jumping

Between 1990 and 1999, Zimbabwe's gross domestic product dropped from around US$8.3 billion to US$6.8 billion. By 2009, it had sunk further to about US$5.6 billion.[29] Together with this negative economic development trend, the 1990s witnessed a rise in political repression, which created an atmosphere of crisis in Zimbabwe. This became particularly so after a series of strikes by civil servants, as well as street protests and demonstrations by numerous civil society organizations and university students, that culminated in the formation of the

Movement for Democratic Change (MDC) in September 1999. Although other opposition parties had challenged ZANU-PF in local government and national elections after it came to power in 1980, the MDC posed the greatest threat to the ruling party's dominance. It enjoyed the support of a cross-section of Zimbabwean society, including the country's small white population, which had largely stayed out of politics since independence. Although other reasons might have caused white Zimbabweans to join the MDC—which also enjoyed the support of the United States, Britain, and other Western governments—it is very likely that most did so hoping to protect their farmlands, which veterans of the 1970s war of liberation had started occupying, with impunity, in 1998.

After the MDC successfully campaigned against a government-sponsored constitutional referendum of February 2000, the ZANU-PF government resorted to the use of coercion, repression, and outright violence to win elections. In this context, the June 2000 general election, in which MDC won 57 of 120 contested seats in the House of Parliament, and the March 2002 presidential election, which the MDC claims its president (Morgan Tsvangirai) won, exposed opposition leaders and their supporters to state-sponsored violence. Closely tied to violence associated with these elections, the country witnessed widespread occupations of white-owned commercial farms as part of the government-sponsored fast-track land redistribution program, which was dubbed the "third Chimurenga."[30] As the chaos in the commercial farms spread to white-owned companies and other sectors of the economy, the United States, Britain, Australia, New Zealand, and other countries imposed different kinds of "targeted" sanctions on Zimbabwe. Together with the collapse of the agricultural sector, which had remained as the only major source of employment after the closure of several manufacturing companies during the ESAP years, sanctions had devastating effects on the country's economy.

After the March 2005 election, which ZANU-PF won without the absence of violence and allegations of vote rigging, the government sanctioned an urban cleanup program, code-named "Operation Restore Order" or "Operation Murambatsvina, which resulted in the destruction of thousands of informal housing units and informal businesses in the country's major towns and cities. The Zimbabwean government justified the cleanup as an operation meant "to deal with crime, squalor and landlessness, and rebuild and reorganize urban settlement and small and medium enterprises (SMEs) in a way that would bring dignity, order and prosperity to the stakeholders and the nation at large." However, the manner in which the program was executed made some analysts to conclude that Operation Murambatsvina was a politically motivated project targeting MDC supporters.[31] For example, the executive director of the United Nations Human Settlements Program, who also served as a United Nations special envoy with responsibility for assessing the damage caused by Murambatsvina, castigated this exercise as "a smokescreen for motives that had little to do with addressing the problem of informal structures and restoring order within urban areas."[32]

The situation in Zimbabwe further deteriorated following the March 2008 elections, which Mugabe lost to Tsvangirai before he reclaimed victory after an even more violent runoff in June of the same year. By that September, when President Thabo Mbeki of South Africa brokered a deal that gave birth to the Government of National Unity (GNU), in which Tsvangirai and Author Mutambara (who led a smaller party made up of former MDC members) occupied the positions of prime minister and deputy prime minister, respectively, while Mugabe retained the presidency. At that time, the inflation rate had risen to more than 7,000 percent, unemployment was above 80 percent, and supplies of medicines, basic commodities, and fuel through official channels had almost dried up. This gave rise to what Jeremy Jones has characterized as the *kiya-kiya* economy, which essentially means that everybody did whatever he or she could do to survive.[33] Although the governor of the central bank tried every trick in the book—including printing bills as large as Z$20 trillion—Zimbabwe's currency completely lost its value, and the majority of people depended on food handouts from a few Western-backed humanitarian organizations that were allowed to operate in the country.

As the number of Zimbabweans leaving the country increased in response to the deteriorating environment during the first decade of the twenty-first century, South Africa gradually softened its handling of migration from its northern neighbor. For example, in 2002 the South African government announced a program, which exempted Zimbabwean civil servants on temporary visits from paying visa fees if they provided proof of employment (particularly pay stubs) along with their visa applications. Although visa fees and deposit charges remained in place for most Zimbabweans, the South African government also dropped off the requirements for letters of invitation and proof of employment for people traveling on short-term holiday visits. Furthermore, through the 2004 Immigration Amendment Act, the South African government made provisions for "corporate permits," which cleared the way for the "legal" employment of unskilled foreigners in the country. Although the South African government scrapped the B1-17 permit arrangement in the same year, several farmers in Limpopo Province took advantage of the corporate permits facility to issue farm-based identification cards to thousands of "undocumented" Zimbabwean workers they employed. As such, despite the fact that South African authorities deported 72,112 Zimbabwean "illegal" migrants in 2004, "undocumented" migrants from Zimbabwe accounted for between 70 and 95 percent of workers on farms in South Africa's Limpopo Province in 2005, altogether between 18,000 and 20,000 people.[34]

Given that many potential travelers struggled to meet most of the requirements for obtaining the South African visa—including the fee of R2,060 (approximately

US$200)—people who were not civil servants bought fake government pay slips, which some "enterprising" Zimbabweans sold or fraudulently printed. A good example is the case of Natalie Peacock, who liaised with Samson Murozvi—a former employee of the Zimbabwe Revenue Authority—who agreed to assist her husband Tristan Peacock in traveling to South Africa as a government employee in January 2005. Tristan's passport had expired, so Murozvi provided him with a fake emergency travel document (ETD), a pay slip, and a letter purporting that he worked for the Ministry of Education as a teacher at Victoria High School in Masvingo. When Tristan presented the documents at the passport control desk at the Beitbridge border post, the immigration officer on duty noticed that although the ETD had the holder's photograph and signature, it did not have some of the standard security features. Following the arrest of the trio, Murozvi pleaded guilty and paid a fine. Although they denied any wrongdoing, Natalie and Tristan were both found guilty and each sentenced to twelve months' imprisonment, with six months suspended on condition of good behavior. Following an appeal against the ruling, it took more than two years for a high court judge to set aside the jail term and impose a fine instead.[35] This and other cases such as *State v. Majiga Atabiya* (Beitbridge Magistrates Court, January 21, 2006) and *State v. Charles Nhope* (Beitbridge Magistrates Court, July 11, 2006) give credence to widespread rumors about the existence of syndicates that printed and sold fake pay slips in Beitbridge Town before the South African government scrapped this facility in 2009.

In related cases, Zimbabwean police detectives operating in many sections of the border post arrested several travelers who attempted to use other people's passports to leave the country. One of the case summaries at the Beitbridge Magistrates Court reveals that on February 6, 2006, a Zimbabwean woman named Abigail Ndlovu who was going to South Africa presented a South African passport belonging to Happiness Ndlovu as her own. Although an attendant at the passport control desk stamped the passport authorizing Ndlovu to proceed, a more attentive police detective checking travelers' documents at the bridge before they crossed onto the South African side of the border post noticed the anomaly and arrested Abigail.[36] While Zimbabwe's principal immigration officer for Beitbridge boastfully stated that officials in his department "intercepted several Zimbabweans for attempting to cross the border while using forged travel documents," such actions did not stop a thriving underground economy of border jumping in the region.[37]

What made the situation complicated was that the majority of Zimbabweans who desired to leave the country through official channels in the early 2000s struggled to obtain passports and other identity documents. This issue came up strongly in a focus group discussion I had with more than thirty Zimbabwean former migrants who returned from South Africa in May 2010 under the auspices of the International Organization for Migration's (IOM's) Voluntary Assisted

Return and Reintegration Program. The issue of greatest concern to the focus group participants was the amount of time it took for people to go through the passport application process at many provincial registry offices in the country. MaNdlovu, a woman in her mid-fifties, recounted how she tried for three days but failed to submit her application for a passport at the Harare passport office (commonly referred to as "Makombe Building") in 2008. Having arrived at Makombe Building around four o'clock one morning, she was surprised to find a long queue of people already waiting to be served. When the passport office opened, four and half hours later (at 8:30 a.m.), a passport office employee gave out some small papers with numbers written on them. When the papers ran out—he was very close to where MaNdlovu stood—he announced that the people who had received the numbers were the only ones who would be served that day and advised the rest to go home and try again the following day. With a voice filled with anger and sorrow, MaNdlovu narrated how she remained in the queue until the following day. "I realized that if I left the queue, I was going to lose my position, and that was going to make it difficult for me to be served the next day," she said.

Despite getting a number the following day, she could not turn in her application because she spent half of the day in another queue waiting for passport officers to hand out the application forms. After filing out the forms, she joined another queue hoping to submit her application the same day, but the office closed before she could turn in her completed forms. She said, "I had to come back at 4 a.m. the following day and join another queue. But when I finally reached the service desk where they took fingerprints, I was told that my pictures were not of the correct type they needed. That broke my back and I gave up."[38] In many ways, MaNdlovu's story resonates with another that appeared in the Zimbabwean weekly *Financial Gazette* on February 26, 2010. The writer of that story, Jupiter Punungwe, says he paid for the "fast track" processing of his passport on December 17, 2008, on the promise that he would get it within four weeks' time, but the passport only became available on December 23, 2009—twelve months after the initial application was made.[39]

After listening to MaNdlovu's story, I asked the participants in the focus group to share what they thought were the causes of the long lines that became a common sight at passport offices throughout the country. At that point the discussion shifted toward allegations of corruption among people working in the registrar general's offices. The entire group, it seemed, was convinced that corrupt officials at Makombe Building and other passport offices in the country deliberately caused the long queues and delays to compel applicants to give out bribes. In line with this, another woman named Sophia, who claimed she traveled back and forth across the Zimbabwe–South Africa border without a passport more than forty times between February 2007 and May 2010, said:

I gave up on getting a passport a long time ago. After applying for a passport in September of 2005, I spent six months visiting the passport office checking for my passport. Every time I went there I was told that the passport was not ready. However, other people who applied after me collected theirs in short periods of time. Some in a single a month. I knew that the staff at the passport offices delayed processing my application because they wanted a bribe from me, so I just forgot it. Nowadays, when I want to travel I just pick up my handbag and board the bus. I do not get bothered about all these things. I have been arrested and deported many times, but I keep going back to South Africa.[40]

Like Sophia, many participants in the group discussion shared stories that showed that they viewed the delays they experienced at various passport offices around the country as an indication that the people who worked there wanted bribes to get things moving.

Gilbert, a former nurse at Kwekwe General Hospital, revealed some tactics that passport officers allegedly deployed to induce people to pay bribes. He said that sometime in August 2006 he visited the passport office in Gweru, where he obtained the necessary paperwork to file his application. After completing the forms, he joined a queue waiting for the passport officer, who was checking each application before he could submit it. It was then that Gilbert encountered what he thought was the officers' trick for asking for bribes: "When the passport officer came to collect the forms, he told me and many other people that we did not complete the forms correctly and instructed us to correct the errors on our forms. . . . I went over my application several times but did not see anything that needed to be corrected, so I went and asked the officer to tell me what I needed to correct. Instead of helping with my forms, the officer shouted at me saying I was not the only person waiting to be served."[41] As Gilbert narrated, he simply went behind the building and pretended to be writing on the forms before rejoining the queue. "When the officer got to me for the second time, he took my form without saying anything. I knew the idea was to frustrate me so I could bribe him," he said.[42] Given that Gilbert's application was approved without making any changes to what he had written on the forms, it is possible that the concerned passport officer indeed wanted him to pay a bribe; however, it is difficult to say for certain that the officer wanted Gilbert to pay a bribe.

Although the focus group participants thought that passport-processing delays were caused by state officials who wanted bribes from applicants, the Registrar General's Office evidently struggled to cope with the sharp increase in demand for travel documents in Zimbabwe during the first nine years of the twenty-first century. At one point in 2006, the Zimbabwean government temporarily stopped issuing passports (and national identity documents) citing shortages of foreign currency to import some of the materials they used in making the documents.[43]

Two years later, the Registrar General's Office attracted wide-ranging criticism after failing to renew the passport of MDC President Morgan Tsvangirai, who was supposed to travel to Lesotho for the interparty talks that resulted in the formation of the GNU. Responding to criticism about the government's handling of Tsvangirai's passport application, President Mugabe's spokesperson argued that the Registrar General's Office did not have the money to import the materials required to produce passports because of economic sanctions imposed by some Western governments.[44] It is very likely that the pro–ZANU-PF senior civil servants in the Registrar General's Office deliberately delayed the processing of Tsvangirai's passport renewal in a bid to frustrate him and his supporters. Nevertheless, perennial queues at the country's registry offices indicated that Zimbabwe struggled to cope with the demand for passports and other types of identity documents.

In addition to the long delays and allegations of corruption, focus group participants criticized the Office of the Registrar General in Zimbabwe for adding new features to birth certificates, national identity documents, and passports in the early 2000s. For example, the A5-sized birth certificates (approximately 5.8 × 8.3 inches) that registry authorities issued to Zimbabweans before the 1990s were no longer accepted as legitimate documents because they did not contain the names and identity numbers of the holder's parents. To obtain a passport in twenty-first-century Zimbabwe, an individual had to produce an unabridged version of his or her birth certificate, commonly referred to as the "A4" or "long birth certificate" (approximately 8.3 × 11.7 inches), along with a national identity document for those aged 18 years and older. Although the government encouraged people with A5-sized birth certificates to apply for A4 ones anywhere in the country, the process presented several challenges for prospective travelers. Getting the A4-sized birth certificate in 2008 cost an average of US$5, but applicants sometimes had to wait for days or weeks (depending on the location of the office they applied to) for their requests to be processed. In most cases, one had to make several trips to the district registration office before obtaining an acceptable birth certificate to file with the application for a passport.

Although people in different parts of the country experienced the situation differently, the scenario in Beitbridge District reflected what transpired in most rural districts. Although the inhabitants of Beitbridge depended on South Africa for almost everything they needed on a daily basis, the district did not have a passport office. The nearest place one could go to apply for a passport was Gwanda Town, more than 150 kilometers (approximately 93 miles) from the border town. Some buses and minivans (commonly referred to as *kombis*) plied the Beitbridge–Gwanda route on a regular basis, but it was rare for people to obtain the necessary forms and file their applications on the same day that they arrived at the Gwanda passport office. Long queues and other delays associated with an overburdened system meant people sometimes needed two or more nights in Gwanda to complete the passport application process.

Those coming from places such as Chikwarakwara, on the eastern side of Beitbridge district, would need much more time to travel to and from Gwanda. Although the gravel road linking Chikwarakwara to Beitbridge Town was in a sound condition compared with other parts of Zimbabwe, no public transportation traveled that route. In such circumstances, people needed about one and half days to walk almost one hundred kilometers between Chikwarakwara and Beitbridge Town before connecting to Gwanda. Given that it sometimes took more than two days for a person to travel from Chikwarakwara to Gwanda Town, several people from that area—which is, on average, five kilometers from the Limpopo River—did not bother to go through the process of applying for travel documents. Only those who needed passports for purposes other than traveling to South Africa took the trouble to go to Gwanda.

Emergency situations, such as those associated with political violence during elections, also made it difficult for some people to obtain passports before going to South Africa. The fact that Zimbabwe had a facility for people in emergency situations to apply for ETDs did not help political activists running away from threats of persecution. Some senior officers in the police and army often issued public statements in support of ZANU-PF, so opposition political activists fleeing the country preferred to avoid contact with state functionaries at all levels until they crossed the border. Consequently, most people in such situations left the country through unofficial routes. In this context, border jumping from Zimbabwe to South Africa continued unabated.

As was the case in previous years, border jumpers escaping the deteriorating environment in Zimbabwe in the early 2000s engaged the services of maguma-guma, who commonly colluded with some members of the South African border patrol units to whom they routinely gave bribes. Commenting on the prevalence of networks that facilitated border jumping across the Zimbabwe–South Africa border, Darshan Vigneswaran argued that as of 2008, "the least expensive of the various smuggling services was wholly run by the South African Police Services. Officials at the Beitbridge border post charge R50 [approximately $5.75] for the undocumented entry to one side of the facility and R50 for unauthorized exit on the other."[45] My observation suggests that the use of informally organized networks tended to be more expensive because several people had to be paid. Such networks usually involved transport operators, sex workers, and state officials who helped travelers cross the border without following official channels. Although a traveler did not need to know anyone ahead of time to be able to utilize these networks, one had to be prepared to pay larger amounts of money than they would if dealing directly with border officials.

Drivers of cross-border buses and trucks played a very important role as contacts in these networks. Negotiations usually began on the way from various departure points to Beitbridge. Some drivers openly advertised their services by asking passengers if they needed help at the border. Others would "help" only when potential clients asked for assistance. To earn the trust of the driver, it was important to allow some time for traveling and talking about other things before introducing the subject. Usually discussions of this nature would not begin until after the traveler and the driver had shared some food, drinks, and a few personal stories along the way. On reaching some agreement to work together, the driver would make arrangements to hand over the travelers to the next group of people on the conveyer belt, usually female sex workers who masqueraded as fruit and candy vendors in the vicinity of the border post. They would connect the travelers with border officials on the Zimbabwean side who provided the clients with gate passes, which they presented if asked to show passports at various points through the border post. Although there were no fixed charges for these transactions, the involvement of layers of "helpers" pushed up the costs of using these networks. On average, each person involved in such a network charged no less than R100, which meant travelers would end up paying at least R300.[46] Regardless of how much travelers paid to illegally cross the border, the involvement of border officials in these networks compromised both countries' efforts to control "clandestine" activities in the border zone.

In an interview that shed more light on the workings of networks of border jumping in this region, Ben Makato, a regular employee at Nottingham Estates (on the Zimbabwean side of the border) who doubled as a guma-guma, said "I have been caught several times by the South African police, but I have never been sent to jail because I always pay them. On two occasions, I gave them all the money I had collected from my clients, but it helped me to know two guards I later met one Sunday afternoon at Bretts Farm [on the South African side of the border] when I went to drink beer with my friends. We talked openly and we exchanged phone numbers, so these days I call them first before I take people across the Limpopo."[47] Makato also pointed out that his eight years of experience living and working on farms on both sides of the border was a huge asset. He knew several holes through which he smuggled travelers into South Africa. He also knew many people who used their cars as "bush" taxis on both sides of the border. Transporters on the Zimbabwean side brought customers to him, and those on the South African side helped Makato move his clients to Musina or the main road (N1), where they got rides to Johannesburg or other areas.

Some travelers worked around the system of migration control by engaging in what they referred to as "pay as you go" or *kudhiza,* which means paying something in return for a favor. This very simple but risky strategy involved border jumpers paying their way through several checkpoints at the Beitbridge border post from the Zimbabwean side to the South African end. As was the case with those who paid maguma-guma to take them across the border, one did not need to make prior arrangements or know anyone at the border. What was important was for the traveler to know the right time to get to the border (usually at night) and to have at least R100 in smaller bills of R10 or R20. The traveler would then walk through the border post with confidence, just like everybody else. If any of the police detectives or other border officials stopped the traveler and asked to see his or her visa, the strategy was to insert a R10 or R20 bill in his or her passport before handing it over. If the concerned official took the cash and returned the passport, the traveler would proceed.[48] Given that the two countries deployed their agents at various points along the border post, this strategy should have resulted in several arrests of border jumpers. However, records at the Beitbridge Magistrates Court did not suggest that a lot of people were charged for giving bribes to the police or other officials at the border post. Many travelers who deployed this strategy probably got away with it because state agents accepted the bribes and let them pass.

As concerns about "illegal migrants" increased in South Africa after the xenophobic violence of May 2008, which resulted in the death of more than sixty-five people and the displacement of thousands of Zimbabweans, Mozambicans, and other African migrants, the Democratic Alliance—the biggest opposition party in post-apartheid South Africa—and other critics of the ANC government called for the re-electrification of the country's northern border fences and the tightening of immigration control policies.[49] Instead of giving into the demands of the opposition, the South African government further relaxed the conditions of entry and temporary stay for Zimbabwean travelers through a visa-free program it announced in April 2009. Rather than having to struggle to meet the visa requirements that had been in place since the mid-1990s, Zimbabweans traveling to South Africa on short-term visits (e.g., shopping trips, visiting relatives) were now required only to produce a valid passport to obtain a ninety-day temporary visitor's permit. In removing the visa requirements for Zimbabwean travelers, the South African government argued that the new approach to migration control was in line with article 4 of the SADC Protocol on the Facilitation of Movement of Persons in the Southern African Development Community. Interestingly, the launch of South Africa's visa-free program for Zimbabweans coincided with the inauguration of the unity government in Zimbabwe.

Zimbabwe's GNU and South Africa's Visa-Free Programs

Although Zimbabwe celebrated the signing of the Global Political Agreement and the birth of the GNU in September 2008, interparty contestations over cabinet posts delayed the inauguration of the unity government for almost five months. It was not until February 2009, barely three months before South Africa introduced a visa waiver program for Zimbabweans, that the GNU began its work. Notwithstanding the new dispensation, the resolution of the political impasse and economic crisis in Zimbabwe did not happen as quickly as had been anticipated. For example, the squabbles over the implementation of electoral reforms—including the drafting of a new constitution—went on for several months. As a result, several companies that left the country or downsized operations as the economy plummeted from the mid-1990s onward did not rush back when the GNU began, and the rate of unemployment in Zimbabwe remained quite high. In addition, the adoption of a multicurrency policy (some say the "dollarization" of the Zimbabwean economy) in February 2009 did very little to help. The removal of the Zimbabwean currency from circulation slowed down the rate of inflation but created a liquidity crunch in the country. Given that the Zimbabwean government had no capacity to print any of the foreign currencies that came into circulation, the country could do very little (if anything) to make sure the majority of people had access to cash. Furthermore, the less than 20 percent of Zimbabweans who were formally employed earned very low wages compared with the cost of living.

In this context, Zimbabweans in search of livelihood opportunities continued to travel to South Africa through unofficial channels even after the latter began implementing a visa-free regime. On December 20, 2009, I witnessed how some people dodged the official systems of controlling migration between the countries when I traveled from Johannesburg to Harare on a bus whose passengers were predominantly Zimbabwean cross-border traders. As the bus approached the Beitbridge border post, a woman who was sitting next to me asked if I knew the border well. When I told her I did not understand what she meant by "knowing the border," she said she wanted me to assist by presenting "her" passport for inspection at the border post because it had a picture of a man. Before I could say anything further, the woman told me she had concluded that I did not know the border at all, so she was going to look for someone else to assist her. As we got off the bus to join the queue for immigration checks at the South African border control point, I saw her handing over a Zimbabwean passport and some money to the bus driver. Before we got back onto the bus, so we could proceed to the Zimbabwean side of the border post, the driver returned the passport and collected more money from her. When we resumed the journey, after spending almost three hours on the Zimbabwean side of the border, where customs officials ordered us to remove every piece of luggage from the bus so they could check for smuggled goods, I asked my seatmate how she had resolved the passport issue. After spending almost ten minutes talking about her experience as a cross-border trader and frequent traveler between Zimbabwe and South Africa, the woman went ahead to reveal that she, in fact, had another passport with her picture in it. The one with a man's picture belonged to her nephew who had traveled to South Africa some three months back. Although he was on a temporary visitor's permit, he had obtained employment and did not plan to go back to Zimbabwe anytime soon, although his permit was due to expire in a few days. To avoid travel expenses and the risk of losing his job, he gave this woman his passport and some money for bribing immigration officers so they could stamp the passport purporting that its owner left the country before the expiry of the visa. Because she succeeded in having the passport stamped, the woman told me she was going to deploy the same strategy, or a different one if necessary, to obtain another visitor's permit for him on her return trip in three weeks' time.

As case records at the Beitbridge Magistrates Court indicate, hundreds of Zimbabweans were arrested and charged for engaging in similar activities. A good example relates to a group of eight people—Felix Makwere (aged 28), Patrick Shumba (49), Caroline Muganhiri (19), Tambudzai Masviba (20), Kelvin Ncube (20), Redemption Murivani (38), Twoboy Muradza (29), and Tinashe Mapedzamombe (35)—who appeared in court March 19, 2010, to answer charges of crossing the border at an undesignated point. The case register reveals that members of SAPS's Border Patrol Unit caught these people as they crossed the border through an undesignated crossing point in the Chitulipasi area. None had a passport or any other form of travel document, and they were fined for departing the country without the required documents.[50] In another case, the police arrested Lisa Dube of Lupane District on March 17, 2010, when she tried to use Patricia Mazikana's passport to enter South Africa. According to the case register, Dube got the passport from Damane Mzingeli, a motorist who had given her a ride from the rural township of Tsholotsho to Beitbridge. The attendant at the control desk who inspected the passport when Dube presented it for stamping noticed that the photograph on it did not match the holder's face and called the police, who arrested Dube.[51]

When I asked the focus group participants to explain why many people were still going to South Africa without following formal channels, they argued that the cost of obtaining a passport in Zimbabwe was beyond the reach of most people who were without jobs. One participant said, "Most of us do not want to be border jumpers. We do that because of the situation at the passport offices in this country. The passport fees are too high for us, especially when you are not working. I would rather jump the border and use that money for other things in South Africa."[52] At the time of the discussion, the Zimbabwe Registrar General's Office was charging a minimum of US$143 for a regular passport, a substantial decrease from around US$340 at the beginning of 2009. However, given that most civil servants and other people in formal employment earned an average of US$100 per month, the fees were too high and many people could not afford them. This situation made it hard for Zimbabweans who would have wanted to take advantage of South Africa's visa waiver policy to actually do so. Consequently, cross-border shoppers and job seekers continued to use unofficial channels to enter South Africa. The activities of the malayitsha, maguma-guma, sex workers, and corrupt state officials who viewed border jumping as business also continued to thrive.

As the South African government continued to search for a way to reduce the rate of border jumping from Zimbabwe, the Department of Home Affairs (DHA) introduced what it called the Zimbabwe Dispensation Project (ZDP) in September 2010. This program was contrary to the demands of government critics who wanted to see the government taking a restrictive approach to border enforcement and migration control. Through the ZDP, South Africa gave holders of valid Zimbabwean passports who entered the country before May 1, 2010, regardless of how they entered, the opportunity to apply for study permits, work permits, and/ or business permits valid for up to four years. To obtain a study permit through this program, one had to produce an official letter of acceptance from an educational institution registered in South Africa. Those who applied for work permits were required to produce proof of employment offers with the employer's contact address, registration, and tax identification number. Those seeking a business permit had to produce proof of self-employment such as a valid business address and registration certificate for their company. Zimbabwean asylum seekers were also eligible to apply for any of the three types of permits under this project; however, doing so meant they had to forgo their refugee application cases.[53]

In developing such a project, the DHA brought back memories of the special employment permits (the zero-twos). However, the ZDP was much broader and multipronged in its objectives. Through it, South African officials wanted to reduce the number of Zimbabwean "illegal" migrants on welfare programs in the country by allowing such people to officially work, study, or trade. In addition, it was hoped that the project would benefit the country through revenue produced by thousands of Zimbabwean border jumpers. Another, perhaps more important objective was to address the issue of fraudulent documents, which border jumpers from Zimbabwe and other countries obtained with the help of corrupt state officials in South Africa. In this respect, the DHA guaranteed amnesty to holders of fraudulent documents who voluntarily surrendered such documents to the Office of the Inspectorate and had case statements and fingerprints taken. By promising amnesty to such people, the South African government hoped to minimize the security risks and revenue losses associated with the use of fraudulent identity documents. However, some Zimbabweans who voluntarily surrendered fraudulent documents ended up in prison (presumably for different cases), making it difficult for others to come forward.[54]

As with the 90-day visitor's permits, the ZDP triggered intense debates in South Africa. For example, the Democratic Alliance issued a statement calling for the ANC-led government to "actively promote the repatriation of Zimbabweans" and stop thinking that "economic and political improvements in Zimbabwe will encourage a lot of Zimbabweans to voluntarily go back home." In the same statement, the party lambasted what it viewed as the South African government's pandering to President Mugabe, which "placed an overwhelming burden on our country and on those Zimbabweans who have been forced to seek refuge within our borders due to President Mugabe's repressive regime."[55] Despite the criticism, the South African government proceeded with the project, which benefited approximately 250,000 Zimbabweans over the course of four years.[56] Interestingly, that period also witnessed some improvements in the political and economic environment in Zimbabwe, although such improvements turned to be short lived.

Maguma-guma, Malayitsha, and Border Violence in the Twenty-First Century

In an interview I had with Tshabeni Ndou in May 2010, he revealed that some travelers who crossed the border at undesignated points during the first decade of the twenty-first century engaged in violent activities as they passed through the border district. In this respect, Ndou argued that because the border people were used to helping "strangers," they felt obliged to provide travelers with information about where it would be safe to cross the Limpopo and locate food supplies and temporary accommodation. Suggesting that border jumpers were the perpetrators of most of the violence in the border zone, he explained that despite the hospitable treatment they received, some travelers ended up abusing or stealing from the people who helped them. Ndou further pointed out that the early 2000s witnessed an increase in travelers who "killed border people for no apparent reason, maybe asking for sexual favors and all that," and adding, "I myself have kept a number of them in my homestead, but in the end they would always steal something, be it a radio or a blanket and disappear."[57] Several other residents of Beitbridge District that I interviewed talked about travelers who broke into people's homes or slaughtered small livestock they came across in the border zone. However, much of the available evidence suggests that travelers were mostly victims and not perpetrators of violence in this area. The routes they followed and the strategies they deployed in attempts to evade official systems of controlling cross-border mobility led not just to the arrest of some travelers but also to various kinds of abuse and even death for many.

For most people who did not possess the required documents, crossing the Limpopo River during the rainy season put them at great risk. This was particularly true for travelers who originated from areas far from the border. Many residents of Beitbridge knew a lot about the Limpopo, which they crossed regularly, whereas most travelers tried to cross the river without any prior knowledge of its flowing patterns. Such people commonly misjudged the depth and strength of the water and drowned as they tried to cross the border. In addition to the

Limpopo River, wild animals in Kruger National Park and Sentinel Ranch on the South African and Zimbabwean sides of the border, respectively, also posed a natural challenge to travelers who tried to use undesignated crossing points. In this respect, the geophysical nature of the borderline became a source of violence against border jumpers. However, the maguma-guma, malayitsha, other self-styled agents, and corrupt state officials who "helped" people cross the border clandestinely were the main perpetrators of violence against travelers.

Between November 2008 and March 2009, the IOM conducted a survey to identify some of the challenges facing Zimbabwean women and children who traveled to South Africa illegally. Among its major findings, the IOM report notes that maguma-guma "took advantage of travelers' impulse towards informal channels of crossing the border as well as their lack of knowledge about South Africa's immigration laws to exact money and abuse people in desperate situations."[58] In addition to stealing travelers' clothes, shoes, cell phones, and cash, maguma-guma also raped, physically assaulted, and even killed people who sought their help with crossing the border. In one of several stories in the report, a group of travelers paid maguma-guma who had offered to help them cross the Limpopo River. As soon as they reached the other side of the river, the maguma-guma asked them to pay more than originally charged. The report notes that "most of the people paid. But there was one man, about 25 years old, who said he had no more money. The magumaguma lifted him out and threw him into the river. He was swept away."[59]

Perhaps the most common form of violence that maguma-guma and malayitsha committed was raping women and girls who either sought their help or were trying to cross the border independently at undesignated points. This occurrence stood out in most interviews and informal conversations I had with people in the border zone. For example, Netsai, a resident of Beitbridge and a former employee at the Medecins sans Frontieres (MSF) office in Beitbridge, narrated a story of an undocumented Zimbabwean woman who was abused by two men who gave her a ride from Beitbridge Town and offered to smuggle her into South Africa in December 2009. After successfully crossing the border, the car stopped at a fuel station in Musina and both men got out to buy drinks. As they proceeded with their journey toward Johannesburg, the driver handed a bottled drink to the woman who accepted without suspecting anything. After taking a few sips the woman lost consciousness. When she recovered, she realized that she was in a hospital in Polokwane (formerly Pietersburg), where she learned that a motorist found her lying unconscious on a roadside and called the police. Although the woman could not recall what happened after she took the drink, she realized that she no longer had a tampon she was wearing when she left her house the previous day. The two men probably drugged and sexually abused the woman before dumping her. In another case, which Netsai narrated, a group of maguma-guma raped a woman while her husband watched and then forced him to have sex with her afterward.[60]

These stories resonate with what I heard during a trial of two women arrested for using other people's passports that I witnessed at the Beitbridge Magistrates Court on April 30, 2010. After both women gave their testimony, admitting to committing the offense and explaining why they tried to cheat the system, the judge warned them and the public in attendance about the risks of abuse while trying to cross the border at undesignated points. He pointed out that he and other court officials felt overwhelmed by complaints from victims of assault, theft, rape, and other acts linked to maguma-guma or malayitsha. He revealed, in particular, that his court had previously dealt with horrendous cases including one in which more than ten men gang raped a woman as she tried to cross the border at Makhakhabule. What the judge did not talk about was that corrupt state officials also abused travelers, especially women, who tried to cross the border through unofficial channels. An interview with Kuda Ndlovu, who was a senior staff member at the IOM reception center in Beitbridge, revealed that the IOM helped several migrants who fell victim to abuse by border officials. One of the cases that Ndlovu talked about involved a South African customs official who took an undocumented Zimbabwean woman into the toilet so he could give her a "border pass" but ended up raping her.[61] Stories such as these say a lot about the vulnerability of people who sought to clandestinely cross the Zimbabwe–South Africa border in the first decade of the twenty-first century. Although border jumping was a major means of livelihood for Zimbabweans who sustained their families through cross-border trading and smuggling, the practice was also a source of great pain for victims of abuse and their families.

In an attempt to mitigate the health risks emanating from the abuse of cross-border travelers, the IOM, MSF, and other nongovernmental organizations operating in the border region provided counseling and other forms of support to victims who reported their ordeals. In June 2010, the MSF clinic in Musina treated more than thirty-five Zimbabwean women with sexually transmitted infections they allegedly contracted after being abused by maguma-guma and/or malayitsha.[62] On the Zimbabwean side of the border, the IOM reception center in Beitbridge Town employed two nurses who provided various kinds of treatment, including the postexposure preventative kits to women who reported being sexually abused within seventy-two hours. Along with offering treatment, the IOM organized several "migration health awareness" workshops in townships and villages in Beitbridge District. At one of the IOM workshops, which I attended as part of my field research, the facilitators encouraged women who planned to cross the border at undesignated points to wear female condoms before embarking on the journey through the "no-man's land" between the two countries. By encouraging Zimbabwean women to pack condoms—as if they were passports they needed for the trips to South Africa—the IOM employees were not being unreasonable. Their argument was that if women travelers could not prevent rape by using safer avenues to cross the border, at least they could minimize chances of contracting HIV and other sexually transmitted infections by wearing condoms. Desperate measures such as this show not only how dangerous the situation was for border jumpers, especially women, but also the extent to which border jumping between these countries stretched the capacity of state and nonstate institutions to control activities in the border zone.

Notes

1. See World Bank, "South Africa at a Glance," https://data.worldbank.org/country /south-africa; and "Zimbabwe at a Glance," https://data.worldbank.org/country/zimbabwe.

2. Lovemore Zinyama, "Who, What, When and Why: Cross-Border Movement from Zimbabwe to South Africa," in *On Borders: Perspectives on International Migration in Southern Africa*, ed. David A. McDonald (Ontario: SAMP, 2000): 72.

3. According to Zimbabwe's Ministry of Public Service Labor and Social Welfare, the number of people retrenched increased from about 1,200 in 1991 to about 14,000 in 1993. See Central Statistical Office, *Labour Statistics* (Harare: Government of Zimbabwe, 2004).

4. Rekopantswe Mate, *Making Ends Meet at the Margins?: Grappling with Economic Crisis and Belonging in Beitbridge Town, Zimbabwe* (Dakar: Council for the Development of Social Science Research in Africa, 2005).

5. Showers Mawowa and Alois Matongo, "Inside Zimbabwe's Roadside Currency Trade: The World Bank of Bulawayo," *Journal of Southern African Studies* 36, no. 2 (2010): 319–37.

6. Elaine Fultz and Bodhi Pieris, "The Social Protection of Migrant Workers in South Africa," (ILO/SAMAT Policy Paper no. 3, International Labor Organization, Pretoria, 1997). In light of the debates surrounding the number of Zimbabweans who lived in South Africa during the "Zimbabwe crisis" from the mid-1990s to around 2009, it is very difficult to verify the accuracy of these figures.

7. Jonathan Crush, *Covert Operations: Clandestine Migration, Temporary Work and Immigration Policy in South Africa* (Ontario: SAMP, 1997); Minaar and Hough, *Who Goes There?*

8. Peberdy, *Selecting Immigrants*, 139.

9. Peberdy, "Imagining Immigration." See also, Ettiene Hennop, Clare Jefferson, and Andrew McLean, "The Challenge to Control South Africa's Borders and Borderline" (Monograph 57, Institute for Security Studies, Pretoria, 2001).

10. Republic of South Africa, "Draft Green Paper on International Migration," *Government Gazette*, 383, no. 18033 (1997), https://www.gov.za/sites/default/files/gcis _document/201409/migrate1.pdf.

11. See Peter Mudungwe, "Promoting Free Movement of People in Southern Africa: A Case for Ratification of the Protocol on the Facilitation of Movement of Persons in the SADC Region" (Research Report 2016/03, African Diaspora Policy Center, Den Haag, July 2015);

Hussein Solomon, "Towards the Free Movement of People in Southern Africa?" (Occasional Paper 18, Institute for Security Studies, Pretoria, 1997).

12. Zinyama, "Who, What, When and Why."

13. McDonald et al., "Guess Who's Coming to Dinner."

14. David Lincoln and Claude Mararike, "Southward Migrants in the Far North: Zimbabwean Farmworkers in Northern Province," in *Borderline Farming: Foreign Migrants in South African Commercial Agriculture*, ed. Jonathan Crush (Cape Town: SAMP, 2000).

15. The Office of the Registrar General in Zimbabwe uses a system whereby the first two or three digits on an individuals' national identity document tally with the number allocated to the district of one's birth. According to that system the number for Beitbridge District is 02, whereas that for Buhera District where I was born is 07.

16. Patrons at MaSibanda's Shebeen, interview with author, Beitbridge Town, May 15, 2010.

17. Blair Rutherford, "Zimbabweans on the Farms of Northern South Africa," in *Zimbabwe's Exodus: Crisis, Migration, Survival*, ed. Jonathan Crush and Daniel Tevera (Cape Town: SAMP, 2010).

18. Republic of South Africa, "Draft Green Paper on International Migration."

19. Vincent Williams and Lizzie Carr, "The Draft Protocol on the Facilitation of Movement of Persons in SADC: Implications for State Parties," Migration Policy Brief no. 18, (Southern African Migration Project, 2006). See also, International Organization for Migration, "Towards Facilitation of the Movement of People in the SADC Region" (Paper presented at the 27th SADC Parliamentary Forum, Livingstone, May 2010); Mudungwe, "Promoting Free Movement"; Solomon, "Towards the Free Movement."

20. International Organization for Migration, "IOM Urges African Countries to Ratify, Implement Protocols on Free Movement," May 6, 2016, https://www.iom.int/news /iom-urges-african-countries-ratify-implement-protocols-free-movement. See also, Mudungwe, "Promoting Free Movement."

21. Crush, "Discourse and Dimensions"; Lyndith Waller, "Irregular Migration to South Africa During the First Ten Years of Democracy" (Migration Policy Brief 19, South Africa Migration Project, 2006).

22. Muromoni Mbedzi, interview with author, Rukange Village, Beitbridge, May 26, 2010.

23. The rand is the monetary unit of South African currency.

24. J. Maramani, interview. Given that the majority of border jumpers who drowned in the Limpopo River every rain season came from areas far away from the border, the inhabitants of Beitbridge referred to people from "up-country" as *vana mvuraivete*. This term is derogatory for people who stupidly think that when the Limpopo River flows smoothly and quietly it is asleep, not knowing that it only does that when the water level is high enough to cover rocks, pools, and other features that normally make flowing water noisy.

25. For more information on this, see France Maphosa, "Transnationalism and Undocumented Migration between Rural Zimbabwe and South Africa," in Crush and Tevera, *Zimbabwe's Exodus*; Vusilizwe Thebe, "The *Malayisha* Industry and the Transnational Movement of Remittances to Zimbabwe," in Crush et al., *Mean Streets*; and "From South Africa with Love: The 'Malayisha' System and Ndebele Households' Quest for Livelihood Reconstruction in South-Western Zimbabwe," *Journal of Modern African Studies*, 49 (2011): 647–70.

26. *Chabane* is a pseudonym used to protect the actual identity of this particular individual, whom the author did not have an opportunity to interview. Information obtained through informal conversation with patrons at MaSibanda's Shebeen, May 15, 2010.

27. Dorica Gada, interview with author, Beitbridge Town, May 15, 2010. *MaHarare* simply means people from Harare. When I conducted field research for this study in 2010, residents of Beitbridge used this term, with contempt, to refer to people from outside the district who "flooded" the border town as they traveled to and from South Africa.

28. Information obtained through informal conversation with patrons at MaSibanda's Shebeen, May 15, 2010.

29. See World Bank, "South Africa at a Glance," and "Zimbabwe at a Glance."

30. The term *Chimurenga*, which means fighting, was used in this case to emphasize the idea that the land reform program was part of a historic fight against imperialism and (neo)colonialism in Zimbabwe. For more detailed discussions of the politics of land reform in postcolonial Zimbabwe see, e.g., Amanda Hammar, Brian Raftopoulos, and Stig Jensen, eds., *Zimbabwe's Unfinished Business: Rethinking Land, State and Nation in the Context of Crisis* (Harare: Weaver, 2003); Sadomba, *War Veterans*; Ian Scoones, Nelson Marongwe, Blasio Mavedzenge, Jacob Mahenehene, Felix Murimbarimba, and Chrispen Sukume, *Zimbabwe's Land Reform: Myths and Realities* (Suffolk: James Currey, 2010); Mahmood Mamdani, "Lessons of Zimbabwe: Mugabe," *London Review of Books* 30, no. 23 (2008): 17–21; Sean Jacobs and Jacob Mundy, eds., "Reflections on Mahmood Mamdani's 'Lessons of Zimbabwe,'" *Concerned Africa Scholars Bulletin* 82 (Summer 2009).

31. *Herald* (Harare), "Response by Government of Zimbabwe to the Report by the UN Special Envoy on Operation Murambatsvina/Restore Order," August 17, 2005; Sarah Bracking, "Development Denied: Autocratic Militarism in Post-Election Zimbabwe," *Review of African Political Economy,* 104, no. 105, (2005): 341–57; Francis Musoni, "Operation Murambatsvina and the Politics of Street Vendors in Zimbabwe," *Journal of Southern African Studies* 36, no. 2 (2010): 301–17.

32. Anna K. Tibaijuka, *Report of the Fact-Finding Mission to Zimbabwe to Assess the Scope and Impact Of Operation Murambatsvina by the UN Special Envoy on Human Settlements Issues in Zimbabwe* (Nairobi: United Nations Human Settlement Program, 2005).

33. Jeremy L. Jones, "Nothing Is Straight in Zimbabwe: The Rise of the Kukiya-kiya Economy, 2000–2008," *Journal of Southern African Studies,* 36, no. 2 (2010): 285–99. For more details on inflation rates, see Reserve Bank of Zimbabwe, "Consumer Price Index, 1979–2007," https://www.rbz.co.zw/index.php/research/markets/inflation.

34. Waller, "Irregular Migration"; Rutherford, "Zimbabweans on the Farms."

35. *State v. Natalie Alice Fenn Peacock and Tristan John Peacock*, Bulawayo Provincial High Court, May 15, 2008.

36. *State v. Abigail Ndlovu*, Beitbridge Magistrates' Court, February 6, 2006.

37. Mashadu Netsianda, "Zimbabweans Are Forging Documents," *Zoutnet News*, http://www.zoutnet.co.za/articles/news/5551/2007-07-20/8220zimbabweans-are-forging-documents8221.

38. Returning migrants group, focus group discussion with the author, IOM Reception Center, Beitbridge, May 17, 2010. To protect the identities of participants in this focus group who jumped the border on their various journeys to South Africa, I use pseudonyms instead of their actual names.

39. Jupiter Punungwe, "Government to Blame for Passport Delays," *Financial Gazette* (Harare), February 26, 2010.

40. Returning migrants group, focus group discussion, May 17, 2010.

41. Returning migrants group, focus group discussion, May 17, 2010.

42. Returning migrants group, focus group discussion, May 17, 2010.

43. See *Zim Online*, "Cash Crisis Forces Harare to Suspend Issuing of Passports," November 29, 2006, http://www.zimbabwesituation.com/old/nov29_2006.html#Z1.

44. *Mail and Guardian Online*, "No Passport, No Talks, Says Tsvangirai," http://mg.co.za /article/2008-10-20-no-passport-talks-says-tsvangirai.

45. Darshan Vigneswaran, "Migration Control, Documentation and State Transformation," *Contemporary Migration to South Africa: A Regional Development issue,* ed. Aurelia Segatti and Loren B. Landau (Washington DC: World Bank, 2011), 113. See also, Forced Migration Studies Program and Musina Legal Advice Office, *Special Report: Fact or Fiction? Examining Zimbabwean Cross-Border Migration into South Africa* (Johannesburg: University of the Witwatersrand, 2007).

46. Returning migrants group, estimates based on information from the focus group discussion with author, May 17, 2010.

47. Nottingham group, author's interview with Ben Makato (pseudonym), Nottingham Estate, Beitbridge, June 27, 2010.

48. Returning migrants group, focus group discussion, May 17, 2010.

49. See, Sakhile Modise, "South Africa-Zimbabwe Border Fences Disappear: Opposition Expresses Fears," *Afrik-News,* July 27, 2009, http://www.afrik-news.com/article15970.html; *News24,* "Sections of SA/Zim Border Fence Stolen," July 24, 2009, https://www.news24.com /Africa/News/Parts-of-SA-Zim-border-stolen-20090724.

50. *State v. Felix Makwere and Seven Others,* Beitbridge Magistrates' Court, March 19, 2010.

51. *State v. Lisa Dube,* Beitbridge Magistrates' Court, March 17, 2010.

52. Returning migrants group, focus group discussion, May 17, 2010.

53. See Union of South Africa, "Zimbabwean Special Permit," http://www.home -affairs.gov.za/index.php/immigration-services/zimbabwean-special-permit-zsp; Immigration South Africa, "Amnesty to Zimbabwean Immigrants" (blog), https://www .immigrationsouthafrica.org/blog/amnesty-for-zimbabwean-immigrants/.

54. Kenichi Serino, "Two Steps Forward, One Step Back for Zimbabweans in South Africa," *Fair Observer,* July 17, 2011, https://www.fairobserver.com/region/africa /two-steps-forward-one-step-back-zimbabweans-south-africa/; Karabo Keepile, "Zimbabwe Dispensation 101," *Mail and Guardian,* September 16, 2010, https://mg.co.za/article /2010-09-16-zimbabwe-dispensation-101.

55. See Democratic Alliance, "Zimbabwean Permits: Minister Either Doesn't Know or Won't Tell," October 7, 2010, https://www.politicsweb.co.za/opinion/minister-in-denial -over-zim-asylum-seekers--da.

56. Riley Dillon, "After the Exodus: The Challenges of Return Migration in Zimbabwe," *Africa Portal* 53 (May 2013); Douglas Mpondi, "The Zimbabwe Diaspora's Narratives and Notions of Return" (Paper presented at the African Studies Association Annual Conference, Indianapolis, November 22, 2014).

57. Tshabeni Ndou, interview, May 17, 2010.

58. International Organization for Migration, *Migrants' Needs and Vulnerabilities in the Limpopo Province, Republic of South Africa* (New York: United Nations, 2009), 4. See also, Forced Migration Studies Program, *Zimbabwean Migration*, and "Report on Human Smuggling."

59. International Organization for Migration, *Migrants' Needs*, 19.

60. Netsai Mudau, interview with author, Beitbridge Town, May 17, 2010.

61. Kuda Ndlovu, interview with author, IOM Reception Center, Beitbridge, May 14, 2010.

62. Phyllis Kachere, "Raped by Omaguma-guma: Heavy Price to Pay for Zimbabwean Women Crossing Border Illegally," *Sunday Mail* (Harare), June 6–12, 2010. See also, Tendai Sean Joe, "Sexual Violence in Limpopo River," *Tendai Joe* (blog), August 14, 2010, https://tendaiseanjoe.wordpress.com/2010/08/14/sexual-violence-in-limpopo-river/; Eva-Lotta Jansson, "Security Doesn't Flow across the River," *Mail and Guardian*, May 3, 2013, https://mg.co.za/article/2013-05-03-00-security-doesnt-flow-across-the-river.

Conclusion

Like many other regions of the world, Southern Africa is currently struggling with movements that seek to evade official channels of migration. Although their nature varies from one border to another, these movements usually manifest in the form of bribes to cross borders through official border posts, fake or fraudulently obtained documents by migrant work seekers and cross-border traders, and border inhabitants' use of unofficial crossing points in regular interactions with kith and kin in different countries. Traffickers and smugglers of human beings, drugs, weapons, and other kinds of goods also use various methods to cross borders through unofficial channels. In using the term *border jumping* to refer to all of these activities, which are often treated as subjects of separate scholarly discourses, this book sought to understand why and how this phenomenon became a salient feature of the Zimbabwe–South Africa border culture by the twenty-first century. I argue that a much longer and more complex history of border jumping exists between the two countries than is usually thought to be the case. The foregoing chapters showed how this phenomenon emerged with the beginning of state-centered controls of cross-Limpopo mobility in the 1890s and evolved over a period of more than 120 years. In that respect, I paid very close attention to issues of time, temporality, and periodization, showing that the Zimbabwe–South Africa border itself and movements across it have meant different things to differently positioned people at different times.

Border jumping from Zimbabwe to South Africa mirrors trends in other regions in that it is commonly associated with people's movements from a less developed country to one with better livelihood opportunities. However, in this book I questioned the tendency to view "illegal migration" as simply a product of poverty, unemployment, and other conditions of insecurity in countries of migrants' origin. Instead, the foregoing chapters have developed a framework for seeing border jumping as a product of multisited contestations over the control of cross-border mobility. In that respect, the book shows that despite working together toward many common interests, state officials in Southern Rhodesia/Zimbabwe and their counterparts in the Transvaal/South Africa deployed conflicting approaches to controlling movements across the border. Meanwhile, interest groups such as mine owners and farmers associations from both sides of the border lobbied for border control policies that favored their competing interests. Taking advantage of this scenario, generations of people from Beitbridge

District and other areas adjacent the Zimbabwean border with South Africa used unofficial channels to travel between the two countries. Similarly, work-seeking migrants and shoppers from other areas north of the Limpopo River deployed various methods to evade state-based efforts of restricting migration across the Zimbabwe–South Africa border.

Rather than viewing border jumpers simply as lawbreakers (which they were in most cases), I sought to understand the structural conditions that made it difficult for people to follow official channels when traveling between the two countries at any given moment between the 1890s and the early 2000s. In doing so, the study viewed border jumpers as rational thinkers who thoughtfully considered their options before making the decision to cross the border using unofficial channels. This is not to say that people who ended up "jumping" the border always had freedom of choice. Some people left their homes because they wanted better paying jobs, whereas others did so to escape forced labor, forced taxation, famine, political violence, unemployment, and other kinds of pressures they experienced in colonial and postcolonial Zimbabwe. The book also revealed that the decision to cross the border through unofficial lines was not always an easy one to make. Given that people knew the risks involved in using unofficial channels—including arrest, abuse by labor recruiters and maguma-guma, or drowning in the Limpopo—most travelers resorted to border jumping only after they found it difficult or inconvenient to use official channels.

The book also argued that although many people participated in border jumping primarily in pursuit of livelihood opportunities, they unintentionally and sometimes intentionally challenged the border's legitimacy and questioned state-centered characterizations of their activities as illegal, criminal, prohibited, or undesirable. Their activities mocked border enforcement regimes. As Hastings Donnan and Thomas Wilson put it, these activities "ignore, contest and subvert state power [even though] they do not seek to overthrow the state, since in some sense their existence depends upon it and, in particular, on the borders which the state seeks to establish and uphold."[1] In this context, the book presented border jumping as a reflection of ordinary people's determination to pursue their goals in defiance of the border's master plan. In addition, the book revealed the complexities surrounding this phenomenon by showing that the resilience of border jumping between the two countries—from the 1890s to the early 2000s—was not just a result of subaltern agency in the form of border jumpers' ingenuity. Other actors, such as labor recruiters, human smugglers, transport operators, corrupt state officials at and away from the border post, and South Africa–based employers also engaged in activities that encouraged, promoted, and sustained this phenomenon.

Furthermore, the book problematized widely held views about the nature of borders and measures of border enforcement in colonial Africa by showing how different border enforcement regimes shaped the dynamics of mobility between these countries before the attainment of independence in Zimbabwe and the construction of an electrified fence on the South African side of the border in the 1980s. It might be true, as John Oucho argues, that "during much of the colonial period the national boundaries [in Southern Africa] were not as rigidly observed as they became after independence, which implies that illegal migration was then an irrelevant concept."[2] Similarly, Jonathan Crush observes that throughout much of the twentieth century, Southern African states were concerned with "monitoring" rather than "controlling" cross-border movements, thus "there were no border posts and people crossed wherever they wanted."[3] However, this book shows that the historical dynamics of the Zimbabwe–South Africa border are far more complicated than that. Although it was possible for people to cross that border almost anywhere before the construction of the fence, the official controls of movements between the two countries began in the 1890s when the newly founded British colonial administration introduced registration certificates and passes for African subjects in Southern Rhodesia in a bid to prevent loss of labor through migration to South Africa. This approach had a huge effect on cross-border mobility in the region. In fact, I argue that border controls not only gave rise to "illegal migration" between these countries but also sustained this phenomenon, which expanded over the course of the twentieth century, as states on both sides of the boundary increased their presence and visibility in the Limpopo Valley.

In analyzing the ways in which the dynamics of border jumping changed after the deployment of armed guards and the construction of South Africa's border fence, I also questioned the view that "illegal migration" is a result of the receiving countries' failure to secure their borders. That view, common among supporters of antiimmigration movements calling for the tightening of border control measures in several countries, misses the complicated dynamics of border jumping and its ability to survive against odds. As we saw in chapters 4 and 5, border jumping from Zimbabwe to South Africa thrived even as it became a much riskier endeavor after the construction of the fence in 1980s. Hundreds of people died as they tampered with the electrified fence in bids to enter South Africa. This does not suggest that tight controls of borders do not work; rather, it shows that such measures do not always provide the solution to the challenges posed by border jumping. Elsewhere, studies of the infamous Berlin Wall and the United States' attempts to "fortify" parts of its border with Mexico also show the limits of such measures, which are usually expensive.[4]

In addition to examining how South Africa's border fence increased the risks associated with border jumping, this book also explored other forms of violence that have been a major part of the Zimbabwe–South Africa border culture. As state-centered controls of migration between these countries became routinized in the first decade of the twentieth century, the border zone became a sanctuary of unlicensed labor recruiters, who used violent methods to recruit migrant workers they "sold" to mine owners and other employers in South Africa. Over the years, violence became entrenched in the border zone as competition among labor recruiters intensified with the increased visibility of state functionaries from both sides of the border. By the late 1990s, the maguma-guma and malayitsha had replaced labor recruiters as the main perpetrators of violence targeting border jumpers, who were technically their clients. Although the magnitude of violence associated with border jumping across the Zimbabwe–South Africa border might not be anywhere close to migration disasters witnessed along the southern shores of Europe over the past decade, both cases suggest that the fortification of borders does not necessarily stop border jumping. Instead, such approaches tend to increase the violence associated with this phenomenon, making it more dangerous.

By presenting border jumping across the Zimbabwe–South Africa border as a product of the British occupation of the Zimbabwean plateau in the 1890s, this book highlights a "forgotten" legacy of the European partition of Africa. Although William Miles and other scholars have examined various "scars of partition" that the African continent continues to grapple with, border jumping has somehow skipped most scholars' consideration as one of those scars.[5] By showing how border jumping is tied to the current system of nation-states in Africa—a product of colonial conquest—I have also suggested that as long as such a system prevails, contestations over the control of cross-border mobility will continue, and it will remain very difficult to eradicate this practice. In other words, it will take complete removal of all forms of restriction of peoples' movements between these countries for border jumping across the Zimbabwe–South Africa border to stop.

Notes

1. Donnan and Wilson, *Borders: Frontiers of Identity*, 88.
2. Oucho, "Cross-Border Migration," 47.
3. Crush, "Migrations Past," 17.
4. Pertti Ahonen, "The Berlin Wall and the Battle for Legitimacy in Divided Germany," *German Politics and Society* 29, no. 2 (2011): 40–56; Mathijs Pelkmans, "Chaos and Order along the (Former) Iron Curtain," in *A Companion to Border Studies*, ed. Thomas M. Wilson and Hastings Donnan (Oxford: Blackwell, 2012); Michael Dear, *Why Walls Won't Work: Repairing the US-Mexico Divide* (Oxford: Oxford University Press, 2013); Nevins, *Operation Gatekeeper*.
5. Miles, *Scars of Partition*. See also Miles, *Hausaland Divided*; Asiwaju, *Partitioned Africans*; Nugent, *Smugglers, Secessionists*; Mahmood Mamdani, *Citizen and Subject: Contemporary Africa and the Legacy of Late Colonialism* (Princeton, NJ: Princeton University Press, 1996).

Bibliography

Archival References

A. National Archives of South Africa (NASA), Pretoria

AMPT PUBS, vol. 45, file CD1894, Reports of the Transvaal Labour Commission, 1904.

BNS, vol. 1/1/377, file 194/74, Immigrants Regulation Act (No. 22) 1913.

BNS, vol. 442, file 146/74, Undesirable Immigrants: Police Views.

BTS, file 14/33, Froneman Commission, First Draft Report (1961).

GNLB, vol. 30, file 3260/11/240, Immigrants Regulation Act (No. 22) 1913.

GNLB, vol. 30, file 3260/11/240 (Part 2), Temporary Removal of Restrictions on Natives Entering the Union Seeking Work.

GNLB, vol. 120, file 1950/13/240, Tropical Natives Evading the Depot at Louis Trichardt.

GNLB, vol. 122, file 1950/13/240, Illegal Recruitment of Rhodesian Natives.

GNLB, vol. 122, file 1950/13/D240, Employment of Tropical Natives on Mines.

GNLB, vol. 123, file 1950/13/240, Emigration of Rhodesian Natives to the Transvaal.

GNLB, vol. 417, file 81/42, Application for Permission: Rhodesian Native Mboya John to Return to Johannesburg.

NTS, vol. 2246, file 564/280, Illegal Recruitment of Tropical Natives.

NTS, vol. 2246, file 603/280, Migrant Native Labour Conference.

NTS, vol. 2252, file 802/117, Recruitment of Natives for the Mines.

NTS, vol. 2061, file 107/280, Rex Versus W. P. de Villiers: Illegal Recruiting of Tropical Natives, (1923–1924).

NTS, vol. 2062, file 112/280 (Part 1), Employment of Tropical Natives.

NTS, vol. 2062, file 112/280 (Part 2), Employment of Tropical Natives.

NTS, vol. 2117, file 225/280, Repatriation of Portuguese Natives.

PM, vol. 32, file 73/14/1907, Labor: PEA for Rhodesia.

B. British Library (BL)

C.S.D.252, Union of South Africa House of Assembly Debates, November 8, 1910.

C.S.D.252, Union of South Africa House of Assembly Debates, February 10, 1911.

C.S.D.252, Union of South Africa House of Assembly Debates, March 13, 1911.

C.S.D.252, Union of South Africa House of Assembly Debates, May 14, 1912.

C.S.D.252, Union of South Africa House of Assembly Debates, May 8, 1913.

C.S.D.252, Union of South Africa House of Assembly Debates, May 14, 1913.

C. National Archives of Zimbabwe (NAZ)

A3/18/30/26, Native Affairs, Labor Recruitment.

A3/18/31/6, Pass Laws.

A3/20/1, Matabele Order-in- Council, July 18, 1894.

NAZ, A3/21/57, Pass Consolidation, 1913–1917.

AOH/46, Amon Makufa Mlambo, interview with Dawson Munjeri, Rhodesdale, December 13, 1978.

F120/IMM/23/4, Control of Southern Rhodesia's Borders.

F138/2, Central Africa Standing Committee Meetings.

F146/12, Central African Proposals for a Migrant Labour Agreement with South Africa, October 7, 1950.

Hansards, Rhodesia Government, House of Assembly Debates, April 11, 1975.

N1/2/2, Chief Native Commissioner's Annual Reports, 1895.

N3/1/21, Rhodesia Native Labour Bureau.

N3/17/5, Pass Laws, 1909–1923.

N3/2/4, Operation of Pass Laws, 1922.

N3/22/4, vol. 1, Employment of Southern Rhodesian Natives in the Union of South Africa, 1914–1923.

N3/22/4, vol. 2, Employment of Southern Rhodesian Natives in the Union of South Africa, 1914–1923.

N3/22/4, vol. 3, Employment of Southern Rhodesian Natives in the Union of South Africa, 1914–1923.

NB/6/1/20, Compound Inspector, Selukwe Division, Report of the Year ended December 31, 1907.

ORAL GL/1, Louis Samuel Glover Interviewed by D. Hartridge, Salisbury, February 4, 1969.

S1042, Emigration of Natives to the Transvaal, 1924–1937.

S1226, Illegal Recruiting of Native Labour, 1925–1951.

S138/203, Emigration of Natives to Bechuanaland, 1925–1929.

S138/4, Native Movements between Adjoining Territories, 1924–1928.

S138/40, Native Labour, Forced Recruitment, 1924–1934.

S138/5, Native Pass Laws, 1927–1932.

S1542/E2/1, Emigration of Natives to South Africa, 1933–1939.

S1542/E2/2, Emigration of Natives to South Africa, 1933–1939.

S1561/4, Minutes of Proceedings of a Meeting of the Standing Committee Held in Salisbury, December 3–4, 1937.

S1561/5, Migrant Labour: Recruitment of Natives in Nyasaland and Northern Rhodesia, 1938–1939.

S1692, Assistant Native Commissioner Beitbridge: Correspondences, 1926–1938.

S2009, Beitbridge Inquests, 1942–1950.

S235/418, Transportation of Natives in Southern Rhodesia to and from the Limpopo.

S246/716, Recruiting of Southern Rhodesian Natives for the Union of South Africa.

S2929/6/1, Report of the Delineation of Tribal Communities in Beitbridge District of Rhodesia, 1966.

S3287/45/48, Repatriation of Africans to and from South Africa.

S480/83, Emigration of Natives to the Transvaal, 1924–1926.

S482/203/39/1, Bridges General.

S482/468/39/1, Emigration and Immigration, 1930–1936.

S482/468/39/2, Emigration and Immigration, 1937–1939.

S482/509/39, Native Labour to the Union, 1944–1948.

SRG 2, Southern Rhodesia: Legislative Council Debates, June 7, 1899.

SRG 2, Southern Rhodesia: Legislative Council Debates, July 16, 1901.
SRG 2, Southern Rhodesia: Legislative Council Debates, November 7, 1902.
SRG 2, Southern Rhodesia: Legislative Council Debates, July 2, 1903.
SRG 2, Southern Rhodesia: Legislative Council Debates, April 28, 1905.
SRG 2, Southern Rhodesia: Legislative Council Debates, May 7, 1907.
SRG 2, Southern Rhodesia: Legislative Council Debates, December 18, 1907.
SRG 2, Southern Rhodesia: Legislative Council Debates, May 25, 1909.
SRG 2, Southern Rhodesia: Legislative Council Debates, May 19, 1909.

D. The Employment Bureau of Southern Africa Archives (TEBA; University of Johannesburg, Doornfontein Campus, Special Collections, and Institutional Repository Department)

WNLA Circular Letters, vol. 2, Secretary of the Transvaal Chamber of Mines Circular to the Chairman and Directors of Mining Companies, May 18, 1901.
File 45B/4, Pad 1, Extract of Findings and Recommendations of the Inter-department Committee in Connection with Bantu Natives in the Republic of South Africa.
File 45A/3, Pad 1, Circular by A. J. Limebeer, Secretary of the Transvaal Chamber of Mines' Gold Producers Committee, September 21, 1939.
File 45A/3, Pad 1, Union Gazette Extraordinary, July 7, 1950.

Court Documents

State v. Abigail Ndlovu, Beitbridge Magistrates Court, February 6, 2006.
State v. Felix Makwere and Seven Others, Beitbridge Magistrates Court, March 19, 2010.
State v. Lisa Dube, Beitbridge Magistrates Court, March 17, 2010.
State v. Natalie Alice Fenn Peacock and Tristan John Peacock, Bulawayo Provincial High Court, May 15, 2008.

Interviews and Informal Conversations (All Conducted by the Author)

Anonymous, Beitbridge Town, May 26, 2010.
Chauke, M., Chikwarakwara Business Center, Beitbridge, June 29, 2010.
Dube, L., Chikwarakwara Business Center, Beitbridge, June 29, 2010.
Firihwa, G., Chasvingo Village, June 29, 2010.
Gada, D., Beitbridge Town, May 15, 2010.
Govhana, P., Mukwakwami Village, Chipinge, June 6, 2013.
Mabhureni, P., Beitbridge Town, June 28, 2010.
Madzive, C., Madzive village, Beitbridge, May 19, 2010.
Makombe group, Makombe Village, Beitbridge, May 25, 2010.
Mapfumo, D., Limpopo Village, Beitbridge, June 15, 2010.
Maramani, J., Limpopo Village, Beitbridge, June 15, 2010.
Marange, W., Musheekwa Village, Chipinge, June 9, 2013.
Matibe, E., Chabili Village, Beitbridge, June 1, 2010.
Mbedzi, L., Rukange Village, Beitbridge, May 29, 2010.
Mbedzi, L., Zezane Business Center, Beitbridge, May 19, 2010.
Mbedzi, M., Rukange Village, Beitbridge, May 26, 2010.
Moyo, M. G., Limpopo Village, Beitbridge, June 15, 2010.

Moyo, S., Chitulipasi Village, Beitbridge, July 12, 2013
Mudau, N., Beitbridge Town, May 17, 2010.
Muleya, N., Malala Business Center, Beitbridge, June 22, 2010.
Muleya, S., Beitbridge Town, May 20, 2010.
Muleya, T., Luthumba Business Center, Beitbridge, May 17, 2010.
Muroiwa, T., Chipise Village, Beitbridge, June 2, 2010.
Musheekwa, J., Musheekwa village, Chipinge, June 9, 2013.
Ncube, A., Chabili Village, Beitbridge, June 1, 2010.
Ncube, E., Makombe Village, Beitbridge, May 25, 2010.
Ndlovu, K. Beitbridge Town, May 14, 2010.
Ndou, T., Beitbridge Town, May 17, 2010.
Ngwaxani, M., Musheekwa Village, Chipinge, June 9, 2013.
Nottingham group, Nottingham Estates, Beitbridge, June 27, 2010.
Patrons at Beitbridge Country Club, May 15, 2010.
Patrons at MaSibanda's Shebeen, Beitbridge Town, May 15, 2010.
Returning migrants group, International Organization for Migration, Beitbridge, May 17, 2010.
Sibanda, L., Chabili Village, Beitbridge, June 1, 2010.
Siyasongwe, D., Malabe Village, Beitbridge, May 31, 2010.
Tapiwa and Tendai, Beitbridge Magistrates Court, April 30, 2010.
Vhomo, S., Makombe Village, Beitbridge, May 25, 2010.
Zezane group, Zezane Village, Beitbridge, May 19, 2010.

Government Publications

Agreement between the Government of the Republic of South Africa and the Government of the Republic of Botswana Relating to the Establishment of an Office for a Botswana Government Labour Representative in the Republic of South Africa, Botswana Citizens in the Republic of South Africa and the Movement of Such Persons across the International Border, December 24, 1973. https://treaties.dirco.gov.za/dbtw-wpd/exec /dbtwpub.dll?AC=GET_RECORD&XC=/dbtw-wpd/exec/dbtwpub.dll&BU=https%3A %2F%2Ftreaties.dirco.gov.za%2Fdbtw-wpd%2Ftextbase%2Ftreatywebsearch.htm&GI= &TN=TreatyWeb&SN=AUTO9568&SE=1844&RN=4&MR=20&TR=0&TX=1000&ES =0&XP=&RF=Printingformat2018&EF=Basic+Record+Form&DF=Web+full+record &RL=1&EL=1&DL=1&NP=1&ID=&MF=&DT=&ST=0&IR=488&NR=0&NB=0&SV= 0&SS=0&BG=&FG=&QS=TReaties+New+Master.

Agreement between the Government of the Republic of South Africa and the Government of the Kingdom of Lesotho Relating to the Establishment of an Office for a Lesotho Government Labour Representative in the Republic of South Africa, Lesotho Citizens in the Republic of South Africa and the Movement of such Persons across the International Border, August 24, 1973. https://treaties.dirco.gov.za/dbtw-wpd/exec /dbtwpub.dll?AC=GET_RECORD&XC=/dbtw-wpd/exec/dbtwpub.dll&BU=https%3A %2F%2Ftreaties.dirco.gov.za%2Fdbtw-wpd%2Ftextbase%2Ftreatywebsearch.htm&GI= &TN=TreatyWeb&SN=AUTO8657&SE=1843&RN=2&MR=20&TR=0&TX=1000&ES =0&XP=&RF=Printingformat2018&EF=Basic+Record+Form&DF=Web+full+record &RL=1&EL=1&DL=1&NP=1&ID=&MF=&DT=&ST=0&IR=483&NR=0&NB=0&SV=0 &SS=0&BG=&FG=&QS=TReaties+New+Master.

Agreement between the Government of the Republic of South Africa and the Government of the Kingdom of Swaziland Relating to the Establishment of an Office for a Swaziland Government Labour Representative in the Republic of South Africa, Certain Swaziland Citizens in the Republic of South Africa, the Movement of Such Persons across the Common Border and the Movement of Certain South African Citizens across the Common Border, and Addendum Thereto, August 22, 1975. https://treaties.dirco.gov.za/dbtw-wpd/exec/dbtwpub.dll?AC=GET_RECORD&XC=/dbtw-wpd/exec/dbtwpub.dll&BU=https%3A%2F%2Ftreaties.dirco.gov.za%2Fdbtw-wpd%2Ftextbase%2Ftreatywebsearch.htm&GI=&TN=TreatyWeb&SN=AUTO10133&SE=1845&RN=5&MR=20&TR=0&TX=1000&ES=0&XP=&RF=Printingformat2018&EF=Basic+Record+Form&DF=Web+full+record&RL=1&EL=1&DL=1&NP=1&ID=&MF=&DT=&ST=0&IR=498&NR=0&NB=0&SV=0&SS=0&BG=&FG=&QS=TReaties+New+Master.

Agreement between the Governments of the Republic of South Africa and Malawi Relating to the Employment and Documentation of Malawi Nationals in South Africa. August 1, 1967. https://treaties.dirco.gov.za/dbtw-wpd/exec/dbtwpub.dll?AC=GET_RECORD&XC=/dbtw-wpd/exec/dbtwpub.dll&BU=https%3A%2F%2Ftreaties.dirco.gov.za%2Fdbtw-wpd%2Ftextbase%2Ftreatywebsearch.htm&GI=&TN=TreatyWeb&SN=AUTO10381&SE=1846&RN=2&MR=20&TR=0&TX=1000&ES=0&XP=&RF=Printingformat2018&EF=Basic+Record+Form&DF=Web+full+record&RL=1&EL=1&DL=1&NP=1&ID=&MF=&DT=&ST=0&IR=429&NR=0&NB=0&SV=0&SS=0&BG=&FG=&QS=TReaties+New+Master.

Central Statistical Office. *Labour Statistics.* Harare: Government of Zimbabwe, 2004.

Republic of South Africa. "Draft Green Paper on International Migration." *Government Gazette* 383, no. 18033 (1997). https://www.gov.za/sites/default/files/gcis_document/201409/migrate1.pdf.

Union of South Africa. "Zimbabwean Special Permit." http://www.home-affairs.gov.za/index.php/immigration-services/zimbabwean-special-permit-zsp.

Newspapers, Magazines, and Internet Materials

Afrik-News. "South Africa-Zimbabwe Border Fences Disappear: Opposition Expresses Fears." July 27, 2009., http://www.afrik-news.com/article15970.html.

Bulawayo Chronicle. "Fined for Selling Passes." January 14, 1944.

———. "Labour Smuggled Over the Border." November 29, 1935.

DefenceWeb. "Africa's Leading Defence News Portal" (Home page). South African National Defense Forces. http://www.defenceweb.co.za/index.php?option=com_content&view=article&catid=55:SANDF&id=1199.

Democratic Alliance. "Secure Our Borders." https://www.da.org.za/policy/secure-our-borders.

———. "Zimbabwean Permits: Minister Either Doesn't Know or Won't Tell." October 7, 2010. https://www.politicsweb.co.za/opinion/minister-in-denial-over-zim-asylum-seekers--da.

"Designated Area." *Africa Research Bulletin, Political Series,* 22, no. 1 (1985).

Dillon, Riley. "After the Exodus: The Challenges of Return Migration in Zimbabwe." *Africa Portal* 53 (2013). https://www.africaportal.org/publications/after-the-exodus-the-challenges-of-return-migration-in-zimbabwe/.

"Electric Fence." *Africa Research Bulletin, Political Series,* 22, no. 1 (1985).

Europe or Die, directed by Milene Larsson (New York: Vice News, 2015), https://www.vice
.com/en_us/article/exqgek/europe-or-die-all-episodes.
Fairbridge, W. E. "Labour for the Mines." *Rhodesia Herald.* August 4, 1900.
Globe and Mail (Canada). "Electrocution Ends Border Crossing." April 2, 1985.
———. "Wall of Razor Wire a Cruel Barrier to Freedom: Fenced in Frightened Mozambican
Refugees Risk Capture, Injury or Death as They Attempt to Cross into South African
Homeland." January 14, 1992.
Herald (Harare). "Response by Government of Zimbabwe to the Report by the UN Special
Envoy on Operation Murambatsvina/Restore Order." August 17, 2005.
Immigration South Africa, "Amnesty to Zimbabwean Immigrants." https://www
.immigrationsouthafrica.org/blog/amnesty-for-zimbabwean-immigrants/.
IRIN News. "South Africa: Troops Reinforcing a Porous and Dangerous Border." May 26,
2010. http://www.irinnews.org/Report.aspx?ReportID=89262.
Jansson, Eva-Lotta. "Security Doesn't Flow across the River." *Mail and Guardian,* May 3,
2013. https://mg.co.za/article/2013-05-03-00-security-doesnt-flow-across-the-river.
Jeppe, Julius. "South African Coal Estates (Witbank) Limited." *Sun and Agricultural Journal
of South Africa* (December 1926).
Kachere, Phyllis. "Raped by Omaguma-guma: Heavy Price to Pay for Zimbabwean Women
Crossing Border Illegally." *Sunday Mail,* Harare, June 6–12, 2010.
Keepile, Karabo. "Zimbabwe Dispensation 101." *Mail and Guardian,* September 16, 2010.
https://mg.co.za/article/2010-09-16-zimbabwe-dispensation-101.
Kennedy, Ray. "Zimbabwe Blacks Ordered to Leave South Africa." *Times,* August 5, 1981.
Laurence, Patrick. "SA to Build Electric Fence on Zimbabwe Frontier/South Africa Reacts to
Cross-border Attacks by ANC rebels." *Guardian* (London), January 13, 1986.
L.K.R. "WNLA in Rhodesia." *Rhodesia Herald,* December 6, 1907.
Mail and Guardian Online. "No Passport, No Talks, Says Tsvangirai." October 20, 2008.
http://mg.co.za/article/2008-10-20-no-passport-talks-says-tsvangirai.
McCullum, Hugh. "South Africa's Fence of Death." *Horizon,* Harare, August 19, 1992.
Minerals Council South Africa. https://www.mineralscouncil.org.za/about/history.
Modise, Sakhile. "South Africa-Zimbabwe Border Fences Disappear: Opposition Expresses
Fears." *Afrik-News,* July 27, 2009. http://www.afrik-news.com/article15970.html.
Monteiro, Tania. "Hundreds Killed by South Africa's Border Fence." *New Scientist,* January
27, 1990.
Murphy, Caryle. "S. Africa sets Ban on Jobs for Zimbabweans." *Washington Post,* August 7, 1981.
Netsianda, Mashudu. "Zimbabweans Are Forging Documents." *Zoutnet,* July 20, 1007.
http://www.zoutnet.co.za/articles/news/5551/2007-07-20/8220zimbabweans-are
-forging-documents8221.
New York Times. "South Africa Border Death." April 2, 1985.
News24. "Sections of SA/Zim Border Fence Stolen." July 24, 2009. https://www.news24.com
/Africa/News/Parts-of-SA-Zim-border-stolen-20090724.
O'Toole, Sean, and Paul Botes. "Porous Border Is Smugglers' Paradise." *Mail and Guardian
Online,* April 4, 2011. http://mg.co.za/article/2011-04-04-porous-border-is
-smugglers-paradise.
Punungwe, Jupiter. "Government to Blame for Passport Delays." *Financial Gazette,* Harare,
February 26, 2010.

Rand Daily. "Banned Natives Enter Union: Immigration Laws Not Enforced: Thousands Cross Northern Border." April 5, 1934.

Reserve Bank of Zimbabwe. "Consumer Price Index, 1979–2007." https://www.rbz.co.zw /index.php/research/markets/inflation.

Rhodesian Herald. "Charter Plane Is Flying Mine Labour to South Africa." January 10, 1975.

———. "Native Labour Conference." December 20, 1907.

Serino, Kenichi. "Two Steps Forward, One Step Back for Zimbabweans in South Africa." *Fair Observer,* July 17, 2011. https://www.fairobserver.com/region/africa/two-steps -forward-one-step-back-zimbabweans-south-africa/.

Sunday Times (Johannesburg). "Police Drive against Border 'Blackbirders': 'Recruiters's Use of Violence in Trade in Human Bodies." March 20, 1949.

Taylor, Stephen. "Mugabe Attitude Blamed for Blacks' Expulsion." *Times,* August 7, 1981.

Tendai Sean Joe. "Sexual Violence in Limpopo River." *Tendai Joe* (blog), August 14, 2010. https://tendaiseanjoe.wordpress.com/2010/08/14/sexual-violence-in-limpopo-river/.

Toronto Star. "Farmers Stand on Guard for South Africa." June 12, 1988.

United Nations. "Peace and Security." https://www.un.org/en/sections/issues-depth/peace -and-security/.

World Bank. "South Africa at a Glance." https://data.worldbank.org/country/south-africa.

———. "Zimbabwe at a Glance." https://data.worldbank.org/country/zimbabwe.

Zim Online. "Cash Crisis Forces Harare to Suspend Issuing of Passports." November 29, 2006. http://www.zimbabwesituation.com/old/nov29_2006.html#Z1.

Dissertations, Reports, and Unpublished Papers

African Union Commission. "Agenda 2063." Final edition. 2015. https://www.un.org/en/ africa/osaa/pdf/au/agenda2063.pdf.

Barstow, Timothy M. "Border Interdiction in Counterinsurgency: A Look at Algeria, Rhodesia and Iraq." Master's thesis, University of California, San Diego, 1995.

Centre for Development and Enterprise. *Migration from Zimbabwe: Numbers, Needs and Policy Options.* Johannesburg: Centre for Development and Enterprise, 2008.

Clarke, Duncan G. "Foreign African Labour Supply in South Africa, 1960–1977." Development Studies Research Group Working Paper 1, University of Natal, April 1977.

———. "State Policy on Foreign African Labour in South Africa: Statutory, Administrative and Contractual Forms." Development Studies Research Group Working Paper 4, University of Natal, September 1977.

Forced Migration Studies Program. "Report on Human Smuggling across the South Africa/ Zimbabwe Border." Migration Research and Monitoring Project Report, University of the Witwatersrand, Johannesburg, March 2009.

———. *Zimbabwean Migration into Southern Africa: New Trends and Responses.* Johannesburg: University of the Witwatersrand, 2009.

Forced Migration Studies Program and Musina Legal Advice Office. *Special Report: Fact or Fiction? Examining Zimbabwean Cross-Border Migration into South Africa.* Johannesburg: University of the Witwatersrand, 2007.

Fultz, Elaine, and Bodhi Pieris. "The Social Protection of Migrant Workers in South Africa." ILO/SAMAT Policy Paper no. 3, International Labor Organization, Pretoria, 1997.

Hanson, Gordon H. "Illegal Migration from Mexico to the United States." Working Paper no. 12141, National Bureau of Economic Research, Cambridge, MA, March 2006.

Hennop, Ettiene, Clare Jefferson, and Andrew McLean. "The Challenge to Control South Africa's Borders and Borderline." Monograph 57, Institute for Security Studies, Pretoria, 2001.

Human Rights Watch. *"Bullets for Each of You": State-Sponsored Violence since Zimbabwe's March 29 Elections.* New York: Human Rights Watch, 2008.

———. *Neighbors in Need: Zimbabweans Seeking for Refuge in South Africa.* New York: Human Rights Watch, 2008.

International Organization for Migration. "IOM Urges African Countries to Ratify, Implement Protocols on Free Movement." May 6, 2016. https://www.iom.int/news/iom-urges-african-countries-ratify-implement-protocols-free-movement.

———. *Migrants' Needs and Vulnerabilities in the Limpopo Province, Republic of South Africa.* New York: United Nations, 2009.

———. "Towards Facilitation of the Movement of People in the SADC Region." Paper presented at the 27th SADC Parliamentary Forum, Livingstone, May 2010.

Kalsheker, A. M. H. "The 1908 Asiatics Ordinance in Perspective." Henderson Seminar Paper, University of Rhodesia, 1974.

Kloppers, Roelof J. "Border Crossings: Life in the Mozambique/South Africa Borderland since 1975." DPhil diss., University of Pretoria, 2005.

Leslie, Robyn, et al. *Migration from Zimbabwe: Numbers, Needs and Policy Options.* Johannesburg: Center for Development and Enterprise, April 2008.

MacDonald, Andrew. "Colonial Trespassers in the Making of South Africa's International Borders, 1900 to c.1950." DPhil diss., University of Cambridge, 2012.

Mavhunga, Clapperton Chakanetsa. "The Mobile Workshop: Mobility, Technology and Human-Animal Interaction in Gonarezhou (National Park), 1850–Present." PhD diss., University of Michigan, 2008.

McNamara, J. K. "Black Workers Conflicts on South African Gold Mines, 1973–1982." PhD diss., University of the Witwatersrand, 1985.

Mpondi, Douglas "The Zimbabwe Diaspora's Narratives and Notions of Return." Paper presented at the African Studies Association annual conference, Indianapolis, November 2014.

Mudungwe, Peter. "Promoting Free Movement of People in Southern Africa: A Case for Ratification of the Protocol on the Facilitation of Movement of Persons in the SADC Region." Research Report 2016/03, African Diaspora Policy Center, Den Haag, July 2015.

Mutandi, Robson. "Locally-Evolved Knowledge in Livestock and Range Management Systems in Southern Zimbabwe's Dry Lands: A Study of Pastoral Communities in Beitbridge District." PhD diss., University of Waterloo, 1997.

Nemudzivhadi, Mphaya Henry. "The Attempts by Makhado to Revive the Venda Kingdom, 1864–1895." PhD diss., Potchefstroom University for Christian Higher Education, 1998.

Owen, Ken. "Foreign Africans: Summary of the Report of the Froneman Committee." Institute of Race Relations, Johannesburg, 1964.

Pierre, Jean, Loren B. Landau, and Tamlyn Monson. *Towards Tolerance, Law, and Dignity: Addressing Violence against Foreign Nationals in South Africa.* Arcadia: International Organization for Migration Regional Office for Southern Africa, 2009.

Solomon, Hussein. "Towards the Free Movement of People in Southern Africa?" Occasional Paper 18, Institute for Security Studies, Pretoria, 1997.

Tibaijuka, A. K. *Report of the Fact-Finding Mission to Zimbabwe to Assess the Scope and Impact of Operation Murambatsvina by the UN Special Envoy on Human Settlements Issues in Zimbabwe.* Nairobi: United Nations Human Settlement Program, 2005.

Van Driel, Nicole. "The ANC's First Armed Military Operation: The Luthuli Detachment and the Wankie Campaign, July-September 1967." Master's thesis, University of the Western Cape, 2003.

Waller, Lyndith. "Irregular Migration to South Africa during the First Ten Years of Democracy." Migration Policy Brief 19, South Africa Migration Project, 2006.

Williams, Vincent, and Lizzie Carr. "The Draft Protocol on the Facilitation of Movement of Persons in SADC: Implications for State Parties." Migration Policy Brief no. 18, Southern African Migration Project, 2006.

Books and Journal Articles

Abraham, Itty, and Willem van Schendel. "Introduction: The Making of Illicitness." In *Illicit Flows and Criminal Things: States, Borders and the Other Side of Globalization,* edited by Willem van Schendel and Itty Abraham, 1–37. Bloomington: Indiana University Press, 2005.

Ahonen, Pertti. "The Berlin Wall and the Battle for Legitimacy in Divided Germany." *German Politics and Society* 29, no. 2 (2011): 40–56.

Alexander, Jocelyn. *The Unsettled Land: State-Making and the Politics of Land in Zimbabwe, 1893-2003.* Oxford: James Currey, 2006.

Alexander, Peter. "Oscillating Migrants, 'Detribalized Families' and Militancy: Mozambicans on Witbank Collieries, 1918–1927." *Journal of Southern African Studies* 27, no. 3 (2001): 505–25.

Allen, Victor L. *The History of Black Mineworkers in South Africa.* Vol. 1, *The Techniques of Resistance, 1871–1948.* West Yorkshire: Moore, 1992.

Anderson, Jens A. "Informal Moves, Informal Markets: International Migrants and Traders from Mzimba District, Malawi." *African Affairs* 105, no. 420 (2006): 375–97.

Andersson, Ruben. *Illegality, Inc.: Clandestine Migration and the Business of Bordering Europe.* Oakland: University of California Press, 2014.

Anene, Joseph C. *The International Boundaries of Nigeria, 1885-1960: The Framework of an Emergent African Nation.* London: Longman, 1970.

Asiwaju, Anthony I. "The Conceptual Framework." In *Partitioned Africans: Ethnic Relations across Africa's International Boundaries, 1884-1984,* edited by Anthony I. Asiwaju, 1–18. New York: St Martin's, 1985.

———. ed. *Partitioned Africans: Ethnic Relations across Africa's International Boundaries, 1884-1984.* New York: St Martin's, 1985.

———. "Partitioned Culture Areas: A Checklist." In *Partitioned Africans: Ethnic Relations across Africa's International Boundaries, 1884-1984,* edited by Anthony I. Asiwaju, 252–259. New York: St Martin's, 1985.

———. *Western Yorubaland under European Rule, 1889-1945.* London: Longman, 1976.

Barnes, Teresa. "Virgin Territory? Travel and Migration by African Women in Twentieth Century Southern Africa." In *Women in Africa Colonial Histories,* edited by Jean Allman, Susan Geiger, and Nakanyike Musisi, 164–90. Indianapolis: Indiana University Press, 2002.

Beach, David N. *A Zimbabwean Past*. Gweru: Mambo, 1994.

Bean, Frank D., and Susan K. Brown. "Demographic Analyses of Immigration." In *Migration Theory: Talking across Disciplines,* edited by Caroline B. Brettell and James F. Hollifield, 67–89. New York: Routledge, 2015.

Betts, Alexander. *Survival Migration: Failed Governance and the Crisis of Displacement.* Ithaca, NY: Cornell University Press, 2013.

Bird, Ed. *Special Branch War: Slaughter in the Rhodesian Bush Southern Matabeleland, 1976–1980.* West Midlands: Helion, 2014.

Blake, Robert. *A History of Rhodesia.* New York: Knopf, 1977.

Bolt, Maxim. *Zimbabwe's Migrants and South Africa's Border Farms: The Roots of Impermanence.* Cambridge: Cambridge University Press, 2015.

Bozzoli, Belinda, and Mmantho Nkotsoe, *Women of Phokeng: Consciousness, Life Strategy, and Migrancy in South Africa, 1900–1983.* Portsmouth, NH: Heinemann, 1991.

Bracking, Sarah. "Development Denied: Autocratic Militarism in Post-Election Zimbabwe." *Review of African Political Economy* 104, no. 105 (2005): 341–57.

Bulpin, Thomas V. *The Ivory Trail.* Cape Town: Timmins, 1954.

Calavita, Kitty. *Inside the State: The Bracero Program, Immigration, and the INS.* New York: Routledge, 1992.

Centre for Development and Enterprise. *Migration from Zimbabwe: Numbers, Needs and Policy Options.* Johannesburg: Centre for Development and Enterprise, 2008.

Cilliers, Jakkie K. *Counter-Insurgency in Rhodesia.* London: Croom Helm, 1985.

Cisneros, Josue D. *The Border Crossed Us: Rhetorics of Borders, Citizenship and Latina/o Identity.* Tuscaloosa: University of Alabama Press, 2014.

Coplan, David B. "A River Runs through It: The Meaning of the Lesotho-Free State Border." *African Affairs* 100, no. 398 (2001): 81–116.

———. "Border Show Business and Performing States." In *A Companion to Border Studies,* edited by Thomas M. Wilson and Hastings Donnan, 507–21. West Sussex: Blackwell, 2012.

———. *In the Time of Cannibals: The Word Music of South Africa's Basotho Migrants.* Chicago: University of Chicago Press, 1994.

Crush, Jonathan. *Covert Operations: Clandestine Migration, Temporary Work and Immigration Policy in South Africa.* Ontario: SAMP, 1997.

———. "The Discourse and Dimensions of Irregularity in Post-apartheid South Africa." *International Migration* 37, no. 1 (1999): 125–51.

———. "Fortress South Africa and the Deconstruction of Apartheid's Migration Regime." *Geoforum* 30, no. 1 (1999): 1–11.

———. "Migrations Past: An Historical Overview of Cross-Border Movements in Southern Africa." In *On Borders: Perspectives on International Migration in Southern Africa,* edited by David A. McDonald, 12–24. Ontario: SAMP, 2000.

Crush, Jonathan, Abel Chikanda, and Caroline Skinner, eds. *Mean Streets: Migration, Xenophobia and Informality in South Africa.* Cape Town: Southern African Migration Project, 2015.

Crush, Jonathan, Alan Jeeves, and David Yudelman, *South Africa's Labor Empire: A History of Black Migrancy to the Gold Mines.* Boulder, CO: Westview, 1991.

Crush, Jonathan, and Daniel Tevera, eds. *Zimbabwe's Exodus: Crisis, Migration, Survival.* Cape Town: SAMP, 2010.

Dauvergne, Catherine. *Making People Illegal: What Globalization Means for Migration and Law*. Cambridge: Cambridge University Press, 2008.

Dear, Michael. *Why Walls Won't Work: Repairing the US-Mexico Divide*. Oxford: Oxford University Press, 2013.

De Genova, Nicholas. "The Production of Culprits: From Deportability to Detainability in the Aftermath of 'Homeland Security.'" *Citizenship Studies* 11, no. 5 (2007): 421–48.

Desmond, Cosmos. *The Discarded People: An Account of African Resettlement in South Africa*. Harmondsworth: Penguin, 1970.

Dodson, Belinda. "Women on the Move: Gender and Cross-Border Migration to South Africa from Lesotho, Mozambique and Zimbabwe." In *On Borders: Perspectives on International Migration in Southern Africa*, edited by David A. McDonald, 119–150. Ontario: SAMP, 2000.

Donnan, Hastings, and Thomas M. Wilson. *Borders: Frontiers of Identity, Nation and State*. New York: Berg, 1999.

Dotson, Floyd, and Lillian O. Dotson. *The Indian Minority of Zambia, Rhodesia and Malawi*. New Haven: Yale University Press, 1968.

Du Toit, Stefanus. J. *Rhodesia: Past and Present*. London: Heinemann, 1897.

Ellis, Stephen, and Tsepho Sechaba. *Comrades against Apartheid: The ANC and the South African Communist Party in Exile*. Bloomington: Indiana University Press, 1992.

Fadahunsi, Akin, and Peter Rosa. "Entrepreneurship and Illegality: Insights from the Nigerian Cross-Border Trade." *Journal of Business Venturing* 17, no. 5 (2002): 397–429.

Feyissa, Dereje, and Markus Virgil Hoehne, eds., *Borders and Borderlands as Resources in the Horn of Africa*. Suffolk: James Currey, 2010.

Flynn, Donna. "We Are the Border: Identity, Exchange, and the State along the Benin–Nigeria Border." *American Ethnologist* 24, no. 2 (1997): 311–30.

Foucault, Michel. *Discipline and Punish: The Birth of the Prison*, translated by Alan Sheridan. New York: Vintage, 1995.

Freund, Bill. "Forced Resettlement and the Political Economy of South Africa." *Review of African Political Economy* 29 (1984): 49–63.

Gaidzanwa, Rudo. *Voting with Their Feet: Migrant Zimbabwean Nurses and Doctors in the Era of Structural Adjustment*. Uppsala: Nordiska Institute, 1999.

Geloin, Ghislaine. "Displacement, Migration, and the Curse of Borders in Francophone West Africa." In *Movements, Borders and Identities in Africa*, edited by Toyin Falola and Aribidesi Usman, 226–237. New York: University of Rochester Press, 2009.

Giles-Vernick, Tamara, and James L. A. Webb, eds. *Global Health in Africa: Historical Perspectives on Disease Control*. Athens: Ohio University Press, 2013.

Giliomee, Hermann B. *The Afrikaners: Biography of a People*. Charlottesville: University of Virginia Press, 2003.

Goodhand, Jonathan. "Epilogue: The View from the Border." In *Violence on the Margins: States, Conflict, and Borderlands*, edited by Benedikt Korf and Timothy Raeymakers, 247–264. New York: Palgrave Macmillan, 2013.

Griffiths, Ieuan. "Permeable Boundaries in Africa." In *African Boundaries: Barriers, Conduits and Opportunities*, edited by Paul Nugent, and Anthony Asiwaju, 68–83. New York: Pinter, 1996.

Guerette, Rob T., and Ronald V. Clarke. "Border Enforcement, Organized Crime, and Deaths of Smuggled Migrants on the United States–Mexico Border." *European Journal on Criminal Policy and Research* 11, no. 2 (2005): 159–74.

Haines, David W., and Karen E. Rosenblum. "Introduction: Problematic Labels, Volatile Issues." In *Illegal Immigration in America: A Reference Handbook,* edited by David W. Haines and Karen E. Rosenblum, 1–12. Westport, CT: Greenwood, 1999.

Hammar, Amanda., Brian Raftopoulos, and Stig Jensen, eds. *Zimbabwe's Unfinished Business: Rethinking Land, State and Nation in the Context of Crisis.* Harare: Weaver, 2003.

Harries, Patrick. "Capital, State, and Labour on the 19th Century Witwatersrand: A Reassessment." *South African Historical Journal* 18, no. 1 (1986): 25–45.

———. *Work, Culture and Identity: Migrant Laborers in Mozambique and South Africa, c1860–1910.* Portsmouth, NH: Heinemann, 1994.

Heyman, Josiah McC. "The Study of Illegality and Legality: Which Way Forward?" *Political and Legal Anthropology Review* 36, no. 2 (2013): 304–7.

Hone, Percy F. *Southern Rhodesia.* London: George Bell & Sons, 1909.

Huffman, Thomas N. *Snakes and Crocodiles: Power and Symbolism in Ancient Zimbabwe.* Johannesburg: Witwatersrand University, 1996.

Iliffe, John. *Honour in African History.* Cambridge: Cambridge University Press, 2005.

Jacobs, Sean, and Jacob Mundy, eds. "Reflections on Mahmood Mamdani's 'Lessons of Zimbabwe.'" *Concerned Africa Scholars Bulletin* 82 (Summer 2009).

Jeeves, Alan H. "Over-Reach: The South African Gold Mines and the Struggle for the Labour of Zambesia." *Canadian Journal of African Studies* 17, no. 3 (1983): 393–412.

Jeeves, Alan H., and Jonathan Crush, "Introduction." In *White Farmers, Black Labor: The State and Agrarian Change in Southern Africa, 1910–50,* edited by Alan H. Jeeves and Jonathan Crush. Portsmouth, NH: Heinemann, 1997.

Jones, Jeremy L. "Nothing Is Straight in Zimbabwe: The Rise of the Kukiya-kiya Economy, 2000–2008." *Journal of Southern African Studies* 36, no. 2 (2010): 285–99.

Jones, Reece. *Violent Borders: Refugees and the Right to Move.* London: Verso, 2016.

Keppel-Jones, Arthur. *Rhodes and Rhodesia: The White Conquest of Zimbabwe, 1884–1902.* Kingston: McGill-Queen's University Press, 1983.

Khosravi, Sharam. *'Illegal' Traveller: An Auto-ethnography of Borders.* Hampshire: Palgrave Macmillan, 2010.

King, Russell, and Daniela DeBono. "Irregular Migration and the 'Southern European Model' of Migration." *Journal of Mediterranean Studies* 22, no. 1 (2013): 1–31.

Klaaren Jonathan, and Jay Ramji. "Inside Illegality: Migration Policing in South Africa after Apartheid." *Africa Today* 48, no. 3 (2001): 35–47.

Klotz, Audie. *Migration and National Identity in South Africa, 1860–2010.* New York: Cambridge University Press, 2013.

Kopytoff, Igor, ed. *The African Frontier: The Reproduction of Traditional African Societies.* Bloomington: Indiana University Press, 1987.

Korf, Benedikt, and Timothy Raeymakers. "Introduction: Border, Frontier and the Geography of Rule at the Margins of the State." In *Violence on the Margins: States, Conflict, and Borderlands*, edited by Benedikt Korf and Timothy Raeymakers, 3–27. New York: Palgrave Macmillan, 2013.

———. *Violence on the Margins: States, Conflict, and Borderlands.* New York: Palgrave Macmillan, 2013.

Kriger, Norma. "The Politics of Legal Status for Zimbabweans in South Africa." In *Zimbabwe's New Diaspora and the Cultural Politics of Survival,* edited by JoAnn McGregor and Ranka Primorac, 77–100. New York: Berghahn, 2010.

Lahiff, Edward. *An Apartheid Oasis? Agriculture and Rural Livelihoods in Venda.* London: Cass, 2000.

Landau, Loren. "Transplants and Transients: Idioms of Belonging and Dislocation in Inner-City Johannesburg." *African Studies Review* 49, no. 2 (2006): 125–45.

Lavenex, Sandra. "Migration and the EU's New Eastern Border: Between Realism and Liberalism." *Journal of European Public Policy* 8, no. 1 (2001): 24–42.

Lentz, Carola. *Land, Mobility, and Belonging in West Africa.* Bloomington: Indiana University Press, 2013.

———. "'This Is Ghanaian Territory!': Land Conflicts on a West African Border." *American Ethnologist* 30, no. 2 (2003): 273–89.

Liesegang, Gerhard. "New Light on Venda Traditions: Muhamane's Account of 1730." *History in Africa* 4 (1977): 168–172.

Lincoln, David., and Claude Mararike, "Southward Migrants in the Far North: Zimbabwean Farmworkers in Northern Province." In *Borderline Farming: Foreign Migrants in South African Commercial Agriculture,* edited by Jonathan Crush, 40–62. Cape Town: SAMP, 2000.

MacGaffey, Janet, and Remy Bazenguissa-Ganga. *Congo-Paris: Transnational Traders on the Margins of the Law.* Bloomington: Indiana University Press, 2000.

Magubane, Bernard. "Introduction to the 1970s: The Social and Political Context." In *The Road to Democracy in South Africa.* Vol. 2, *1970–1980,* edited by South African Democracy Education Trust, 1–36. Cape Town: Zebra, 2007.

Mamdani, Mahmood. *Citizen and Subject: Contemporary Africa and the Legacy of Late Colonialism.* Princeton, NJ: Princeton University Press, 1996.

———. "Lessons of Zimbabwe: Mugabe." *London Review of Books* 30, no. 23 (2008): 17–21.

Mann, Kristin, and Richard Roberts, eds. *Law in Colonial Africa*London: James Currey, 1991.

Maphosa, France. "Transnationalism and Undocumented Migration between Rural Zimbabwe and South Africa." In *Zimbabwe's Exodus: Crisis, Migration, Survival,* edited by Jonathan Crush and Daniel Tevera, 346–60. Cape Town: SAMP, 2010.

Martinez, Oscar J. "The Dynamics of Border Interaction." In *Global Boundaries: World Boundaries.* Vol. 1, edited by Clive H. Schofield, 1–15. London: Routledge, 1994.

———. *Troublesome Borders.* Tucson: University of Arizona Press, 2006.

Massey, Douglas S., Joaquin Arango, Graeme Hugo, Ali Kouaouci, Adela Pellegrino, and J. Edward Taylor. "Theories of International Migration: A Review and Appraisal." *Population and Development Review* 19, no. 3 (1993): 431–66.

Mate, Rekopantswe. *Making Ends Meet at the Margins? Grappling with Economic Crisis and Belonging in Beitbridge Town, Zimbabwe.* Dakar: Council for the Development of Social Science Research in Africa, 2005.

Mavhunga, Clapperton C. "Navigating Boundaries of Urban/Rural Migration in Southern Zimbabwe, 1890s to 1920s." In *African Agency and European Colonialism: Latitudes of Negotiation and Containment: Essays in Honor of A.S. Kanya-Forstner,* edited by Femi J. Kolapo and Kwabena O. Akurang-Parr,121–39. Lanham, MD: University Press of America, 2007.

———. *Transient Workspaces: Technologies of Everyday Innovation in Zimbabwe.* Cambridge, MA: MIT Press, 2014.

Mawowa, Showers, and Alois Matongo, "Inside Zimbabwe's Roadside Currency Trade: The World Bank of Bulawayo." *Journal of Southern African Studies* 36, no. 2 (2010): 319–37.

Mbembe, Achille. "At the Edge of the World: Boundaries, Territoriality, and Sovereignty in Africa." *Public Culture* 12, no. 1 (2000): 259–84.

McDonald, David A., and Jonathan Crush, eds. *Destinations Unknown: Perspectives on the Brain Drain.* Pretoria: Africa Institute and SAMP, 2002.

McDonald, David A., Lovemore Zinyama, John Gay, Fion de Vletter, and Robert Mattes. "Guess Who's Coming to Dinner: Migration from Lesotho, Mozambique and Zimbabwe to South Africa." *International Migration Review* 34, no. 3 (2000): 813–41.

McGregor, JoAnn. *Crossing the Zambezi: The Politics of Landscape on a Central African Frontier.* Suffolk: James Currey, 2009.

McGregor, JoAnn, and Ranka Primorac, eds. *Zimbabwe's New Diaspora: Displacement and the Cultural Politics of Survival.* New York: Bergham, 2010.

McKeown, Adam M. *Melancholy Order: Asian Migration and the Globalization of Borders.* New York: Columbia University Press, 2008.

Mechlinski, Timothy. "Towards an Approach to Borders and Mobility in Africa." *Journal of Borderlands Studies* 25, no. 2 (2010): 94–106.

Megoran, Nick, Gael Raballand, and Jerome Bouyjon, "Performance, Representation and the Economics of Border Control in Uzbekistan." *Geopolitics* 10, no. 4 (2005): 712–40.

Miles, William F. S. *Hausaland Divided: Colonialism and Independence in Nigeria and Niger.* Ithaca, NY: Cornell University Press, 1994.

———. "Postcolonial Borderland Legacies of Anglo-French Partition in West Africa." *African Studies Review* 58, no. 3 (2015): 191–213.

———. *Scars of Partition: Postcolonial Legacies in French and British Borderlands.* Lincoln: University of Nebraska, 2014.

Minaar, Anthony, and Mike Hough. *Who Goes There?: Perspectives on Clandestine Migration and Illegal Aliens in Southern Africa.* Pretoria: HSRC, 1996.

Mlambo, Alois S. "A History of Zimbabwean Migration to 1990." In *Zimbabwe's Exodus: Crisis, Migration, Survival,* edited by Jonathan Crush and Daniel Tevera, 52–76. Cape Town: SAMP, 2010.

Moodie, Dunbar, *Going for Gold: Men, Mines and Migration,* with Vivienne Ndatshe. Berkeley: University of California Press, 1994.

Moodie, T. Dunbar. *The Rise of Afrikanerdom: Power, Apartheid, and the Afrikaner Civil Religion.* Berkeley: University of California Press, 1975.

Moore, Donald S. *Suffering for Territory: Race, Place, and Power in Zimbabwe.* Harare: Weaver, 2005.

Mpofu, Busani. "'Undesirable Indians,' Residential Segregation and the Ill-Fated Rise of the White 'Housing Covenanters' in Bulawayo, Colonial Zimbabwe, 1930–1973." *South African Historical Journal* 63, no. 4 (2011): 553–80.

Msindo, Enocent. *Ethnicity in Zimbabwe: Transformations in Kalanga and Ndebele Societies, 1860–1990.* Rochester, NY: University of Rochester Press, 2012.

Mtisi, Joseph, Munyaradzi Nyakudya, and Teresa Barnes. "Social and Economic Developments during the UDI Period." In *Becoming Zimbabwe: A History from the*

Pre-colonial Period to 2008, edited by Brian Raftopoulos and Alois S. Mlambo, 115–40. Harare: Weaver, 2009.

Munochiveyi, Munya B. *Prisoners of Rhodesia: Inmates and Detainees in the Struggle for Zimbabwean Liberation, 1960–1980.* New York: Palgrave Macmillan, 2014.

Murray, J. F. "History of the South African Institute of Medical Research." *South African Medical Journal* (April 1963): 389–95.

Murray, Martin J. "'Blackbirding' at 'Crooks' Corner': Illicit Labour Recruiting in Northeastern Transvaal, 1910–1940." *Journal of Southern African Studies* 21, no. 3 (1995): 373–97.

———. "'Burning the Wheat Stacks': Land Clearances and Agrarian Unrest along the Northern Middelburg Frontier, c. 1918–1926." *Journal of Southern African Studies* 15, no. 1 (1988): 102–22.

———. "Factories in the Fields: Capitalist Farming in the Bethal District, c.1910–1950." In *White Farmers, Black Labor: The State and Agrarian Change in Southern Africa, 1910–50*, edited by Alan H. Jeeves and Jonathan Crush. Portsmouth, NH: Heinemann, 1997.

Mushongah, Josphat, and Ian Scoones. "Livelihood Change in Rural Zimbabwe over 20 Years." *Journal of Development Studies* 48, no. 9 (2012): 1241–57.

Musoni, Francis. "The Ban on 'Tropical Natives' and the Promotion of Illegal Migration in Pre-apartheid South Africa." *African Studies Review* 61, no. 3 (2018): 156–77.

———. "Contested Foreignness: Indian Migrants and the Politics of Exclusion in Early Colonial Zimbabwe." *African and Asian Studies* 16, no. 4 (2017): 312–35.

———. "Cross-Border Mobility, Violence and Spiritual Healing in Beitbridge District, Zimbabwe." *Journal of Southern African Studies* 42, no. 2 (2016): 317–31.

———. "Operation Murambatsvina and the Politics of Street Vendors in Zimbabwe." *Journal of Southern African Studies* 36, no. 2 (2010): 301–17.

Muzondidya, James. "*Makwerekwere*: Migration, Citizenship and Identity among Zimbabweans in South Africa." In *Zimbabwe's New Diaspora and the Cultural Politics of Survival*, edited by JoAnn McGregor and Ranka Primorac, 37–58. New York: Berghahn, 2010.

———. "The Zimbabwean Diaspora: Opportunities and Challenges for Engagement in Zimbabwe's Political Development and Economic Transformation." In *Zimbabwe in Transition: A View from Within*, edited by Timothy Murithi and Aquilina Mawadza, 112–58. Auckland Park: Institute for Justice and Reconciliation, 2011.

Nattrass, Nicoli, and Jeremy Seekings. "The Economy and Poverty in the Twentieth Century." In *The Cambridge History of South Africa*. Vol. 2, *1885–1994*, edited by Robert Ross, Anne Kelk Mager, and Bill Nasson. Cambridge: Cambridge University Press, 2011.

Nevins, Joseph. *Operation Gatekeeper: The Rise of the "Illegal Alien" and the Making of the US–Mexico Boundary.* New York: Routledge, 2002.

Newbury, David. "From 'Frontier' to 'Boundary': Some Historical Roots of Peasant Strategies of Survival in Zaire." In *The Crisis in Zaire: Myths and Realities*, edited by Georges Nzongola-Ntalaja, 87–97. Trenton, NJ: Africa World, 1986.

Ngai, Mae M. *Impossible Subjects: Illegal Aliens and the Making of Modern America.* Princeton, NJ: Princeton University Press, 2004.

Nicol, Heather, and Julian Minghi. "The Continuing Relevance of Borders in Contemporary Contexts." *Geopolitics* 10, no. 4 (2005): 680–87.

Nugent, Paul. "Arbitrary Lines and the People's Minds: A Dissenting View on Colonial Boundaries in West Africa." In *African Boundaries: Barriers, Conduits and Opportunities,* edited by Paul Nugent, and Anthony Asiwaju, 35–67. New York: Pinter, 1996.

———. *Smugglers, Secessionists and Loyal Citizens on the Ghana-Togo Frontier: The Lie of the Borderlands since 1914.* Oxford: James Currey, 2002.

Nugent, Paul, and Anthony I. Asiwaju, eds. *African Boundaries: Barriers, Conduits and Opportunities.* New York: Pinter, 1996.

———. "Introduction: The Paradox of African Boundaries." In *African Boundaries: Barriers, Conduits and Opportunities,* edited by Paul Nugent, and Anthony Asiwaju, 1–17. New York: Pinter, 1996.

Nyagumbo, Maurice. *With the People: An Autobiography from the Zimbabwe Struggle.* London: Allison & Busby, 1980.

Nyamnjoh, Francis B. *Insiders and Outsiders: Citizenship and Xenophobia in Contemporary Southern Africa.* Dakar: Council for the Development of Social Science Research in Africa, 2006.

Nyamunda, Tinashe. "Cross-Border Couriers as Symbols of Regional Grievance? The Malayitsha Remittance System in Matabeleland, Zimbabwe." *African Diaspora* 7, no. 1 (2014): 38–62.

Oucho, John O. "Cross-Border Migration and Regional Initiatives in Managing Migration in Southern Africa." In *Migration in South and Southern Africa: Dynamics and Determinants,* edited by Pieter Kok, Derik Gelderblom, John Oucho, and Johan Van Zyl, , 47–70. Pretoria: Human Science Research Council, 2006.

Owen, Ken, and Gabriël Francois van Lingen Froneman. *Foreign Africans: Summary of the Report of the Froneman Committee, 1963.* Johannesburg: South Africa Institute of Race Relations, 1963.

Packard, Randall M. "The Invention of the 'Tropical Worker': Medical Research and the Quest for Central African Labor on the South African Gold Mines, 1903–36." *Journal of African History* 34 (1993): 271–92.

Pallitto, Robert, and Josiah Heyman, "Theorizing Cross-Border Mobility: Surveillance, Security and Identity." *Surveillance and Society* 5, no. 3 (2008): 315–33.

Palmer, Robin. *Land and Racial Domination in Rhodesia.* London: Heinemann, 1977.

Patel, Hasu H. *Indians in Uganda and Rhodesia: Some Comparative Perspectives on a Minority in Africa.* Denver: Center on International Race Relations, 1973.

Paton, Bill. *Labour Export Policy in the Development of Southern Africa.* London: Macmillan, 1995.

Peberdy, Sally A. "Border Crossings: Small Entrepreneurs and Cross-Border Trade between South Africa and Mozambique." *Tijdschnft voor Economische en Social Geografie* 91, no. 4 (2000): 361–78.

———. "Imagining Immigration: Inclusive Identities and Exclusive Policies in Post-1994 South Africa." *Africa Today* 48, no. 3 (2001): 15–32.

———. *Selecting Immigrants: National Identity and South Africa's Immigration Policies, 1910–2008.* Johannesburg: Wits University Press, 2009.

Pelkmans, Mathijs. "Chaos and Order along the (Former) Iron Curtain." In *A Companion to Border Studies,* edited by Thomas M. Wilson and Hastings Donnan. Oxford: Blackwell, 2012.

Phimister, Ian. *An Economic and Social History of Zimbabwe 1890–1948: Capital Accumulation and Class Struggle*. London: Longman, 1988.

Pikirayi, Innocent. *The Zimbabwe Culture: Origins and Decline of Southern Zambezian States*. Walnut Creek, CA: AltaMira, 2001.

Platzky, Laurine, and Cherryl Walker. *The Surplus People: Forced Removals in South Africa*. Johannesburg: Ravan, 1985.

Polzer, Tara. "Adapting to Changing Legal Frameworks: Mozambican Refugees in South Africa." *International Journal of Refugee Law* 19, no. 1 (2007): 22–50.

Pophiwa, Nedson. "Mobile Livelihoods—The Players Involved in Smuggling of Commodities across the Zimbabwe-Mozambique Border." *Journal of Borderlands Studies* 25, no. 2 (2010): 65–76.

Prince, Ruth J., and Rebecca Marsland, eds. *The Making and Unmaking of Public Health in Africa*. Athens: Ohio University Press, 2014.

Ralinala, Rendani Moses, Jabulani Sithole, Gregory Houston, and Bernard Magubane. "The Wankie and Spolilo Campaigns." In *The Road to Democracy in South Africa*. Vol. 1, *1960–1970*, edited by South African Democracy Education Trust, 479–540. Cape Town: Zebra, 2004.

Ralushai, Nkhumeleni M. N. "Further Traditions Concerning Luvhimbi and the Mbedzi." *Rhodesian History* 9 (1978): 1–12.

Ralushai, Nkhumeleni M. N., and J. R. Gray. "Ruins and Traditions of the Ngona and Mbedzi among the Venda of the Northern Transvaal." *Rhodesian History* 8 (1977): 1–11.

Ranger, Terence O. *The Invention of Tribalism in Zimbabwe*. Gweru: Mambo, 1985.

———. *Voices from the Rocks: Nature, Culture and History in the Matopos Hills of Zimbabwe*. Oxford: James Currey, 1999.

Ranke, W. "Down the Limpopo." *South African Geographical Journal* 15, no. 1 (1932): 35–44.

Richardson, Chad, and Michael J. Pisani. *The Informal and Underground Economy of the South Texas Border*. Austin: University of Texas Press, 2012.

Richardson, Chad, and Rosalva Resendiz. *On the Edge of the Law: Culture, Labor, and Deviance on the South Texas Border*. Austin: University of Texas Press, 2006.

Roitman, Janet. "The Ethics of Illegality in the Chad Basin." In *Law and Disorder in the Postcolony*, edited by Jean Comaroff and John L. Comaroff, 247–72. Chicago: University of Chicago Press, 2006.

———. *Fiscal Disobedience: An Anthropology of Economic Regulation in Central Africa*. Princeton, NJ: Princeton University Press, 2005.

———. "A Successful Life in the Illegal Realm: Smugglers and Road Bandits in the Chad Basin." In *Readings on Modernity in Africa*, edited by Peter Geschiere, Birgit Meyer, and Peter Pels, 214–20. London: International African Institute, 2008.

Rupiah, Martin R. "The History of the Establishment of Internment Camps and Refugee Settlements in Southern Rhodesia, 1938–1952." *Zambezia*, 22, no. 2 (1995): 137–52.

Rutherford, Blair. "The Politics of Boundaries: The Shifting Terrain of Belonging for Zimbabweans in a South African Border Zone." *African Diaspora* 4, no. 2 (2011): 207–29.

———. "Zimbabweans Living in the South African Border-Zone: Negotiating, Suffering and Surviving." *Concerned African Scholars Bulletin* 80 (2008): 35–42.

———. "Zimbabweans on the Farms of Northern South Africa." In *Zimbabwe's Exodus: Crisis, Migration, Survival*, edited by Jonathan Crush and Daniel Tevera, 244–66. Cape Town: SAMP, 2010.

Sadomba, Zvakanyorwa W. *War Veterans in Zimbabwe's Revolution: Challenging Neo-Colonialism and Settler and International Capital.* Harare: Weaver, 2011.

Samatar, Said S. "The Somali Dilemma: Nation in Search of a State." In *Partitioned Africans: Ethnic Relations across Africa's International Boundaries, 1884-1984,* edited by Anthony I. Asiwaju, 155–93. New York: St Martin's, 1985.

Schoettler, Gail S. "The Sotho, Shona and Venda: a Study in Cultural Continuity." *African Historical Studies* 4, no. 1 (1971): 1–18.

Scoones, Ian, Nelson Marongwe, Blasio Mavedzenge, Jacob Mahenehene, Felix Murimbarimba, and Chrispen Sukume. *Zimbabwe's Land Reform: Myths and Realities.* Suffolk: James Currey, 2010.

Scott, James C. "Everyday Forms of Peasant Resistance." *Journal of Peasant Studies* 13, no. 2 (1986): 5–35.

——. *The Moral Economy of the Peasant: Rebellion and Subsistence in Southeast Asia.* New Haven, CT: Yale University Press, 1976.

——. *Weapons of the Weak: Everyday Forms of Peasant Resistance.* New Haven, CT: Yale University Press, 1985.

Segatti, Aurelia. *Of Myths and Migration: Illegal Immigration into South Africa.* Pretoria: University of South Africa, 2003.

——. "Reforming South African Immigration Policy in the Post-apartheid Period (1990–2010)." In *Contemporary Migration to South Africa: A Regional Development Issue,* ed. Aurelia Segatti and Loren B. Landau), 31–66. Washington, DC: World Bank, 2011. Solomon, Hussein. *Challenges to Global Security: Geopolitics and Power in an Age of Transition.* London: Tauris, 2008.

Spener, David. *Clandestine Crossings: Migrants and Coyotes on the Texas-Mexico Border.* Ithaca, NY: Cornell University Press, 2009.

Staudt, Kathleen. *Border Politics in a Global Era: Comparative Perspectives.* Lanham, MD: Rowman & Littlefield, 2018.

Staunton, Irene. "Sosana Marange." In *Mothers of the Revolution: The War Experiences of Thirty Zimbabwean Women,* edited by Irene Staunton, 11–26. London: James Currey, 1990.

Stayt, Hugh A. *The Bavenda.* London: Cass, 1968.

Swindell, Ken. "Serawoolies, Tillibunkas and Strange Farmers: The Development of Migrant Groundnut Farming along the Gambia River 1848-95." *Journal of African History* 21, no. 1 (1980): 93–104.

Tapela, Henderson M. "Labour Migration in Southern Africa and the Origins of Underdevelopment in Nyasaland, 1891–1913." *Journal of Southern African Affairs* 4, no. 1 (1979): 67–80.

Taylor, Ian. "The Ambiguous Commitment: The People's Republic of China and the Anti-Apartheid Struggle in South Africa." *Journal of Contemporary African Studies* 18, no. 1 (2000): 91–106.

Thebe, Vusilizwe. "From South Africa with Love: The 'Malayisha' System and Ndebele Households' Quest for Livelihood Reconstruction in South-Western Zimbabwe." *Journal of Modern African Studies,* 49 (2011): 647–70.

——. "The *Malayisha* Industry and the Transnational Movement of Remittances to Zimbabwe." In *Mean Streets: Migration, Xenophobia and Informality in South Africa.* Cape Town: Southern African Migration Project, 194–206.

Thom, Derrick J. *The Niger-Nigeria Boundary, 1890–1906: A Study of Ethnic Frontiers and a Colonial Boundary*. Athens: Ohio University Center for International Studies, 1975.

Thomson, Harry C. *Rhodesia and its Government*. London: Smith, Elder, 1898.

Toktas, Sule, and Hande Selimoglu, "Smuggling and Trafficking in Turkey: An Analysis of EU-Turkey Cooperation in Combating Transnational Organized Crime." *Journal of Balkan and Near Eastern Studies* 14, no. 1 (2012): 135–50.

Torpey, John. *The Invention of the Passport: Surveillance, Citizenship and the State*. Cambridge: Cambridge University Press, 2000.

Touval, Saadia. "Treaties, Borders, and the Partition of Africa." *Journal of African History* 7, no. 2 (1966): 279–93.

———. *The Boundary Politics of Independent Africa*. Cambridge, MA: Harvard University, 1972.

Tshuma, Lawrence. *A Matter of [In]Justice: Law, State and the Agrarian Question in Zimbabwe*. Harare: SAPES Trust, 1997.

Vail, Leroy, ed. *The Creation of Tribalism in Southern Africa*. Berkeley: University of California Press, 1989.

Van Dijk, Han, Dick Foeken, and Kiky van Til. "Population Mobility in Africa: An Overview." In *Mobile Africa: Changing Patterns of Movement in Africa and Beyond*, edited by De Bruijn, Mirjam, Rijk A. van Dijk, and Dick Foeken, 9–26. Leiden: Brill, 2001.

Van Houtum, Henk. "The Geopolitics of Borders and Boundaries." *Geopolitics*, 10, no. 4, (2005): 672–79.

Van Onselen, Charles. *Chibaro: African Mine Labour in Southern Rhodesia, 1900 to 1933*. London: Pluto, 1976.

Van Warmelo, Nicolaas J. *Anthropology of Southern Africa in Periodicals to 1950: An Analysis and Index*. Johannesburg: Witwatersrand University Press, 1977.

———. *Contributions towards Venda History, Religion and Tribal Ritual*. Pretoria: University of South Africa, Department of Native Affairs, 1932.

Vigneswaran, Darshan. "Migration Control, Documentation and State Transformation." In *Contemporary Migration to South Africa: A Regional Development Issue*, edited by Aurelia Segatti and Loren B. Landau, 105–19. Washington, DC: World Bank, 2011.

Vigneswaran, Darshan, Tesfalem Araia, Colin Hoag, and Xolani Tshabalala. "Criminality or Monopoly? Informal Immigration Enforcement in South Africa." *Journal of Southern African Studies*, 36, no. 2 (2010): 465–81.

Von Sicard, Harald. "The Origin of Some of the Tribes in the Belingwe Reserve." *NADA*, (1952): 43–64.

White, Luise. *Unpopular Sovereignty: Rhodesian Independence and African Decolonization*. Chicago: University of Chicago Press, 2015.

Wilks, Ivor. "On Mentally Mapping Greater Asante: A Study of Time and Motion." *Journal of African History* 33, no. 2 (1992): 175–90.

Wilson, Francis. "International Migration in Southern Africa." *International Migration Review* 10, no. 4 (1976): 451–88.

———. *Labour in the South African Gold Mines, 1911–1969*. Cambridge: Cambridge University Press, 1972.

Yoshikuni, Tsuneo. *African Urban Experiences in Colonial Zimbabwe: A Social History of Harare before 1925*. Harare: Weaver, 2007.

Zamindar, Vazira Fazila-Yacoobali. *The Long Partition and the Making of Modern South East Asia: Refugees, Boundaries, Histories.* New York: Columbia University Press, 2010.

Zinyama, Lovemore. "Who, What, When and Why: Cross-Border Movement from Zimbabwe to South Africa." In *On Borders: Perspectives on International Migration in Southern Africa,* edited by David A. McDonald, 71–85. Ontario: SAMP, 2000.

Zolberg, Aristide. *A Nation by Design: Immigration Policy in the Fashioning of America.* New York: Russell Sage, 2006.

Index

African Manpower Conference (1943), 88–89
African National Congress (ANC), 108, 114, 137–38
Alfred Beit Bridge, 83, 96, 98–99, 104n7
Aliens Control Act (1991), 137–38
Aliens Registration Act (1939), 110
Al-Qaeda, 1
Andersson, Ruben, 3
anticolonial liberation movements, 11, 108–9, 114–16, 119–20, 122, 125, 126–27
apartheid, 107–8
Asiwaju, Anthony I., 33
Axon (African worker), 99

B1-17 permits, 140–41, 144
Barnard, Cecil, 72
Bechuanaland. *See* Botswana
Beitbridge, 140, 142, 143–44; concentration camps in, 119, 120–21; dependence on South Africa, 150
Beitbridge border post, 1, 86, 111; and B1-17 permits, 140, 144; bribery and corruption at, 144, 151, 152–53; control measures at, 83–84, 121–22, 147
Ben Bella, Ahmed, 115
Berlin Act of 1885, 9
border controls: in apartheid South Africa, 26–29, 84, 110–12, 121–23, 127–28; beginning of cross-Limpopo, 26–29, 38, 167; at Beitbridge border post, 83–84, 121–22, 147; and border control units, 13, 83–84, 122, 138, 142–43, 144, 151, 155; border jumpers' evasion of, 3, 5, 12, 15, 34–35, 69–73, 92–100, 123–24, 129–30, 141–44, 157; in Botswana, 83, 111–12; calls for tightening, 1, 56–57, 137–38, 153, 167; and colonial borders, 8, 9–10, 166–67; and contested borders, 7–11; and cross-border trade, 154–55; governmental

agreements for, 84–87, 113–14, 122–23; and "illegal migration" prevention, 1, 3, 90, 167; militarized, 13, 114–22, 124, 128–29; in Mozambique, 122–23, 127–28; in post-apartheid South Africa, 137–40, 153; in Rhodesia, 5, 26–29, 49, 83–87, 92–100; and surveillance, 8, 83–84, 116, 138; travel and identity documents in, 8, 36, 95, 122–23, 148–50

border jumping: and border control evasion, 3, 5, 12, 15, 34–35, 69–73, 92–100, 123–24, 129–30, 141–44, 157; and bribing officials, 143–44, 148–49, 151, 153, 155; and colonial borders, 8, 9–10, 33–34, 166–68; as concept and term, 2–3, 4–7, 165; criminalization of, 8–9, 137; false identities and documents used in, 36, 71–72, 95, 147–50, 165; governmental agreements against, 84–87, 113–14, 122–23; and human smuggling, 36–40, 142–44; by liberation forces, 124–25; and maguma-guma, 1–2, 142–44, 151, 158–59, 168; motivations for, 11–12, 67–68, 92–93, 165–66; networks used in, 94–95, 97–98, 99–100, 151–52; as rational decision, 12, 13–14, 166; by refugees, 7, 125–26; Rhodesian efforts against, 5, 26–29, 49, 84–87, 92–100; rise of Zimbabwe-to-South Africa, 33–36; routes in, 13, 37, 71, 72, 82, 83, 84, 96, 97, 98, 123–24; South Africa's implicit promotion of, 87–92; statistics on, 70, 87; strategies used in, 12–14, 15, 71–72, 86, 94–100, 123–24, 125–26, 129, 141–44, 147–50, 152–53; trains used in, 95–96, 97–98; and "tropical workers" ban, 46–47, 69–73; vehicles used in, 13, 96–97, 151–52; violence against, 157–60; violence by, 100; women and, 95–96; and Zimbabwean crisis, 135–60

FRANCIS MUSONI is Associate Professor of History at
the University of Kentucky.

ſ

CPSIA information can be obtained
at www.ICGtesting.com
Printed in the USA
BVHW031001190320
575442BV00001B/14